EXPLORING
green roads & lanes of
Great Britain

EXPLORING
green roads & lanes of
Great Britain

by Ian Thompson

Foulis

Haynes

ISBN 0-85429-691-3

A **FOULIS** Motorcycling Book

First published November 1988
Reprinted 1993

Published by
Haynes Publishing Group Ltd
Sparkford, Yeovil, Somerset BA22 7JJ, England

Haynes Publications Inc
861 Lawrence Drive, Newbury Park, California 91320
USA

British Library Cataloguing in Publication Data
Thompson, Ian
    Exploring green roads & lanes of
    Great Britain. (General motorcycling).
    1. Great Britain. Rural regions.
    Description & travels.
    I. Title   II. Series.
    914.1'04858
    ISBN 0-85429-691-3

Library of Congress Catalog Card Number
    88 82508

Printed in England by J.H. Haynes & Co. Ltd.

Section of map on front cover reproduced by courtesy
of George Philip & Son Ltd. Crown copyright reserved.

Contents

Preface

Rambling in the countryside has been an acceptable pursuit for about two centuries. It was made popular by the poet William Wordsworth, who wandered, not usually lonely as a cloud, but in the company of other famous poets or his sister, in the West Country and, in particular, in the Lake District.

Before Wordsworth, any traveller worth his salt rode a horse to do his or her exploring. Celia Fiennes journeyed extensively for pleasure in the late seventeenth century and wrote colourfully of the ordinary things she found. William Cobett used his *Rural Rides* of 1821 to comment on the state of the nation as he found it.

My rambles on an iron horse have not transformed me into a great poet or a successful political commentator, but they have given me great pleasure.

I started my career as an engineer at Cambridge University, subsequently working first in Derby, then in London. I retrained as a teacher in Exeter, and have taught in Wiltshire, Avon and now Cornwall. My work has given me the opportunity to ramble over a large part of Britain on my motorcycle. While living in Somerset, I became embroiled in the rights of motorcyclists to ramble in the countryside. I also acted as membership secretary for the Trail Riders Fellowship, the national organisation dedicated to conservation and use of green roads.

The majority of people living in the Western World understand ordinary roads to be tar-sealed highways with curb stones, white lines and road signs. But this is a long way from the truth. More than eighty per cent of the world's ordinary roads are loose surfaced, rough, potholed and rutted.

What is the ordinary road for the rest of the world has become exceptional in this country only recently. Britain's main roads were tarred after the First World War, but the intricate network of minor roads were still receiving their first coat of tar in the 1950s and 1960s.

The few untarred roads that are left in Britain are there to be explored. Their soft surfaces are best suited to a lightweight vehicle such as a motorcycle. Properly silenced, the motorcycle is the modern equivalent of the horse used by the pre-pedestrian explorers of our countryside.

This book tells of some of my adventures in nearly twenty years of poking my front wheel down little used lanes. I hope that you will not only enjoy reading it, but that you will feel encouraged to try a ramble or two for yourself.

This is a main road in Morocco. Its surface is hard-packed dirt. In Britain it would be called a "green road" because it has no waterproof tarmac layer. Most of the World's roads are green roads. (G. Wilson)

Foreword

As Patron of the Trail Riders Fellowship I was delighted to be invited to write a foreword to Ian Thompson's book on Exploring Green Roads. Green roads are not only a source of pleasure to the variety of travellers who use them but are very much part of our British Heritage and must at all costs be preserved. It is interesting that a hundred years ago all roads were green roads and only towards the end of the last century were the road stones bound together with tar to cope with the demands of the motorcar. Tarred Macadamised roads spread slowly at first and it was not till the 1920s that County Councils slowly took over road maintenance from Parish Councils at a time when minor roads were still untarred. We owe a great debt to the parishes who had looked after the county roads since the reign of Elizabeth I.

Cecil Alden in his book of hunting and horses entitled *'Exmoor. The Riding Playground of England'* published in 1935, says that if you were lost on Exmoor, you rode south until you came to a tarmac road. Since there was only one such road on the whole of Exmoor you knew where you were! A study of green lanes in 1977 stated that almost all minor tarred roads are 'destroyed green lanes'. In spite of this about 5000 miles of green roads remain, a pathetically small mileage compared with the 120,000 miles of rights of way discussed in the Countryside Commission's document 'Recreation 2000' which came out last year. By tradition pedestrians and horses have always used green roads. These have more recently been joined by motorcyclists and drivers of 4 wheel drive vehicles who also love the countryside but, owing to the nature of their transport, noise is a problem. The Autocycle Union and the Trail Riders Fellowship strive to ensure that motorcyclists ride responsibly and their management policies have been successful. One of the more pleasant aspects of using green roads is the serenity and the chance to get away from teeming hordes of people. The personal nature of travelling thus, makes it easier for people to pass the time of day together when they do meet, whether they be riders, pedestrians or motorcyclists.

Ian Thompson takes us into this pleasant world with his great experiences of travelling from Scotland to Land's End, from Dover to the wilder parts of Wales and most parts between. He tells of the people he has met and places he has seen in a relaxed and very readable style which will encourage many readers to follow his example even if only on a lesser scale! By writing this book, Ian Thompson has done a great service for all those who love the countryside in general and the green roads in particular.

Strathcarron

Strathcarron

Introduction to the 1993 Reprint

I was pleased and excited when the publishers told me that the first batch of this book was sold out and they wanted to reprint it.

We discussed what would need changing, and agreed that there was very little. This book is an account of my experiences of exploring green roads and lanes throughout Great Britain. As such, it is as accurate now as when it was first written. However, if you plan to follow in my wheel tracks, you will need to appreciate how insecure the future of our green routes actually is. Even before the first copy of this book reached the shops, many Welsh green roads of great antiquity were closed to vehicles. I rode them before they were closed and my account appears in the following pages. It is an accurate account, but no-one can now follow in my wheel tracks without defying the law.

In some cases, it is physically impossible to follow my tracks. They have been ploughed out. Walls and hedges constructed centuries ago have been grubbed up by modern earth movers. Miles of history have ceased to exist. This had been the case in many counties in the South and East of England. The South Downs Way in Sussex has been closed to vehicles for much of its length, despite a long courtroom battle to save it. Yet another public enquiry was instigated in 1993 to stop vehicles using the Great Ridgeway in Wessex.

Using green roads and lanes in Britain involves a constant struggle to maintain our right to ride. Perhaps you will be one of those who leads this fight in the courts. If not, please think of those who are. They cannot fight to preserve your right to countryside access and enjoyment if you abuse that right.
Ride with care.
Ride with consideration for others.
Remember noise annoys. Keep it quiet.
Ride with a thought to the future.

The situation is not as gloomy as all this might suggest. Riders and archive researchers are rediscovering forgotten lanes. Careful restoration and sensible use can save these lanes from the oblivion of neglect. For every lane lost to the law courts or the plough, there is at least one forgotten lane waiting to give delight for the future.

How do you find out the up to date position in your area? Your County Council will let you look at their maps, which should be up to date and accurate. They may not always give you a warm welcome. They do not usually regard green roads as a very high priority. Your local Trail Riders Fellowship group will have all the latest information. They are experts and will be happy to take you under their wing and show you the local lanes. To contact them you must first join the national Trail Riders Fellowship. Details of the Trail Riders Fellowship can be obtained by writing to the Trail Riders Fellowship, 34 Oak Road, Barton-under-Needwood, Burton-on-Trent, DE13 8LR.

I am asked what to ride and what to wear for green road exploration. The simplest answer is whatever you like, as long as it is quiet and street legal. This applies to bikes and clothes.

The quality of bikes suited to green roads continues to improve. Suspension and chassis design in particular have developed to meet the needs of green roads. Small, water-cooled two stroke engines produce power with a minimum of noise and smoke. Four strokes provide more torque and fuel economy. Whatever you choose, weight is the most important factor to consider. The more demanding the lanes you plan to explore, the lighter your bike should be. The 'super-trail' bikes popular on the Continent for long distance touring are generally too heavy for all but the gentlest green lanes. And they have large areas of vulnerable plastic, easily damaged in a tumble.

For riding gear, I go for layers of clothing. You will be warm on green roads, travelling slowly, working hard. It is good to be able to peel off a layer when the going gets tough, and put extra layers on for the cold ride home at the end of the day. I find a lightweight nylon anorak, bought cheaply in a chain store, gives excellent protection from the rain if worn over the traditional waxed cotton motorcycle suit. If it should stop raining (this does happen occasionally) the anorak can be rolled up and stowed in a pocket.

You need strong, waterproof boots to cope with fords and a stout pair of gloves to protect your hands from stray brambles from the hedge. Helmets need to keep you cool. Open face styles are still best value. There are some excellent full face helmets designed for off road competition use which will give better protection. The open face helmet has the advantage when you meet someone on a green lane. If they can see a human face inside all your protective riding gear, their reaction will always be friendlier than when confronted with the comic strip spaceman's plastic skull of a fully enclosed helmet. If you do opt for full face protection, take it off when you meet other lane users.

That is enough advice for an introduction, You will find plenty more, based on first-hand experience, scattered through the chapters that follow. I hope you enjoy exploring the green roads and lanes of Great Britain.

Ian Thompson

Ian Thompson
1993

On behalf of my fellow members of the Motor Cycle Association – the industry's trade association – and especially its off-road members, I congratulate Ian Thompson on filling a much-needed niche in the motorcyclist's library with this informative new publication.

Much has been said about green lane riding but apart from contributors' columns in the motorcycle press, little has been available in such a concise form. This is more than ever necessary now because of the pressures being exerted upon the use of green lanes, and the need for preserving them for future generations. Concerned motorcyclists can play a very important part in preserving our rights to the use of ancient tracks by responsible behaviour at all times.

For those who have yet to savour the freedom of riding the ancient tracks, you have a great treat in store!

Motorcycling's traditional freedom is further enhanced when spectacular areas of unspoiled countryside otherwise inaccessible by road are opened up to trail riders.

Ride safely, preserve the countryside!

Charles Smart
Off-Road Marketing Group
Motor Cycle Association of GB Ltd

Acknowledgements

I would like to thank the many people who have helped to make this book possible.

I am particularly grateful to Ian Roscow, Bevis Billingham, John Higgin, Colin Patient, Terry Jolley, Pete Wildsmith, Ann Wilks and Bill Riley for their invaluable assistance in devising a green road route from Dover to Land's End, and to Gareth Richards for his companionship in preliminary exploration.

Alan Kind, John Gillett, Gordon Thackray and Dave Giles proved splendid guides along the green roads of northern England, and Brian Smith provided excellent hospitality at a time when it was very welcome.

Photographs were provided by Alan Kind, Geoff Wilson, Dave Giles, Rosie Marston and Mike Cowling. Their pictures serve to illustrate the rich variety of green roads with which our island is endowed.

Above all, I must thank the thousands of people, many known to me and even more unknown, who are working tirelessly to keep Britain's green roads and lanes open and available for us all to explore.

Finally, to my wife, I owe a deep debt for her support and patience during my many years of exploring and researching green lanes, and, more particularly, for her contribution to the photographs in the book.

Ian Thompson

St. Columb Minor
Cornwall
July 1988

Chapter One

Green Lanes

The history of green lanes in Britain is as old as Man's occupation of these islands. It is a long story which starts with the animal trails followed by Stone Age hunters in search of prey. Much new evidence about our roads is still being discovered by the latest techniques in archeology. The history of a road can be very complex and there are thousands and thousands of roads.

Green lanes are a by-product of road improvements in this century. The Motor Age brought high speed vehicles and the pneumatic tyre which destroyed the surface of our road system faster than it could be repaired in the traditional ways. From the start of this century, tar was used to provide a durable, car-proof surface. Tarmac has slowly covered most of our roads, so that roads without tarmac are now rare in Britain. Indeed, some people have the idea that if a road is not tarmacadamed it is not a road at all!

The surviving, non-tarmac roads are what we now call ''green lanes''. They are the remnants of roads from many different periods of our social and economic development. The green lanes which have been saved from the tar provide a microcosm of the history of all our roads for the knowledgeable observer to study at first hand.

An ancient green lane in the North of England. Over the centuries, traffic has worn the surface down below the surrounding ground level. (A. Kind)

Some green lanes are clearly prehistoric in origin. A track like the Great Ridgeway, which runs along the chalk escarpment through Berkshire, Oxfordshire and Wiltshire is at least as old as the stone circles at Avebury and nearby Stonehenge and is lined with burial mounds as well as the smaller remains of early Britons – flint tools traded in the Stone Age, Bronze Age pottery, Iron Age weapons. Such roads have been used by succeeding generations right up to the present day and it is not possible to give a precise date to when they were first used. The original inhabitants of Britain have left few visible traces of their passing. Yet there is evidence, revealed by modern archeological techniques, that the whole of Britain was covered with a network of roads and tracks, used for both local and long distance travel, throughout the Stone Age. It is certain that such an infrastructure existed in the Bronze and Iron Ages.

The Romans superimposed their own roads on the existing network when they conquered Britain. These were straight, smooth surfaced, well-drained, military roads – the motorways of the ancient world. They were designed to speed the movement of troops about a land prone to rebellion. They were laid out and built under the supervision of miitary engineers. Their design was impressive. The roadbed was of carefully graded rocks, becoming progressively smaller towards the top surface. Deep drainage ditches were dug on either side and the road was cambered to help rainwater run off. The Roman surveyors followed straight lines as the shortest and therefore the fastest route for marching troops to follow. If you look at a modern road map of almost any part of England you can still see the straight lines of Roman roads, now used for modern traffic.

No-one who followed ever built roads to such high standards or with such pure engineering excellence as the Romans. The Dark Ages which followed the collapse of the Roman Empire brought wave after wave of invaders to Britain's shores. New peoples inhabited our islands and followed new trails as well as adapting the old roads to their new needs. Several long distance tracks are attributable to this period. These are the Here paths, Hare paths or war paths. They are believed to be Saxon military roads and would have been used by the rulers of Saxon kingdoms to tour their territories to keep an eye on and protect their subjects.

Here paths were not built in any way equal to the Roman roads. In fact there is no evidence to suggest that they were 'built' in the accepted sense at all. Yet they were, undeniably, clearly defined and recognised roads. In addition, many of our smaller, short distance, country lanes have their origin at least as far back as the farming communities of the Dark Ages. Examples of this period are the high-banked, sunken lanes so typical still of the West Country. In the Midlands, the Medieval villages, with their open field system, developed their own type of local lanes. They twist and turn, the way that the cows came home, around the irregular edges of long lost fields. The fields were cleared and fenced into great sheep enclosures in the eighteenth century, but the wandering English road remains.

After the Wars of the Roses, the stable, national government of the Tudors developed a system of road maintenance which, for hundreds of years, resulted in appalling difficulty for travellers. The descriptions of travel during this period are amazing. Roads on Exmoor,

Roman roads run straight for miles and miles. This Wiltshire road barely survives the encroaching plough. (D. Giles)

for example, were "so steep, narrow and encumbered with large, loose stones that it was dangerous even for horses." Britain is a wet country. Ground which is firm and dry in summer can become a sticky quagmire in winter. There are tales of carriages being stranded in the streets of London, because the mud came over the axles so that the horses could not move. Stories like these can be found right up to the eighteenth century.

After 1555, roads were supposed to be maintained by the parishes through which they passed. This resulted in long distance roads which changed complexion from parish to parish, depending on how badly each parish maintained its section of the road. The road mender of this period, from sixteenth to eighteenth century earned little, if anything. In the early days of the system, parishes were required to provide labour for road repairs free of charge. Only hand tools were used, with perhaps a basket to carry stones to fill the worst potholes. Inevitably the work was done poorly, if at all.

Many parishes owned a huge 'road plough', a device pulled by a team of eight or ten horses or oxen, which levelled the road surface each spring by ploughing it! I know from experience how hard it is to walk across ploughed land. Imagine trying to drive a coach or waggon along a freshly ploughed road!

Roads were usually waterlogged due to poor drainage. Some were given a camber to drain them, but the camber was often so steep that carriages were in danger of overturning. Others used water to maintain the roads. This resulted in the hollow ways which are common throughout the country. The road was made slightly concave, so that a stream could be made to flow down the road to wash the surface clear of mud and debris to the lowest point where men with spades would clear it away. The constant washing away of the surface made the road gradually sink below the surrounding land.

The eighteenth century turnpikes transferred responsibility for the upkeep of many through roads from the parish to private enterprise. Turnpike Trusts, usually made up of local landowners and business men, were set up by Acts of Parliament to control and supervise the maintenance of particular stretches of road. The Turnpike Trusts provided houses for the keepers of their tollgates. These were designed to give a clear view of the road in both directions so that the gate keeper could see potential customers approaching. Many of these strange little houses can be seen on modern trunk roads throughout the country.

New stretches of road were built to make travel easier. For example, two parallel stretches of turnpike road were built to carry traffic to the West Country round the northern tip of the Quantock Hills in Somerset. An earlier road, known locally as The Great Road or the Old Coach Road, climbs over the Quantock ridge from East to West, with a change of horses at the top at the Bicknoller posting station. John Cary's map of Somerset, published in 1805, shows the Great Road as the main road to the West. Later maps, such as Greenwood's county map of 1820, while showing the Great Road, show the new turnpikes as the main route. The Great Road, is clearly

Seeingsyke Road, a byway in Weardale. When the land was enclosed, roads often gained walls to define their route. (A. Kind)

the old main road. It is shown on an estate map, drawn on sheepskin in 1687, with a coach and horses travelling the Great Road. This map is in Court House, East Quantoxhead. Today the Great Road is a green lane, with a view over the surrounding countryside and across the Bristol Channel to Wales which is enjoyed by thousands of people every year, while the trunk road scurries round the turnpike route, seeing nothing, taking the buses and caravans to Minehead and all points West.

Thousands of miles of roads were turnpiked and they did provide improved long distance travel. They promoted trade and greatly increased the amount of traffic using roads. Unfortunately, since the Turnpike Trusts still used the same methods as the parishes to maintain their roads, the road surface did not keep pace with the increased traffic. In many cases, travelling on turnpikes was no easier than on other roads, merely more expensive because of the tolls charged.

It is important to note that only a fraction of the roads in the country were turnpiked. Many thousands of miles of holloways and drove roads continued into the Twentieth Century in their ancient form, untouched by the turnpike era.

It was not the advent of the turnpikes, but of the first road engineers at the end of the eighteenth century, which changed the nature of travel. Thomas Telford, who improved the London to Holyhead road, the modern A5, during the 1820s, made roads with meticulous care. His technique was described by a contemporary, Robert Southey : "First level and drain; and then lay a solid pavement of hard stones, the round or broad end downwards; the points are then broken off, and a layer of stones broken to about the size of walnuts, laid over them so that the whole are bound together."

It was not Telford, but McAdam who became a household name. Telford's roads were excellent, but too expensive. John Loudon McAdam also took great care to level and drain. He also graded the stones for the top dressing to a uniform size, but he saved money by omitting the costly foundation of large stones. The first macadamised road in England was made between Bath and Bristol in 1816. It was McAdam's cheap, long lasting roads that transformed travel on the main highways and heralded the beginning of the short, but glorious heyday of the mail coaches and stage coaches which flew along the fast roads between the major cities of the land.

The coming of railways stopped further developments for long distance roads, although local roads became even busier, supplying the railways with passengers and goods. At the start of this century, few people travelled far by road. The railways provided long distance transport for all. Sherlock Holmes consulted his timetable before journeying to the far corners of the country to solve insoluble mysteries. The Royal Train took Her Majesty Queen Victoria, ruler of the greatest empire the world has ever known, from the capital of her Empire, London, to her Scottish holiday retreat, Balmoral. Everyone travelled everywhere by train.

All this British railway travel was soon to be spoiled by foreigners. A couple of Germans had produced horseless carriages, propelled by internal (infernal?) combustion engines. During the infant years of the twentieth century, the French, the Germans and the Americans led the field in a race to produce reliable, long distance motor transport.

McAdam built beautiful bridges as well as cost-effective roads. This one is near Whitfield in Northumberland.
(A. Kind)

The motor car and the motorcycle started their careers as toys for the aristocracy. Henry Ford in America and motorcycle manufacturers on both sides of the Atlantic had, by the 1920s, turned them into transport for the masses. A new Age had arrived – the Motor Age.

Green lanes are a creation of the twentieth century. At the same time, green lanes are as old as civilisation. This paradox has produced confusion, not just for ordinary people, but for the best legal brains in the land, who are still debating how to define a 'true' green lane.

Roads in Britain had been neglected for long distance travel during the century when the railway was king. The Motor Age demanded a cure for the choking, blinding dust sucked up and spewed out by pneumatic tyres in a way unknown in the iron tyred horse drawn ages before. Dust coats, gauntlets and goggles were not mere items of fashion for early motorists. They were essential to protect them from the dust. A solution to this problem was found which created the green lanes of today. The dust was controlled by tar. A layer of hot tar was spread over the main roads of Britain to seal the surface and prevent the dust storms of the early motoring years.

By the end of the 1940s, the majority of roads, from trunk routes to minor lanes, were plastered down with tar. Some roads escaped. Byways in country districts little used to the motor car still had heavily trafficked, untarred roads. Carts and waggons, horse drawn omnibuses, in some places even stage coaches used these untarred 'green' roads and are well-remembered by people alive today.

The tar is still spreading, aided by bitumen and by concrete. Green lanes are becoming rarer and rarer. They are an endangered species. It is often hard to believe that, less than a century ago, all our roads were green.

Chapter Two

Trail Riding

The history of roads in the United States was very different to the developments just described in Great Britain. Early motor vehicles in America replaced horse-drawn transport with the enthusiasm of a young nation. American cars went everywhere a wagon could go. American motorcycles went everywhere a horse could go. Roads followed the settlers westwards. The old covered wagon trails became part of a vast network of new roads which linked together the new land.

The affluence of the post-war period saw Americans travelling in luxurious automobiles, a world away from Henry Ford's tough, go anywhere, Tin Lizzie Model T.

The latent pioneering sense of adventure beneath this veneer of soft living was fertile ground for the Japanese motorcycle industry. Americans were persuaded to rediscover their pioneering roots on a Japanese trail bike.

I picture the first American 'trail riders' as staid family men who have just discovered a new hobby, more exciting than golf or squash, even better than jogging. They would take their family out of the city into the desert, unload the new, lightweight trail bikes from the back of the pick-up, and the whole family would ride around in the desert for the day. This gave fresh air and exercise, a

The pioneering days of motorcycling are re-enacted each year by the Motor Cycle Club in a series of classic "reliability trials". Here a flat tank Triumph wrestles with a steep green lane in the Edinburgh Trial. (G. Wilson)

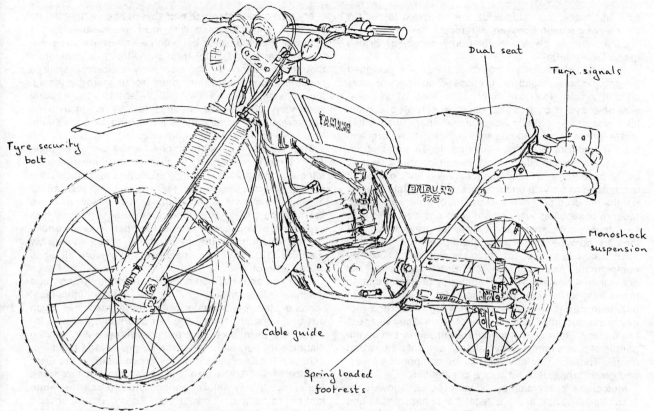

Dual seat

Turn signals

Tyre security bolt

Monoshock suspension

Cable guide

Spring loaded footrests

1977 Yamaha DT175. Made in Japan. This was the sort of bike that made "trail riding" popular, first in the United States and then in Britain.

look at nature, and a lot of pleasure for everybody (especially the motorcycle manufacturers).

I have the impression that these first trail riders were well-paid middle-class citizens who could afford to indulge themselves a little. They were not necessarily experienced motorcyclists. They accepted the Japanese offerings of 'special' trail bikes, without really considering the difference between these and ordinary road bikes.

Trail riding has gone from strength to strength in America. Today it is a well-established pastime, with a strong voice at local and national government level. Different states have different policies, but the general trend is to create vast trail riding parks, with well sign-posted routes as part of the National Parks and wilderness areas, owned and managed by state governments.

Trail bikes for the American market are now very special lightweights with lots of low gears and little weight, designed to transport fishermen or hunters into the depths of the wilderness to enjoy their sport. The old type of trail bike has developed into the Enduro bike, for high speed travel along the well-signed routes in the trail parks. For competition, these Enduro bikes have been further modified by increasing engine size and adding massive fuel tanks for long distance desert racing. None of these types of motorcycle, all manufactured in Japan, are really ideal for the green lanes of Britain.

Riding green lanes in Britain is very different to trail riding in America. We have much less land to play on. Our very limited access to the countryside is confined to the ever-decreasing number of old roads which were not

given a layer of tar during the twentieth century explosion in road transport.

The typical British trail rider has considerable experience of motorcycles. He has usually had several road bikes before contemplating buying a trail bike. Because of the scarcity of green lanes, he chooses his trail bike to cope with tarmac roads as well as green lanes. The British trail bike must comply with all the requirements of the Road Traffic Acts, where the American bike has no such restrictions placed upon it. Because of these more difficult circumstances, it was much harder to sell trail bikes in this country than in America, and I feel that British importers did not try very hard.

The average superbike is not designed for green lanes. Its great weight means that if it gets stuck it is very difficult to move. If the rider is confident that he will not get stuck, then let him use a 1000 cc roadster. In my opinion, weight is the really important factor. A maximum of 300 pounds weight seems to be about the limit for most bikes suitable for regular green lane use. Look at a stage coach and see how it, too, was designed to be light yet strong.

In the winter, many lanes become too muddy for road bikes. Wheels become choked with mud, it is difficult to find grip and the bike becomes difficult to control. Here a 'trail bike' is needed. Apart from styling, which is by far the most prominent feature of a trail bike, it has a number of real advantages over the average lightweight road bike. The most important is a set of dual purpose town and country tyres which provide better grip in the mud than ordinary road tyres. It is also much more stable over loose surfaces; its suspension is designed to ride over ruts and rocks; the mudguards are designed to reduce the risk of becoming choked with mud.

Other, similar bikes are not really suited for British green lane riding:

Trials bikes, as distinct from trail bikes, are designed for competitions based on low speed agility over very difficult terrain. They can climb cliffs, leap fallen trees, scramble over boulders. No obstacle can stop a trials bike ridden by a really competitive rider. Such bikes tackle green lane surfaces effortlessly. There are two main drawbacks. First, they must be ridden standing up. The seat is a token affair, about as comfortable as sitting on the bare frame. Second, the fuel tank is far too small. It is intended to provide enough for a lap of a trials course, not the hundred plus miles used in a day's green laning. Modern trials bikes are well-silenced and equipped with road legal lights. They can be used for green lanes, but they are favoured by very few green lane riders.

Enduro bikes are for high speed, cross-country competition. They can make good green lane bikes, but are rather expensive. All too often they prove unreliable in the long term. They are intended for a season's hard use, with careful maintenance between each race, not day in day out riding for a number of years. They wear out too quickly. Their speed cannot be utilised in the gentle pursuit of green lanes. Above all they cultivate the wrong image. They look so obviously to be competition bikes, and green laning is in no way a competition.

Motocross or scrambles bikes are not allowed on green lanes. They are not legal on public roads, and green lanes are public roads. They are noisy, highly-tuned racing machines, designed to be ridden very fast. They are in completely the wrong environment pottering along green lanes.

My personal preference has always been a lightweight roadster. This can cope with most green lanes in the summer, not with ease but with perseverance. Where a trials bike would skip through without a moment's thought or effort by its rider, my roadster requires concentration, persuasion, often some sturdy pushing, and considerable time. Yet I still prefer it to a trials bike. I see much more of the countryside and obtain a much greater sense of achievement at reaching the end of each lane than could any trials bike rider.

The roadster has its limitations. I also have a trail bike. This is the most popular form of green lane transport, although the number of new models available on the market seems to reduce each year. The few minor modifications from a conventional road machine make the modern trail bike a good dual purpose mount. It is capable of a satisfactory tarmac road performance and is rugged enough for the demands of green lanes. My Yamaha XT250 trail bike enables me to explore all lanes at any time of year.

The Yamaha trail bike is my ultimate green lane machine. This makes my Honda CB125 lightweight roadster the penultimate green lane machine. Such devious logic christened the Honda Penny, the penultimate. My third bike is a bronze-yellow BMW, a long distance touring bike rather than a green lane machine, although it can cope with many green lanes in the drier months. The BMW's size and shape gave it the name Buttercup. It was natural enough then to call the white tanked Yamaha trail bike Daisy. Penny, Buttercup and Daisy – not so much a stable as a cow shed of bikes.

The trail bike craze in America was pioneered by firms like Hodaka as long ago as 1963. The first Hodaka was a 90 cc lightweight, designed for the dry, desert conditions

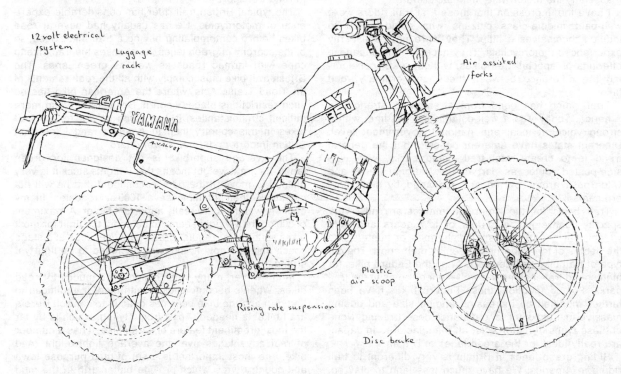

12 volt electrical system

Luggage rack

Air assisted forks

Plastic air scoop

Rising rate suspension

Disc brake

1988 Yamaha XT350. Arguably the best genuine green lane bike of its day. The XT350 combines many practical features with a large helping of styling.

Kawasaki KL650, developed from long distance desert racers, this large capacity, single cylinder, four stroke copes well with the gentler sort of green lane.
(G. Wilson).

of California. The major Japanese manufacturers took some time to realise the potential of the trail bike market. It was not until 1968 that Yamaha led the way by introducing the 250 cc DT1 in America. By the spring of 1971 trail bike sales were booming. In America thirty-two manufacturers and importers offered no fewer than one hundred and twenty-four different models to the trail rider.

In Britain the trail bike 'boom' was very slow in starting. In the spring of 1972, the British *Bike* magazine declared that there were now "over ten trail bikes on offer" to the British buyer. What a contrast to America!

The first Japanese trail bikes to reach Britain were called Suzuki Trail Cats. They were fitted with dual-ratio gearboxes, small wheels and rather odd-looking frames. I think they were probably sold here because they could not compete in the American market. It was not until late in 1972 that the real Japanese trail bikes started to arrive in Britain and even then there was little attempt at the hard selling so successful across the Atlantic.

Trail riding is as old as motorcycling itself. When bikes were first sold there were no tarmac roads. All riding was what we, today, call trail riding. All motorcyclists were expected to cope with rough, muddy lanes as well as cobbled city streets. A friend of mine in Wiltshire found that his 1930s vintage BSA 500 single was well-suited to the mud and ruts on his local green lanes. With the manual ignition control set retarded, the BSA would pull through anything – because it was designed to.

This is a trail rider. The clothing is new, clean, tidy, protective but . . . to the uninitiated she looks more like a space robot than a young lady with a deep concern for and love of the countryside. (D. Giles)

These are green lane riders. Their clothing is also clean, tidy and protective, but they look like people enjoying recreation in the countryside, not an alien threat to its future. (D. Giles)

The earliest motorcyclists in Britain revelled in the challenge of the open road. They sought out steep roads, long roads, the most difficult roads they could find, to test themselves and their machines. Many competitions were devised, but the annals of those early years are full, not only of competition success, but of the joy of conquering a lone hill, or of a long ride along difficult roads.

Trail riding is certainly not a new pastime in Britain. However the Japanese industry has created the trail bike and made it a very desirable commodity to own. Having been tempted into buying one, the new owner then asks where can he ride his trail bike. Where are the trails, the green lanes of Britain?

Trail riding in England and Wales is limited to public rights of way. You cannot ride open moorland, fields or woodland. Understanding public rights of way is straightforward enough. The beginner can easily aquire the basics. To go beyond the basics is another matter entirely and I shall make no attempt to cover more than the most rudimentary points here.

First buy an Ordnance Survey map of the area you wish to ride. The best maps for trail riding are the 1:50 000 scale maps, which usually have a pink cover. These are readily available from bookshops and newsagents. Various classes of rights of way are shown in red on these maps. The different classes are detailed in the map

key. Of the different types of rights of way, you can definitely ride "byways open to all traffic" and you can usually ride "Roads Used as Public Paths '(RUPPs)'. These two classes carry vehicular rights by the way in which they were established in each county. Some counties got RUPPs wrong so beware. You cannot ride on footpaths nor can you ride on bridleways, which are the other two classes of public rights of way.

There are exceptions to this simple classification. Some RUPPs have been closed by the magistrates' court to all vehicles. Some bridleways and some footpaths have been proven to have public vehicular rights of way. The beginner should steer clear of both bridleways and footpaths, unless he has consulted an expert on the individual lane to be ridden. The experts in Britain are the Trail Riders Fellowship, the national watchdog on all matters relating to green lanes. If you are going to take trail riding seriously, you will have to join the TRF.

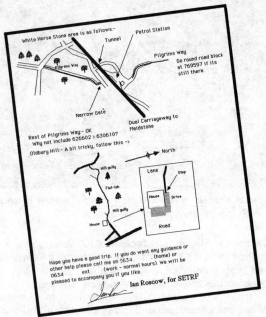

In addition to the rights of way shown on the Ordnance Survey map there is a considerable mileage of untarmaced County Roads. The map shows many tracks as uncoloured (white) roads or as a series of black dashes. Some, but definitely NOT all, of these are public County Roads which you can ride. Many are private roads which you have no right to ride. The way to find out which are public County Roads is to visit the County Roads Department of the County Council. Telephone them in advance. Explain what you want to do and make an appointment. When you get to County Hall you can mark up your copy of the Ordnance Survey map from the Department's six inch or two and a half inch maps. It will take more than a day to mark all the County Roads in a County. An alternative is to contact your local Trail Riders Fellowship group who will have sets of Ordnance Survey maps marked with Byways, RUPPs and County Roads, from which you can mark up your own maps. With your maps accurately marked, you can be sure you have a legal right to be where you are, provided you read the map correctly.

If I am challenged on a green lane, I stop and state my case clearly and calmly. I usually find that I am better

Honda's view of the all-purpose bike. This is the 600cc V-twin "Transalp" – an interesting concept. (R. Marston)

informed than anyone who challenges me on rights of way. I explain that I am on a legal public right of way and that I have every right to be there. If my challenger is too stubborn or too aggressive to listen to me, I ask for his name and address and withdraw gracefully. I see no point in forcing my way through if he is determined to stop me. I do not wish to run the risk of criminal assault charges being brought against me. Any challenge should be followed up with a letter to the County Council. They are usually only too willing to follow up unlawful obstructions. Start at the top. Write to the Chief Executive of the County Council. He can then delegate to the appropriate Council officer.

Beware of signs. Signs are all too often misleading. It is much better to rely on your map. Do not be put off by incorrect signs. Signposting is improving, and you can help by reporting incorrect signs to the County Council.

Mark your maps up accurately and ride with confidence.

I started riding green lanes nearly twenty years ago on an NSU Quickly moped. I graduated to a Honda CB125, a Yamaha 350 twin and then, reluctantly, to a series of Japanese "trail" bikes. All these have provided enjoyment and many miles of green laning.

There is a subtle difference between "green laning" and "trail riding", and an insidious shift all too often takes place from one to the other.

"Green laning" is what everyone used to do. In the old days, twenty years ago, we used to potter down the old, unmetalled roads on our, perhaps lightly modified, road bikes. Converting a road bike to green lane specification entailed fitting Trials Universal tyres, the equivalent for a motorcycle of Land Rover tyres on a car. Some riders did not even go this far. The bike we rode on green lanes was also the bike we rode to work every day. Some of us would take the same bike on holiday abroad. Minor roads in France and Spain were still "green", but tackled by the locals in a family saloon car as a matter of course. The

"ordinary road" in much of Europe was a green road, untarmaced. It would amaze me, not where I could go on a bike, but where Europeans went in their cars.

"Trail Riding" is taking over. It requires specialist machinery to make light work of obstacle after obstacle, any one of which would have a green laner fighting for breath. The trail rider flies over mud, rocks, wash-outs with his long travel suspension, lightweight frame and specially tuned engine. He sees little but the next pothole. If he is to complete his planned route in the planned time he must hurry. He needs his specialist bike. The old green lane bike just won't make the grade.

I often stop and wonder which I am – a green laner or a trail rider. I know which I want to be, but is a compromise possible. Can you be a green laner and ride a trail bike? As I rode up to the campsite, I began to wonder whether "trail riding" had taken over completely from "green laning".

I knew I was in the company of trail riders, rather than green laners when my 120 mile tarmac ride with tent and gear piled on the pillion seat was regarded as an eccentricity by my companions. Their bikes travelled on trailers. (Is this why they are called trail bikes?) They "camped" in a guest house for our camping weekend.

It seems we are all undergoing this subtle change from green laner to trail rider. I use a trailer myself in winter for starting points more than fifty miles from my home. I stayed in a guest house on my last "camping" weekend.

Many would say it is silly to handicap yourself with a road bike on green lanes, but I argue that green lanes are roads and should be ridden by road bikes. I would not insist that everyone rode a giant heavyweight machine, but green lane bikes should be seen to be road bikes.

When a petrol tank is designed to hold enough for one lap of an enduro race, when we don't ride our bikes on tarmac because they will wear out too quickly (Some, I hear, need a rebore after 2000 miles!), when our bikes look like (or are) competition machines, with loud paintwork, competition number plates and tyres stamped "not for highway use", we should all stop and think. We should think not just about what we are doing, but what other people who see us think we are doing.

If manufacturers brought out a trail bike that looked like a road bike rather than a motorcross racer, would I be the only buyer? There is a little bit of engineering and an awful lot of styling which distinguishes a roadster from a trailster. Unfortunately, the major manufacturers tailor their designs to meet the current styling fashions rather than as a practical, go anywhere means of transport, and as the years go on, this seems to be more and more the case.

The ideal motorcycle should be a machine for ALL roads, civilised enough for the tarmac main roads, tough enough for the unmetalled roads which are, in fact, in the majority in the world. The overall weight, power, fuel consumption, suspension and reliability would need to cope with all conditions. Such a vehicle is possible, but it has yet to be put into production.

Chapter Three

In The Beginning

My passion for green lanes started when I went to university.

I was looking forward to three years studying at Birmingham Universty. I had been up to have a look around. I had sorted out accommodation. Then I heard my school examination results. I just could not believe I had done so well! With results as good as those, I had to try for a place at Cambridge.

And I made it! I read for the Engineering Tripos at St Catharine's College, Cambridge.

The experience changed my life completely. University graduates are different to other people. It is not surprising. Three years at the start of adulthood, surrounded by hundreds of other spoilt brats with nothing much to do but enjoy themselves, is bound to alter your perspective of the world.

I did work hard at Cambridge, and I also tried to take part in as much as I could. It was three years not to be

These days there are Wheels Parks in most large towns, where youngsters can learn the basics of machine control in a safe environment.

For details of Wheels Parks, contact your local Road Safety Officer.

wasted. I joined lots of clubs and went to all sorts of lectures from Buddhism to industrial management. I tried hard at rowing in an eight, I went to see weird foreign films, dressed up in clothes mother would not approve, I enjoyed myself.

Rules at Cambridge were called tradition, and were enforced because they were old as much as because they were relevant. All students were required to wear flowing black gowns for meals and tutorial sessions. Engineers were excused gowns at lectures, because they might become entangled in the machinery. This was a marvellous confidence trick by the Engineering Department, since a lecture in Engineering was no more hazardous and no more exciting than a lecture in Law or Geography.

You were not allowed to walk on the college lawns as an undergraduate. The fine was six shillings and eight pence per step. Running across the grass could prove expensive. Once you had graduated, you were allowed on the lawns for free. At the bun fight after the graduation ceremony we joyfully walked back and forth on the hallowed turf, mentally clocking up the cost of such an activity if we had tried it before graduation.

All these petty rules were anachronistic fun. They made you feel different to other universities run on a more logical basis. But there was one rule that came hard to me. There was one regulation which was too much for an enthusiastic young motorcyclist. The only transport you were allowed was a pedal cycle! Student cars and motorcycles were banned within a twenty mile radius of the city.

This was a big blow to me. I was looking forward to riding my aged and decaying Velocette 500 around the city and making excursions into the surrounding countryside. It was one of the first Venoms made, replacing the MSS model in 1956. It leaked oil rather too much and had lost much of its performance, thanks to my clumsy maintenance, but it made a lovely noise and was quite an eye catcher.

Unfortunately this massive lump of polished alloy, chrome and black paint could not readily be disguised as a pedal cycle. Nor, with its unique style of fishtail silencer and beautifully distinctive exhaust note, could I hope to escape being identified by the University's private police force, called the Bulldogs.

There were two loopholes in the vehicle regulations. One was to join a college team or sporting club, when you were allowed a motor vehicle to transport you to training sessions and so on. However I was not really good enough at sport to quality for this. The other loophole was to find digs on the outskirts of Cambridge, where you were too far away, so the Bulldogs reasoned, to be able to cycle in each day. Then they would allow you a moped. Great! This was it!

No it wasn't. I secured digs as far away as possible, but they were not far enough. The only way I was to get even a moped up to Cambridge was through a club. I opted to join the Cambridge University Automobile Club, feigning a passion for car rallies, and so, at last, gained permission to ride a moped.

(To be fair, the car club was good fun. I enjoyed rally navigation in night time events, and marshalling at the club's annual sprint at Snetterton gave me the chance of a couple of laps of the circuit on the ancient Velo.)

The moped I brought to Cambridge was five pounds worth of NSU Quickly. The NSU Quickly was very sophisticated for its day. The top of the range model had a three-speed, hand-change gear box, rear swinging arm suspension and a dual seat. Mine was the two-speed model with no rear suspension and a solo saddle. How I longed for a three-speed model, as my two speeder struggled to maintain its maximum of 22 mph on the flat fen roads around Cambridge.

The brakes and front suspension, common to all Quickly models, were interesting. The rear brake worked by pedalling backwards. Once the technique was acquired, the rear wheel could be locked even on dry tarmac. The rear brake was very effective. The front brake was conventionally operated from the right handlebar lever but did little to slow the moped down. When the front brake was applied, the leading link front forks would try to climb up and over the front wheel. Both brakes therefore required some expertise. Stopping an NSU Quickly was interesting to say the least.

I was restricted to a moped at Cambridge University. It was on this two-speed NSU Quickly that I first discovered the joys of green lanes.

It was shortly after acquiring my moped that I first heard about trail riding. An article in a motorcycle paper told me of the fun that could be had on green roads. It told me that green roads were shown on Ordnance Survey maps under the bizarre title of Roads Used as Public Paths, marked as a string of red T's across the map. There was a new club for green road riders called the Trail Riders Fellowship. I decided that I would like to give this a try.

Accompanied by Walter on his trusty Suzuki 50 and armed with the Ordnance Survey Tourist Map of Cambridge, I headed for the Gog Magog Hills, south east of the city, where the map showed a long string of red T's indicating a green road. The great adventure had begun!

Twenty two mph on the road on an NSU Quickly is really boring, but 5 mph on the Gog Magog green lane was terrifyingly exciting. The front wheel chattered over loose stones. The front suspension banged against the bump stops in each pothole. The handlebars jerked and writhed in my grip. The rear wheel felt like a wooden cartwheel, jolting me from the saddle. My feet were bounced from the pedals and I coasted to a halt, almost totally out of control. This was great!

Regular practice over the next few months improved my riding technique. I tried standing up like trials riders do to gain better balance and control. However, standing on the pedals put too much weight on the gearbox bearings which howled loudly in protest. Sitting down was made safer and more bearable by the purchase of a dual seat.

I didn't seem to fall off! As my confidence grew, I explored further. I found several green lanes within a few miles of Cambridge and rode them as frequently as academic work would allow. I persuaded others that this was near the ultimate in moped excitement! Walter on his Suzuki and Harry on a single speed Raleigh moped were my usual companions.

In the winter, disaster struck. We were enjoying the soft snow filled lanes, much safer than the grit and slush filled main roads, where mopedists were continually showered with filth from passing vehicles. The now white, green lanes were trodden only by rabbits, foxes and us. The snow was fun, but when the ice came this was not. The lanes froze into rock-hard ruts and battered the rear wheel of my NSU Quickly to death. The wheel hub stayed in the right place, but the rim could move an inch sideways. All the spokes had worked loose, though none had broken. The spoke threads were too badly corroded to be adjusted. Trail riding was abandoned temporarily while a replacement wheel was sought.

Spring brought salvation in the form of a giant twenty-six inch wheel to replace the shattered twenty-three inch one. The big wheel was very old, but free and came with a tyre. It was fitted post haste and trail riding resumed in slithery spring mud. With this giant back wheel it was rather like riding a penny farthing backwards. I felt very unstable and my footwork developed to an art form as I used legs to force the moped in the correct direction almost as much as the engine. The back wheel found little grip in muddy ruts, and feet on the ground gave a greater sense of security, as well as providing the main propulsion in the muddiest bits.

During the summer vacation, I worked for Rolls-Royce Aero Engine Division in Derby. Trusty Velocette took me to work each day, but I longed to explore green lanes. With money in my pocket from the four pounds ten shillings a week I earned as an undergraduate apprentice, I scanned the small advertisements in the local paper.

I spent two weeks' wages on a fifteenth-hand BSA Bantam, bought from two lads in a back street of Derby. They had tried to convert it to a chopper by buying high, wide handlebars and painting the entire bike with Dulux red and a yard brush. They had stripped the engine down, then spent all their savings getting the local bike shop to put it together for them. I bought it on condition that one of them rode it to my digs, ten miles to the north of Belper. They looked at each other doubtfully. It seemed that this would be asking a lot of the bike. But the lure of money was strong, and one brave lad volunteered. I chuffed off on the Velo and the Bantam clattered along in my wake as best it could. Having proved its ability to travel ten miles, I was happy that it was a wise investment. I parted with the cash and pointed the lad down the cobbled lane to the bus stop. All that remained was to convert the Bantam to a trail bike.

Around the standard Bantam chassis, engine and wheels, I designed my idea of a trail bike. Since I changed almost no important parts, it was purely a cosmetic job, and even that looked a bodge, but I enjoyed doing it. Aluminium mudguards were bought – much

A BSA Bantam provided the basis of my "green lane special". In standard trim it was a nice little bike.

lighter than the standard deep-valanced steel ones in the pre-plastic age. A smaller, lighter seat was fabricated from wood and foam rubber. The lights were stripped off, partly to save weight, but also because they didn't work. I bought a high level exhaust to lift the standard silencer out of the way, like the Bantam Bushman, which was then still in production.

The red, then pale yellow, then bright green, then dark red paint was stripped off. The frame was painted black. The tank was scarlet, with a rakish white stripe copied from an American magazine picture of a Suzuki trail bike. I fitted a trials tyre on the back and put the studded back tyre on the front. This, and the fitting of a much larger rear sprocket to gear the engine low enough to pull through mud was the nearest I approached to serious improvements on the basic Bantam.

The engine was left untouched. The three speed gearbox would have to cope. The suspension system, aptly referred to as "shockers" rather than shock absorbers, remained standard. My first "serious" trail bike was ready to hit the trail.

I spread out the Ordnance Survey one inch sheet 111 on the bedroom floor of my digs, searching for Roads Used as Public Paths. There didn't seem to be any. Then I noticed a little coloured square in the bottom margin of the map. It was headed "Public Rights Of Way" and showed the "Extent of available information" shaded in pink. There was a bit of pink in the bottom left hand corner and a few tiny smudges near the top right, but the rest of the square was blank. Clearly the "extent of available information" was almost zero in Derbyshire. I could not believe that this meant there were no green lanes. I tucked the map in my pocket and pointed the Bantam towards the nearest likely looking uncoloured or "white" road on the map. We had used "white" roads in a Car Club rally, so I knew they could be "interesting".

Just west of Belper, running parallel to a tarmac lane to Belper Lane End, I found what I was looking for. A muddy lane, full of loose stones scambled upwards and then levelled out into a gentle grassy track. Bantam and I reached the top, very hot and rather muddy. This was REAL trail riding! The old NSU Quickly could never have climbed up that!

The following Sunday I headed north to the moors above Sheffield, looking for more to test the green lane Bantam. The journey north was slow, since the big rear sprocket reduced the Bantam's top speed from fiftiesh to about thirty-five miles an hour, but we persevered.

Bantam and I climbed onto Beeley Moor and followed a little gravel track across the heather for half a mile between two tarmac roads. This was tame stuff. Then Hell Bank Plantation lay before the front wheel. Bare rock and loose shale slabs descended between high, dry stone walls. With a name like Hell Bank it had to be good! I had never ridden on rocks before. Come to that I had never ridden downhill before. There are no rocks and hardly any hills in Cambridgeshire. Slowly, with feet hovering an inch above the ground in case of a slip, I worked my way down the lane. I realise now, just how easy this lane really was, but, at the time, it was a great challenge and I felt elated when I reached the bottom unscathed.

In Birchill Bank Wood I met another trail rider! This was the first one I had ever seen. I kept reading bits in *Motor Cycle News* about trail riding, and John Ebbrell's articles in *The Motor Cycle* were an inspiration, but I had been puzzled that no-one else seemed to be out in the lanes. This chap was on a proper trials bike and made my Bantam bodge-up look very amateurish. What is more he could ride standing on the footrests, something I still lacked the confidence to try. He greeted me cheerfully, warned me of a muddy stream crossing ahead and was off. Still, he did exist. I was not the only one trail riding. And if he could ride through the muddy stream, so could I.

Twenty minutes later, after the muddy stream crossing, I called it a day and headed south again. This was my last weekend in Derby. I was to spend the rest of the summer holiday at my parents' home in Northamptonshire.

The lightweight Bantam coped well with Cambridgeshire clay. You could always get off and push when it got really muddy.

My older brother was a road racer. He won races, first on a Bantam racer, later on a 650 Triumph production bike. He was pretty good. Where I couldn't go round corners on a pedal cycle, he flew along the road like Mike Hailwood. Brother's practice course was called Banbury Lane, which ran to the south of our home in Litchborough for miles and miles through the quiet Northampton countryside.

I discovered later that Banbury Lane is part of an ancient road called the Jurassic Way which ran from Lincoln, via Stamford, Northampton, Banbury, Stow-on-the-Wold and Bath to Glastonbury. Most of the Jurassic Way is now followed by modern tarmac roads, but just south of Moreton Pinkney it is still a green lane. A school friend of mine from Moreton Pinkney knew of the Banbury Lane as the old drovers' road bringing sheep to market in Northampton. It was certainly the main road between Banbury and Northampton in medieval times.

One very hot August morning, I set out to explore the green lane part of Banbury Lane. There are two green sections. One is very short, a couple of hundred yards of rutted grass. The other is long – over three miles of hedged green lane. Northamptonshire is a very fertile country. Wild flowers grow in profusion on the quieter lanes. Banbury Lane was so quiet that the wild flowers had taken over. I rode through a jungle of nettles and cow parsley, towering above me. The Bantam's oil leaks were plastered over with grass seeds. The handlebars and footrests were strewn with knapweed and bindweed. I was drowning in sweat. I stopped at a tiny clearing by a farm gate in the hedge, leaned the Bantam against the gate post (the centre stand had been removed for lightness) and peeled off jacket, helmet and gloves.

This was the first and the only time I ever saw a signpost saying "Green Lane". There had been no signs at the start of either of the green bits of Banbury Lane, but here, halfway along Banbury Lane, pointing through the gateway and across the meadows was a cast iron, green-painted fingerpost with white lettering announcing "Green Lane to Moreton Pinkney". I expect this was where my school friend's family had herded their animals to join the drove road to market in Northampton in years gone by. It would have been a long walk and Banbury Lane must have been alive with animals on a market day. Now, they loaded them into a cattle truck and drove them to market and were home again in time for tea.

I wondered what the Banbury Lane must have been like in the old days. I found a book tucked away in a secondhand shop and bought it for a few pence. *The Roadmender* by Michael Fairless is a fascinating observation of what is now social history. My copy was the twenty-fifth impression, dated 1910. It gives an insight into country life in southern Britain around the start of this century. The poet Fairless took on the job of roadmender for a year and declared that he had "attained his ideal!"

The job of roadmender was about the lowest paid, meanest job anyone could have. For a few pence each week the roadmender sat by the roadside with a pile of stones and a hammer. One by one he would break the stones into small pieces and then use the broken stones to fill the potholes in his stretch of road. Roads were quiet then. They carried mainly local traffic. Long distance travel, before the motor car, was by railway. The lot of the

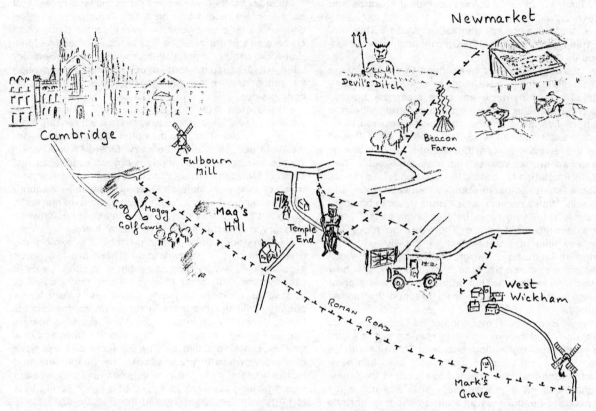

Sketch map of the first Cambridge University Motor Cycle Club green lane ride. I led a very motley crew from the university city to Newmarket.

roadmender was a solitary one which may well have suited a contemplative poet like Fairless. It did not suit others who described it as hammering your heart out for a bit of bread and a pipe of tobacco.

Roadmending was one step better than the workhouse. The workhouse was the worst fear of all poor folk at the turn of the century. I recall my own parents talking of it with loathing. Before the days of a state pension, if you were too old to work on the land, and your children could not afford to keep you, then you trudged off to the workhouse to end your days. Fairless recounts with poignant detail the old folk he encountered who walked his stretch of road on the one-way journey to the workhouse.

He also tells of happier times, when the road was a whirl of dust as, throughout a long hot day, animals were driven to the Cattle Fair in the main market town. He describes the drover and his lad in dusty blue coats driving a flock of sheep. Then a herd of bullocks, going unwillingly with lowered heads and wild eyes, as if they knew they were bound for the slaughterhouse. Then ''a squadron of sleek, well-fed cart-horses, formed in fours, with straw braid in mane and tail''. These were the pride of the farms, but were being replaced by steam traction at the time Fairless wrote. Strings of shaggy young horses, as yet unbroken, were driven by young boys along the white road. As the dust settled, a line of carts followed, carrying pigs, chickens, geese and ducks. Then all was quiet again as evening came on.

Was this the scene on Banbury Lane a few years ago. To look at it now, wild and overgrown, it would not seem possible, but for perhaps seven hundred years Banbury Lane carried the traffic Fairless describes, each market day, bound for the hungry town of Northampton.

The unequal battle between my buzzing Bantam and the wild undergrowth scarcely conjured up images of placid days gone by, when the green lanes were disturbed only occasionally by the passage of a farm wagon, creaking along at walking pace. Clear the lane of undergrowth, though, and Bantam and I would potter along as gently as any dog cart in the old days. On that hot August Sunday, covered in dust, grass seeds, goose grass and perspiration, I was glad to head home for an iced drink and an evening relaxing in the cool of our cottage garden.

Back at Cambridge, the new term saw the re-forming of the University Motorcycle Club. This had been defunct since the Second World War. Before the war there had been annual inter-university motorcycle competitions between Oxford and Cambridge, much like the annual boat race which is still held. The Cambridge University Motorcycle Club had once thrived among the ivory towers of academe, and a handful of enthusiasts were determined to revive it.

I was lucky enough to be in at the start, not wholly because the Club met in the pub behind my College. We established our credentials with the University authorities, elected a committee and wondered what to do next.

Obviously, said I, the first official event should be a green lane run. I was unanimously delegated to lead it!

So the first motorcycle event I had ever organised came to pass. One bright morning, at the start of the Gog

Riding in line astern, a typical trail riding group potters down a quiet green lane. (A. Kind)

Magog road, a gaggle of motorcyclists gathered to do battle with the Cambridgeshire terrain. Gordon rode a Yamaha 125 commuter bike, complete with leg shields. There was a heavy looking Norton twin, whose proud owner was determined that it could do anything and go anywhere, simply because it was a Norton. There was a Bridgestone two-stroke twin, a rare and powerful machine produced by the giant Japanese tyre manufacturer. And there was me on the Bantam.

We rode in line astern, south-eastwards down the road the Romans had used. We reached the first crossroads without mishap. Then Gordon decided this was all a bit tame and set his Yamaha to climb a grassy bank in the lane, diagonally. He fell off, of course, but got to his feet with a laugh. He pressed the electric starter button on his bike and the engine purred back to life.

The Bridgestone was fast and light, and easily kept pace with my Bantam on the dry, bumpy going, but the Norton was proving a bit of a handful. Gordon and the Norton owner were holding their own competition to see who fell off the most times.

Just before Horseheath the road gets very muddy. I waited for the others to catch up, then showed them the way through. This was no trouble at all for the Bantam with its grippy trials tyre. The Bridgestone could find little traction and came through mainly sideways with some pushing. Gordon's Yamaha came on with great style, but stuck halfway across and needed pushing out. We manhandled the Norton round the edge of the mud with a dead engine. It was not worth trying to ride it through. Looking back, this all seems quite ludicrous. How could one patch of mud cause us so much trouble? But it undoubtedly did, and it made the rest of the outing that much more of an adventure, because we had made it through the mud.

We turned north, through Balsham and a green lane behind West Wratting Grange. The others were gaining confidence now, and we sailed serenely along this one. At the end of the lane, my throttle jammed wide open and the nipple came off the clutch cable. With engine pulling maximum revs and no way of disengaging the drive, I aimed at the bank, trying to avoid plummeting into the tarmac road ahead. Fortunately the Bantam stalled. Thank heaven for gutless, under-powered two-stroke engines!

After much consultation, the throttle cable was unjammed and a solderless nipple was found to repair the clutch cable. This was the only breakdown of the day. Everybody else's bikes were in fine fettle. The Bantam really was a heap. It was amazing that it kept going.

We rode the Street Way and the lane from Bungalow Hill at right angles to it. These were the lanes that had destroyed the rear wheel on the NSU Quickly last winter. The ruts were just as hard this time, but dry rather than frozen.

The final lane was the Beacon Course which would take us to the outskirts of Newmarket. The start began as a jumbled mess of bumps and ruts, baked rock hard, which had even the Bridgestone struggling. While the others throttled back and took it slowly, I attacked the bumps on the Bantam and bounced victoriously onto smoother ground. It was not a stylish manoeuvre, but my determination not to let the lane beat me was an indication of what was to come in future years.

They held a second green lane ride the following year, but by then I had graduated from University and was working in London. The Bantam had gone, and was replaced by a string of Japanese road bikes, all of which sampled a few green lanes, as well as taking me thousands of road miles throughout Britain and Europe.

This was how I began trail riding. I daresay it is not dissimilar to the antics of many others as they start to explore our national network of green lanes for the first time. Perhaps the rest of this book will give some guidance to make the entry of others to the select band of green lane cognoscenti smoother than was my own.

Chapter Four

The Great Ridgeway

After my time at Cambridge, I took up a job with a firm of chemical engineering contractors in central London. Central London may not seem the most suitable place to pursue a hobby like trail riding. It isn't.

I enjoyed London, I liked the anonimity of the crowded streets, the excitement of the cosmopolitan variety of people from all over the world jostling for places in the queues that were everywhere. You queued for the bus, you queued for the tube, you queued for lunch, you queued for the cinema.

I liked the museums and the art galleries. There may be better displays of treasure in other parts of the world, but I have seen nothing better than those in London. The treasure houses of continental Europe have given me nothing compared with the paintings and sculptures of the Tate Gallery or the magnificent collections of the Nationary Gallery. Nowhere have I seen paintings so well displayed. You can really relax and drink them in.

Of course the Mecca for a graduate of engineering is the Science Museum. I have spent days there. It has so much to offer of man's ingenuity. There is the staggeringly detailed collection of ship models, some carved by French prisoners of the Napoleonic wars, others the original models used to design the full size ships in Britain's dockyards. Then there is the collection of giant stationary engines from the dawn of the Industrial Revolution, the selection of historic transport, the civil and chemical engineering galleries.

The two high spots of any visit are at opposite ends of the Science Museum. In the basement is the Children's Gallery. This is essential for all visitors. It is packed with things for you to do. There is a whole galaxy of scientific conjuring tricks for you to perform. There seem to be new ones every time I visit.

In the attic is the collection of historic aircraft from Bleriot to Concorde. Full size aircraft buzz around your head in every direction above the cases of models and mock up cockpits.

London's chief ingredients are people and noise. The background traffic noise passes unnoticed after a while, but it worried me at times. Nowhere in the streets of London could I hear the sound of my own feet on the pavement. My footfall was lost amidst millions of others. It made me feel too insignificant.

The rush of cars and taxis and buses and taxis and taxis became the norm, but the exhaust fumes took

In the winter, lush grass can conceal a treacherous layer of very wet mud. Concentration is essential. (A. Kind)

longer to get used to.

At least once every month I tried to escape. The parks of London were a great help, but they were not the real countryside. I would ride south-east to find the Pilgrim's Way, meandering quietly under the trees beside green fields. Best of all, I would go west to find the Great Ridgeway striding across the hilltops of the chalk downlands. Here you can forget the noise and the crowds and enjoy space and fresh air.

The Great Ridgeway, which curves in a huge arc from the extreme edge of London's sprawl, round the rim of Salisbury Plain and finally dips its toes into the sea at Dorset, is without any question THE DEFINITIVE Green Road.

Everyone interested in ancient roads should travel the Great Ridgeway at least once in their lifetime. Its sense of history is overpowering. Despite the surrounding modernity of ever-increasing prairie farming, the Ridgeway

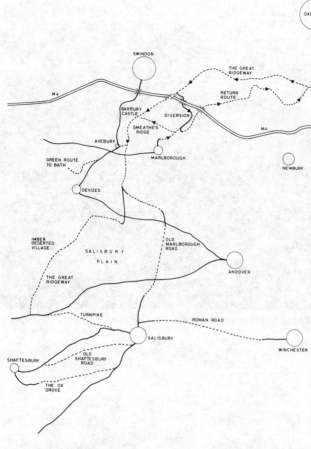

Map of the Great Ridgeway and linking road networks.

oozes antiquity from every pore of its surface. It seems immortal, interminable and yet it is totally fragile. It is a mere scratch across a chalky landscape which could be wiped away by one large plough.

The Ridgeway Long Distance Path was created in the early 1970s. It is now heavily waymarked and much tramped. Even more, it is much picnicked upon and MUCH fought over. For years and years the Ridgeway has been the battleground of recreation in the countryside. Throughout the nation, walker and motorcyclist co-exist and rarely upset each other, but the Ridgeway is a flashpoint between them. The Ramblers Association want it for a footpath alone. They seek a Ridgeway exclusively for ramblers. The Trail Riders Fellowship see the loss of the Ridgeway as the beginning of the end for their hard-won network of green lanes. If they cannot save the Ridgeway, what can they save?

A geological map of England does much to reveal the ancient importance of the Ridgeway. The high chalk ridges provided the earliest settlers with dry routeways away from the heavy clay of the valleys. In the south-east, the North and South Downs provided communications which linked up with the great chalk plateau of Salisbury Plain. Running along the northern and eastern edges of the Plain as a prehistoric orbital motorway ran the Ridgeway, which also joined up to a chalk ridge routeway, the Icknield Way, running north-east into East Anglia, the best agricultural land in pre-Roman Britain. The whole civilisation of prehistoric South and East Britain was based on roads along the chalk ridges, and the main road was the Great Ridgeway.

Despite its status as a long distance path, I would not like to walk the Ridgeway. There is not enough up and down. I like the challenge of a hill to climb every now and then. The Ridgeway provides an endless undulating trudge. You rarely seem to get to the top of anything significant, and the road always stretches endlessly on ahead. I admire anyone with the tenacity to walk the entire length. The views are much less spectacular than one might anticipate. The Ridgeway shelters just beyond the north facing scarp slope and misses the panorama to the north for too long for my liking. On a bike you can put up with the lack of landscape because you know you will soon come to something more interesting, but at the toiling pace of a long distance walk it must be dreary at times.

There are various ways to ride the Ridgeway. The most usual is to start at the London end and ride west, returning home at the end of the day on modern roads. I got to know the Ridgeway best when I lived halfway along it for two years. I would ride east or west from my central starting point as the mood took me. The last time I rode it was from Avebury going eastwards and then returning west on a parallel green lane route south of the Ridgeway. Although all the fuss concentrates on the Ridgeway, there is a tremendous network of surviving green lanes to the south which provides, in many ways, better riding than the Ridgeway itself.

Suppose we opt for the most popular approach and start at Streatley, north-west of Reading, in Berkshire. Here the River Thames carves a gap in the chalk uplands which must be crossed. This is the eastern end of the true Great Ridgeway. You can pick out a green route further east. I did link the Ridgeway up, on the map at least, with green lanes as far as the Pilgrim's Way in Kent and then down to Dover. The Long Distance Path goes north-east from Streatley in the direction taken by the Icknield Way. Part of the Icknield Way is still a green road and can be ridden.

But we intend to ride west not east.

Just north of Streatley, The Great Ridgeway climbs out of the Thames Valley past Thurle Grange and onto Thurle Down. After a steady climb of two miles, the top of the chalk downland is reached. Here it soon becomes

Summer scene on the Ridgeway. The cars parked in the background mark where a tarmac road crosses. (D. Giles)

apparent that the Ridgeway is only part of a network of green lanes. Turnings to the left, turnings to the right, all invite you to follow them. Careful map reading is required to avoid taking the wrong turning, although LDP status means that the route is liberally sprinkled with acorn signs in wood or concrete to guide the mapless walker.

There is not much to see at the Roman temple on Lowbury Hill, but it is a good viewpoint on a clear day and worth a slight detour. On Compton Downs the Ridgeway crosses over the Didcot to Newbury railway. The railway engineers forced a diversion on the road travellers to fit in with where they built their bridge. The railway has been long gone, only the bare trackbed remains, but the diverted Ridgeway continues to be used. Roads have outlasted railroads.

Go south-west over Compton Downs, turn right at the crossroads and go north-west across Several Down. You can then go straight across the A34 on Gore Hill and just ride and ride and ride.

Lower down the chalk scarp, running parallel to the Ridgeway, you can pick up scraps of earth bank. This is Grim's Ditch, a Saxon boundary marker extending for miles along the lower slopes of the chalk, used to fix the edge of a Saxon chieftain's territory. Although a substantial earthwork this was never intended as a rival to Hadrian's Wall. Perhaps it did carry a wooden pallisade, but it was never garrisoned in the way the Romans garrisoned their Wall across the North of England. Grim's Ditch was a border, telling travellers that they were now entering ''foreign'' territory.

There is a second scarp slope below the high chalk scarp which carries the Ridgeway. On the lip of this second scarp the Icknield Way from Cambridgeshire parallels the Great Ridgeway westwards at least as far as Wantage. This paralleling of routes is not uncommon. The lower road would provide richer grazing in summer than the drier soil higher up, but would become thick with

This stretch is naturally surfaced with flints. Note how wide the road is between the wire fences. This width was important when herds of cattle were driven to London's markets before the railways took over. (D. Giles)

Green crossroads on the Ridgeway. The wooden signpost shows the waymarked Long Distance Path and distances to landmarks. (D. Giles)

heavy mud in the winter. The higher road would give an all-year round road, while the lower road provided a drover's "summerway", as it became known. Beyond Wantage the B4507 hugs the base of the chalk escarpment until it turns off for the high market at Old Swindon above the modern industrial town. The B4507 was once the Icknield Way and the "summerway" for drovers using the Ridgeway in the seventeenth and eighteenth centuries.

Sandwiched between the Icknield Way and the Ridgeway, south of the village of Harwell, is the Atomic Energy Authority's Research Establishment. This sprawl of blank buildings is hemmed in on every side by green lanes. It would be a good place to work if you were an expert in atomic energy and a trail rider! If not, then you'd best hurry past in case you get irradiated!

Clumps of beech trees sprout along the ridge top, perhaps planted to give cover for foxes in this wide open hunting country. If the foxes have nowhere to go to earth, they cannot offer much sport, so the theory goes. I think these beech spinneys may obscure older hilltop adornments. All too often I have found the man-made hillock of a burial chamber beneath the tall beeches. Whether these monuments were deliberately hidden by the planting of the trees, I cannot say, but it seems to occur too often to be mere coincidence.

After miles without sight of a tarmac road, the Ridgeway crosses the B4494 Newbury road. Continue straight on along the ridge. In a mile turn left to pass by Whitehouse Farm and reach the A338. Here there is a staggered junction. Go right and then left to bypass Angeldown Farm and come up to Segsbury Camp.

Segsbury is the least impressive of the Ridgeway hillforts. Its site is too level and its ramparts too low to dominate the surrounding countryside in the way of the forts further west. These hillforts, built in the Iron Age,

are thought to be tribal centres rather than settled villages. Clearly they were inhabited by a part of the local population, and usually by a local chieftain, but most of his followers must have lived in lesser enclosures in the surrounding countryside, retreating to the chieftain's stronghold in times of danger.

Excavation has shown that many of the hillforts were taken by storm at various times in history. The Romans captured many by direct assault during their conquest of the south of Britain, while others surrendered to them without a struggle. Some forts were re-used after the Roman era, providing safe haven for both Saxon and Viking in their struggle for the kingdom of England.

The old green road continues on, between thin hawthorn hedges and barbed wire fencing. Beyond Rats Hill the view to the north improves. The Devil's Punchbowl is worth a detour on foot, if you have the time for such a diversion. This will depend very much on the time of year of your Ridgeway ride. In the short days of winter, struggling with the phenominally slippery chalk mud of these parts as well as the ruts and long deep puddles for which the Ridgeway has become all too notorious, you will probably decide to push on. But in the long, lazy summer, with dry but dusty going underfoot, a stroll round the natural scoop in the hillside that is named after the Devil would provide a welcome break from trying to navigate rock hard ruts.

The next section marks a significant chapter in the modern battle for use of the Ridgeway. This was the part that was closed to recreational vehicles for an experimental period in 1975.

Here would be a good point to pause and look at the chronology of the war of words between the lobbyists and between politicians, but hardly ever between folk actually on the Ridgeway itself.

In September 1973, the Countryside Commission designated the Great Ridgeway as part of their Ridgeway Long Distance Path. Their publicity leaflet of the time declared that "from Overton Hill . . . to Streatley the Ridgeway Path provides a continuous right of way for walkers, cyclists and horse riders." This was true, but the omission of the equally continuous rights for motorcyclists to use the Ridgeway was deliberate.

In the winter the Ridgeway becomes surfaced with a thin layer of very slippery chalk mud.

April 1974 saw the reorganisation of county boundaries. This moved much of the Berkshire Ridgeway into Oxfordshire. For the first time Oxfordshire County Council could have a say in the Ridgeway's affairs. They did not waste time.

November 1974: Oxfordshire proposes a temporary ban on the two mile stretch of Ridgeway between Woolstone Hill Road and Pigstrough Bottom.

June 1975: Oxfordshire County Council conduct a survey of Ridgeway users. I was stopped and quizzed by a surveyor at the end of June. Her questions showed the future intent behind them quite clearly: "Did I use the Ridgeway in the winter?" (They were looking for at least a summertime ban.) "Did I object to vehicles using the Ridgeway?" (One of the main aims of the survey was to establish a public dislike of vehicular use.)

The Council's Planning Officer confirmed my interpretation of the survey, though not quite in the same words, when I wrote to him. He also emphasised the erosion caused by vehicular use.

July 1975: The temporary van on vehicles is imposed for two months. A thousand objections were sent in to this closure, mainly by motorcyclists. I photographed the Ridgeway surface before and after the ban, looking for signs of recovery of the surface. I found no such signs, since the surface was being damaged by massive agricultural vehicles, not by motorcycles or private cars. Agricultural vehicles were exempt from the temporary ban!

May 1976: Oxfordshire announce proposals for a permanent ban on their part of the Ridgeway.

The Inspector's report on the temporary ban made nonsense of a permanent ban. He concluded that the Ridgeway "is suitable for use by persons on horseback and on foot. Owing to its width of 37 feet at its narrowest part, I do not regard it as specially so; it is however specially suitable for those who are trail riders and indeed this is the only kind of road which is suitable for such recreation as trail riding. Compared with the facilities available to walkers, trail riders have few routes suitable for their recreation and they are becoming fewer. The same problem may arise so far as horse riders are concerned if bridleways continue to be degraded to footpaths. It is not in my opinion expedient to make the Order."

All was quiet for a while.

January 1978: The Countryside Commission undertake a National Green Lane Survey.

June 1978: House of Lords debates the Ridgeway and finds no reason for action against recreational vehicles.

June 1979: The National Green Lane Survey is published, showing scant evidence of conflict between walkers and motorcyclists, but concern over the neglect and loss of green lanes in some parts of the country. No evidence was found of surface damage by recreational vehicles. Surface damage to green roads is caused by agricultural vehicles, which get bigger, heavier and more powerful every year. If one of these monsters gets stuck in mud it carves the most enormous holes in the ground when it extricates itself. Surface erosion by recreational vehicles was dropped from the argument for closing the Ridgeway after the National Green Lane Survey was published.

July 1979: The Ramblers' Association offer a secret deal to the Trail Riders Fellowship: close the Ridgeway in exchange for support for a new Wildlife and Countryside Bill governing rights of way. Deal rejected.

December 1979: Countryside Commission announce proposal for traffic ban on the whole Ridgeway. They are bombarded with objections from vehicular users.

July 1980: Countryside Commission make formal application for a Traffic Regulation Order to ban all vehicles.

September 1980: Wiltshire County Council officially oppose the Countryside Commission's application.

November 1980: Countryside Commission postpone their application for a Traffic Regulation Order.

July 1981: Countryside Commission appoint a Ridgeway warden, except for Wiltshire.

February 1982: Trail Riders Fellowship put forward a voluntary restraint on vehicular use on Sundays from May to October, when there is the heaviest use by walkers.

September 1982: Wiltshire put forward a Traffic Regulation Order on their bit of the Ridgeway. This was the result of a militant group within the Council. The full County Council rejects the proposal.

January 1983: Countryside Commission officially abandon the idea of a total ban on recreational vehicles following their warden's report on the effect of the period of voluntary restraint. Voluntary restraint agreed for the following summer on the same basis as before – Sundays and Bank Holidays from May to October.

May 1984: Report on voluntary restraint shows that motorcycle use fell by 54% from 1982 figures. Now 2% of total use – "a very small number of vehicles."

June 1984: Countryside Commission ask Berkshire, Wiltshire and Oxfordshire to put forward Traffic Regulation Orders for Sundays from May to October. In consequence, the Trail Riders Fellowship refuses to accept voluntary restraint for 1984.

October 1984: Rider fined for riding Ridgeway, a public road, without tax and insurance. Ramblers publicise this as a reason to close the Ridgeway to vehicles.

November 1984: Remembrance Sunday invasion of Ridgeway by motorcyclists. A day to be regretted by all who fight to keep the Ridgeway open.

June 1985: Berkshire propose a permanent ban on vehicles. Wiltshire refuses to apply for a Traffic Regulation Order.

October 1985: Berkshire do not fix a date for a Public Enquiry about their vehicular ban. The *Sunday Times* features the Ridgeway and emphasises the enormous waste of public money on surveys and proposed traffic bans over the years.

October 1986: Having failed to persuade the Counties to apply for Traffic Regulation Orders, the Countryside Commission makes its own application.

Oxfordshire County Council publish a new *Ridgeway Guide* which again ignores vehicular rights. Price 50p.

The saga continues. Who knows how long the pressure to close will continue and how long the motorcyclists' resolve to fight will last? By the time you read this the Ridgeway may be lost.

Blowingstone Hill is the start of the best bit of Ridgeway. If you want to see the Blowing Stone itself, you must drop off the ridge to the village of Kingston Lisle where the stone is mounted in a wall. It is thought to have been a sort of warning trumpet, but I cannot make it give a sound of any sort.

Back on the ridge, the wide, rutted green way continues in a sweeping arc over Ram's Hill to reveal Uffington Castle moulded into the hillside. Stop here, if it is not overrun by day trippers. On a clear autumn morning it is the most marvellous viewpoint. A vast panorama of English Countryside stretches northwards across the Vale of White Horse, the upper Thames valley to the dreamy spires of Oxford – university, town and motor city.

The banks and ditches of Uffington Castle are well worth exploring on foot, especially the steep north facing side. Seeing how high and steep the banks are now, they must have been formidable in their prime, topped with a palisade and defended fiercely.

You can walk down the hillside to the Uffington White Horse. There are many carvings in the chalk hillside throughout Wessex. Most are relatively modern, but this one is the original. Its strange outline has something of Modern Art about it. It is mentioned in documents at Abingdon Abbey in the twelfth century and gave its name to the Vale of White Horse at the time of the Domesday Book, in the reign of William the Conqueror. The chalk outline, cut into the steep turf hillside, is 365 feet long from ear to tail tip, and 130 feet high. It is enormous. It is shown on gold coins of the Iron Age and on the metal rim of the Marlborough Bucket in Devizes Museum. It is at least as old as Uffington Castle, if not older still.

The Horse has been maintained by regular cleaning down the centuries. Since at least the seventeenth century, there has been a festival to celebrate the Scouring of the Horse every seven years. Now this duty has been taken from the local villagers and the maintenance of the Horse is by the Government. You will probably find it fenced off.

Just beyond the Castle, a tarmac lane drops down the hillside. Go down and have a look at the peculiar little Dragon Hill and see if you can make any sense of its earthworks. You will need to go north as far as Uffington village before you can be far enough away to look back and obtain a true idea of the shape of the White Horse. The further away you go the more impressive the Horse becomes. It overawes the surrounding country, and must have been a powerful symbol of ancient tribal dominance. I used to see it every day from my classroom window in Highworth, seven miles away, unless it was raining hard, or snowing.

Just along the Ridgeway again is Wayland's Smithy. This is a massive, Neolithic, long barrow. The entrance is guarded by giant slabs of uncut boulder, and the barrow stretches for an amazing distance through a clump of towering beech trees. For real atmosphere, you should visit the Smithy late on a misty evening. Then remember the legend that gave it its strange name. Wayland the Smith is reputed to have made the shoes for the White Horse here, and any traveller whose horse casts a shoe has only to leave a silver coin on the capstone of the Smithy overnight to find his animal mysteriously shod again. Wayland was a pre-Christian deity popular among Berkshire tribes before Christianisation.

The Smithy has been excavated. It is said to be a splendid example of a type of burial chamber found from here to the Cotswolds. Burial chamber it may be, a common type at that, but I still see it as the home of the metalworking god. I wonder if he is any good at mending footrests, bent by the hard, summer ruts?

This stretch of Ridgeway, as far as the inn on Fox Hill is a popular route for sponsored walks. It is a shattering experience to encounter one of these vast armies of jolly young folk, after miles of solitude. I remember "helping" with one organised by my school in Highworth. The other teachers manned checkpoints, feeding stations and watering holes along the route. The school minibus cruised the Icknield Way below the scarp to pick up the exhausted and blistered drop-outs. I was to be course opening and closing vehicle, buzzing along the ridge on my little Suzuki roadster. However, just beyond the Smithy, I met a couple of friends who were out for a gentle ride and had been brought to a halt by our horde of schoolchildren. One of my friends, a long-retired engineer, I knew as a collector of vintage motorcycles. I had been privileged to sample a Scott, a Velocette and a delightful two-stroke Levis along the farm track behind his house only a few days before. He was on the Ridgeway on a Villiers-engined Greeves and urged me to try it. While pleading the importance of my marshalling duties, I allowed myself to be persuaded and pottered off down a quiet green lane southwards away from the crowds.

The Villiers engine was smooth and powerful after my Japanese bike. There seemed nothing it would not pull through with hardly any revs. The suspension was amazing. I was used to bouncing over the smallest stone on my undamped, over-stiff "shock absorbers" and short travel telescopic front forks, but the leading link forks of the Greeves noticed nothing. They coped effortlessly, even when driven across the ruts, something I would not dare to try on the Suzuki. When you put on the brakes, the front end of the Greeves came up to meet you! After my initial shock, this could be seen as a much better idea than the nose dive of telescopic forks. Why has no-one developed the leading link fork arrangement further?

I reluctantly returned the Greeves to its owner, and bounced off on the Suzuki after the last of the weary walkers, fast disappearing into the sunset.

The sponsored walk ended at the inn on Fox Hill. At the foot of Fox Hill the Ridgeway crosses the Ermin Way, a main Roman road, hurtling north-west to the important Roman town of Cirencester. The Ridgeway loses the scarp edge here and becomes a tarmac road for four miles, passing below the towering ramparts of Liddington Castle, another Iron Age hill fort.

Near Chiseldon Camp, the Ridgeway leaves the tarmac once more, but the next mile or so is miserable. The well-drained scarp is lost in a confusion of spurs to the south, and the Ridgeway struggles across flat, wet ground. Ruts are dug deep into the mud by heavy farm vehicles through the winter. The sides of the ruts dry hard in the summer but leave mud in the bottom of each wheel track. Clinging, heavy gunge traps you in ruts at least a foot wide and usually over a foot deep. This is not a pretty part of the Ridgeway. It is hard slog all the way to Barbury Castle.

There is a nice detour to avoid the mud if you turn left at the crossroads with the Ermin Way. Follow the Roman road south-east under the M4 motorway, then turn south on a green road from Peaks Downs to Aldbourne. This takes you to the heart of the village, alongside the church. Aldbourne was famed for its bell foundry for two centuries, but this closed in 1824.

Once you leave the Great Ridgeway, the roads become much greener. (D. Giles)

South of the village, take the tarmac Stock Lane past Lewisham Castle and pick up the green lanes again to Whiteshard Bottom. The name Stock Lane implies that this was a diversion used in the great droving days of the Ridgeway, when herds of cattle and flocks of sheep, grazing on the hoof on their way east to the markets of London, would also take a detour to avoid the muddy stretch of Ridgeway.

Lewisham Castle, a Norman motte and bailey this time, not an Iron Age stronghold, was occupied by the troops of Louis, the Dauphin, heir to the French throne, in 1215.

Whiteshard Bottom is an important crossroads of green lanes. With careful navigation you can pick up the road northwards to Ogbourne St George, where you cross another Roman road heading for Cirencester.

From Ogbourne St George you climb up to the Ridgeway along Smeathe's Ridge. This is a fresh, breezy ride along a grassy whale's back of chalk, with a fine view to the north of industrial Swindon. Not being the Ridgeway, Smeathe's Ridge is not a mess of deep ruts, and provides excellent going. It is very exposed, rather too fresh and breezy at times. A walk along here in February, with the frozen hard wind gnawing and snatching at your clothes, is something to be endured more than enjoyed.

The green road through Barbury Castle is closed to vehicles. The castle is now a "Country Park". This sounds great. It rings of the parkland that surrounds so many of our stately homes in Britain. But it is a deception. It really means Country (Car) Park – an area of hardstanding with a neat wooden fence, litter bins, and maps and signposts to show you how to cover the two hundred yards from the car park to the hill fort.

This sounds a harsh judgement on an amenity which has undoubtedly improved the general public's access to the countryside. But I remember Barbury Castle before it became a Country Park. I remember riding the green lane through the gap in the great earth ramparts and entering the vast enclosure within the castle – green and empty, but still echoing with the voices of its past.

No carts and wagons rumble through the courtyard now as they did in ancient times. Children play on the battlements and grown-ups picnic on the grass. It is a beautiful spot for a family outing, but the disappearance of the road through the castle has taken away some of its obvious significance, and the Country Car Park has destroyed much of the lonely magic of the place.

Go north on the tarmac road from the car park to pick up the Ridgeway running west below the banks of Barbury Castle. In the fields to your right, in 556 AD, was fought the battle of Beran Byrig, when, the West Saxons decisively defeated the Britons in a fierce engagement to take over another part of our island and drive the Britons further westwards. Beran Byrig has become Beranburh on the Ordnance Survey map, and has been further corrupted to give Barbury its name.

On Hackpen Hill, the Ridgeway swings southwards in a four mile arc, following the curve of the high ground. On the lower land below, it is again paralleled by a summer way, now part of the A361 from Swindon to Devizes. But for a three mile stretch the summer way is green, though almost invisible under modern cultivation.

In a swirling tumble of downs, scattered about like driftwood on a stormy beach, lie hundreds of Grey Wethers, stranded sandstone slabs on chalky slopes stretching away in every direction. "Wether" is an antique word for sheep. On a murky day it is very difficult to tell from a distance which grey lump in the field is a sheep and which is a stone. It was here that the great, unhewn blocks were found to build Wayland's Smithy. Did the White Horse pull them across the downs from this stone field?

The biggest stones were hauled, heaven knows how, to dance on their toes in a circle at Avebury. The pick of the crop form the main circle of Stonehenge. Here, the massive stones have been chipped to a regular shape by hand, and great stone lintels have been placed across their tops, held in place by mortice and tennon type joints more suited to carpentry than architecture.

Through the middle of the fields of Grey Wethers, also known as Sarsen stones, ran the old main road from London to Bath. Where this road crosses the Ridgeway, its surface changes from faint ruts in the open downland to a fenced, well-used dirt road. It runs west from the Ridgeway into the very centre of the great circle of stones at Avebury.

Samuel Pepys, the famous diarist, travelled this road on his return to London from a holiday "taking the waters" at Bath. I quote from his Diary of 15th June 1668 describing his coach journey from Bath to Marlborough:

"In the afternoon came to Avebury where seeing great stones like those of Stonehenge standing up I stopped and a countryman showed me a place trenched in like Old Sarum almost, with great stone pitched in it some bigger than those at Stonehenge in figure to my great admiration and he told me that most people of learning coming by do come and view and that the King did so.

"I did give this man one shilling. So took coach again. But about a mile on it was prodigious to see how full the downes are of great stones and all along the valley stones of considerable bigness, most of them growing certainly out of the ground so thick as to cover the ground, which makes me think less of Stonehenge for hence they might undoubtedly supply themselves with stones as well as those at Avebury. In my way did give to the poor and menders of the highway three shillings."

Avebury is THE place to end a trip into Wessex. In 1648, John Aubrey declared that the ancient monument of Avebury "did as much excell Stonehenge as a cathedral does a parish church". Sir John Betjeman thought Avebury was the place where British architecture began.

The great henge monument of Avebury is the largest of its kind in Europe, covering an area of twenty-eight and a half acres and enclosing most of the present village, with the Saxon church just outside its bank and ditch. The site is surrounded by a huge earthwork with a deep ditch on its inside face. Entrances pierced the bank from the north, south, east and west. Inside the ditch stands the Great Circle of sarsen stones, the largest one weighing over forty tons. Within the fourteen hundred foot diameter Great Circle are the remains of two other circles, known as the Central and South Circles.

Avebury remains an impressive and timeless spectacle, despite the attention of centuries of weather and stone-robbers. A medievel stone-robber was crushed beneath a falling sarsen. His remains can be seen in the little museum near the church. Some of the stones were removed to add to Stonehenge. Although the first stages of Stonehenge are as old as Avebury, about 2600 BC, Stonehenge came to predominate as the centuries rolled forwards.

While Avebury fills me with awe, it does less for other people. Bill proved a good riding companion and a great one for bringing me back to the ordinary world. When we stopped for a snack on the bank overlooking the Great Circle and I gazed in wonder at the ritual significance of the monument before me, Bill thought it would make a great trials course. He wondered if the standing stones were the forerunners of modern plastic cones, since he was convinced that this had once been used as a test centre for learner chariot drivers!

Avebury was, in fact, part of a larger monument. From its southern entrance runs an avenue of pairs of standing stones which march across the fields for a mile to the top of Overton Hill. Here they reach the site of The Sanctuary, now isolated from its stone avenue by the busy A4 trunk road. There used to be a stone circle at the Sanctuary, too, but it was destroyed in the nineteenth century. The Sanctuary is probably much older even than Avebury.

The Sanctuary is back on the Ridgeway, and opposite the Ridgeway Cafe, a monument to modern transport services. The cafe is also a popular place to finish a ride along the Ridgeway, perhaps after the detour to Avebury.

There is one more prehistoric site, less than a mile west from the Ridgeway Cafe. Silbury Hill is the largest man-made mound in Europe. It is 130 feet high and covers an area of five acres. It dates from the same era as the Avebury circles, but no-one knows what it was for. It is not a burial mound. Perhaps it served some ritual purpose. Perhaps it was used in astronomy. We do not know. It remains a mystery.

The Ridgeway continues south, but loses much of its excitement until it rises once more to a chalk scarp, skirting the northern edge of Salisbury Plain.

Either at Avebury or at the Ridgeway Cafe, you will pause and decide what to do next.

If you have travelled this far in the winter, you will be exhausted by the wet, muddy, slippery going, you will feel a great sense of achievement, and you will be fit for little except to collapse into a hot bath. You will also have run out of daylight, so it will be time to make your way home in the dark.

If it is the summer, then you will be eager for more to explore. There are several attractive alternatives,

Experienced green laners carry tyre patches and a bicycle pump. A puncture is the commonest breakdown and can leave you marooned in the countryside unless you go prepared. (D. Giles)

depending in part on where you live and which way you must travel home when you finally decide it is too dark to go on any further. I give three alternative route sketches below, together with some grid reference numbers on the Ordnance Survey maps.

1. Go West

You can pick up a few more miles of the high chalk on your way to Bath, Bristol or South Wales. Take the Devizes road, the A361, and turn off through a farm gate onto the green stuff at 057674. Go past Baltic Farm and take the loop to Roundway 013640. A splendid finish to the day can be had by riding Heddington Steps 007640 to 981663. There is an easy route down the steps and a difficult/impossible route. Take your pick. You will see what I mean when you get there.

2. Go South

Continue south along the course of the Ridgeway as far as you can, then turn onto the tremendous network of green lanes that radiate from Salisbury across Salisbury Plain.

The Ridgeway goes from 120671 to 115638, then you round the foot of Knap Hill from 115638 to 127624.

Once you are south of the A342 on the Ordnance Survey 1:50000 map sheet 184, the choice seems limitless.

Try the Old Marlborough Road 203536 to 188447.

There is more of the Ridgeway. Half a dozen green lanes climb south onto the rim of Salisbury Plain, then you circle the army firing ranges to Joan a Gore's Cross at 009509. A largely green route can be plotted west from here to the Westbury White Horse. The Ridgeway goes south west from Joan a Gore's Cross to Heytesbury, but it crosses forbidden army land around the deserted village of Imber.

Imber is in the middle of a battlefield. It may not be visited except by permission of the Ministry of Defence. The tarmac Ridgeway through Imber is open to traffic on Bank Holidays, unless there are military exercises taking place. When the army evicted the villagers in 1943, they promised that they would be allowed to return, but they never have. The houses have been blown up many times over, now. The shell of the church still stands, but the old houses have long been replaced by concrete facades, used for training troops in street fighting.

You can go round the Imber ranges on the tarmac roads and pick up another stretch of green Ridgeway from Tytherington, but it would be more enjoyable to head south and east into the great maze of old roads that cross the chalk plain to the city of Salisbury.

3. Go East

A string of green lanes can be used south of and more or less parallel to the Ridgeway to take you back to the starting point of the day's ride at Streatley. If you take this route, you will wonder why you bothered with the

Winter mud needs grippy tyres. These "universal" pattern tyres are a good compromise for all year use on the Ridgeway. In deep mud a larger block tread can give better traction, and cause less surface damage by reducing the wheel's tendency to spin and dig in.
(J. Higgin)

Ridgeway in the first place, since this route is quieter, green and altogether more enjoyable, although of lesser historical significance.

Take the main road to Marlborough, then the A345 northwards to Ogbourne Maizey.
187716 over Poulton Downs to Whiteshard Bottom (again) and on to Stock Lane.
241733 Ewin's Hill to 264754 Aldbourne.
281781 Baydon, through Lambourn to 390802 Fawley.
393813 to 423820 Farnborough.
437819 to 473789 Stanmore.
483787 over Shrill Down to 509819 then north of the Roman temple to finish along the Fair Mile at Kingstanding Hill 573837 on the A417, just north of Streatley where the Ridgeway ride started.

From Streatley to Avebury along the Ridgeway is about forty-five miles, including about four miles of tarmac. This is not bad for a single green lane. From Avebury the alternative routes listed can give you as many more miles as you want. There are so many green lanes between the Ridgeway and Salisbury that you are totally spoilt for choice. Long may it remain so.

The Ridgeway Route

The following is a brief summary of the route of the Great

Ridgeway to help you plot it out on the Ordnance Survey maps. Recommended maps are the 1:50000 series sheets 174 and 173, and if you plan to go further, sheet 184.

589814 On the A417 just north of Streatley, sheet 174.
508818 Turn left from south-west to north-est above East Isley.
490833 Cross A34 Newbury to Oxford road.
417841 Cross B4494 Newbury to Wantage road.
300862 Uffington Castle and White Horse.
281853 Wayland's Smithy.
274843 Cross B4000 Lambourn road.
232814 Fox Hill Inn. Start of tarmac section of Ridgeway.

183784 to 159768 Muddy section of Ridgeway.
Or take diversion:
263790 to 264758 to Aldbourne.
238738 Stock Lane to 203743 Ogbourne St George.
192746 Smeathe's Ridge to 157759 Barbury Castle Country Park.
End of diversion.
159768 Ridgeway.
128747 White Horse on Hackpen Hill.
125708 Turn right for Avebury on the old Great West Road.
103699 Avebury.
100685 Silbury Hill. (Not on a green lane but well worth a look.)
118680 The Sanctuary and the Ridgeway Cafe.

Chapter Five

Wales

Within fifty miles of Bristol, Birmingham or Liverpool lies a foreign country, whose inhabitants speak another language and who feel themselves, in every way, to be a separate nation. Despite fifteen centuries of pressure from the English, and of the eventual union between England and Wales hundreds of years ago, the Welshness of the Welsh is still so distinct that an Englishman can feel as much a foreigner in Wales as he can in France or Spain.

Wales is physically different from its English neighbour. The landscape changes at the border. Wales is always hilly, remote, and, especially in the north, usually mountainous.

The oldest rocks in Wales are in Anglesey in the far north-west. Pushed up against these is the wild, twisted jumble of peaks and sharp-edged ridges of Snowdonia. Beneath the craggy tops are the remnants of the once wealthy slate quarries. Today they are a mixture of modern machinery still hammering away at the mountainside and deserted ghost villages where the quarrymen of old once dwelt. Roads tremble beneath the giant wheels of dumper trucks thundering to and from the working quarries, or are silent and grass-grown, empty of the twice-daily trudge of working men's feet. Rusty, corrugated iron covers the working plant, while stone grey, roofless houses mark the passing of the old families of quarrymen.

South of Machynlleth, the mountains are rounded and green. The centre of Wales is empty of everything but sheep and green hills. This area has never seen industry. Throughout history it has never had a population of more than a few herdsmen. The wide, wind-whipped, wet hilltops are the great desert of Wales.

Tucked away in the centre of this bleak wilderness is one of the great centres of Welsh culture. The Cistercian Abbey of Strata Florida (its name means "the way of the flowers") was at the heart of sheep farming in central Wales. It was a commercial centre. But it is also the burial place of Dafydd ap Gwilym, the greatest of all Welsh poets. It was at Strata Florida that the monks worked their lives away, copying the poetry, the chronicles, the romances that enabled Welsh literature to survive the Dark Ages. It is to the monks of Strata Florida that we are indebted for the richness of the modern Welsh culture.

Today the hills are changing. Afforestation is covering

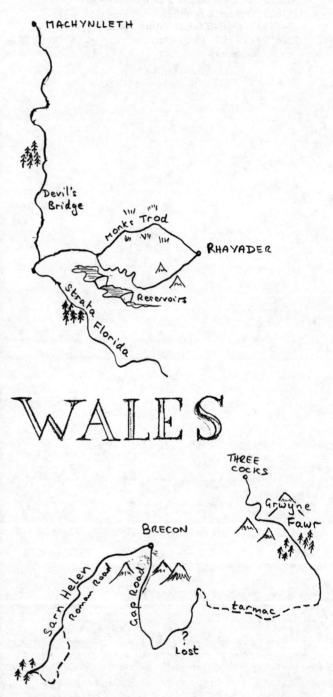

Map showing the Welsh Green Lanes described. There are lots more.

the sheep walks. The creeping conifer plantations are spreading like a dark disease over the open spaces of central Wales. First comes the heavy machinery – giant tractors deep ploughing to break up the subsoil – earth movers to build the ubiquitous, Forestry Commission, dirt roads. Then come the trees. The scenery is buried beneath hectares and square kilometres of pinewood – pulp trees, grown to feed the paper mills and the chipboard factories.

Much of mid-Wales is still wide open and dramatic. Green roads, built by the monks, still thread their way to the ruins of Strata Florida. The really wild area is quite small, and steadily shrinking. Its edges merge into lower, gentler ground – west to the Welsh coast and east into England. Stone walls bound ploughed fields, and crops are grown in the milder lowland climate.

South lie the Black Mountains and the Brecon Beacons – a rampart of wild, lonely Wales before the bowl of the South Wales coalfields. Beyond the rampart are the narrow valleys of terraced houses below the black spoil heaps and the tall winding towers at the pitheads of Wales' wealth. In these valleys live and work two thirds of the country's population. At the end of each street rise the steep moorland foothills that beckon northwards towards the mountains.

The Welsh trace their ancestry to the pre-Roman inhabitants of these islands, the Celts. The Celts were a race of aristocratic warriors. Their lives revolved around fighting and raiding. They loved nothing better than to listen to the bards tell of their bravery in battle. They fought with sword, shield and chariot, all beautifully covered with the flowing designs of their decorative art. They were great story-tellers, generous, quick-tempered, friendly, honouring the smiths who made their weapons and the bards who sang their praises.

The religious leaders of the Celts were the Druids and North Wales was a centre of the Druidic faith. Young men were sent to Anglesey from all over the Celtic lands, from Britain and even from distant Gaul to study religion, history, philosophy and poetry. However, Tacitus wrote of the dark side of the Druids. He described how they "smeared alters with blood from their prisoners and sought the will of the gods by exploring the entrails of men."

The Roman armies destroyed the Druids in Anglesey. They occupied Wales and enmeshed it in a web of forts and roads. When they left and the Dark Ages began, the Welsh emerged as the race which survived. Under the Romans, England and Wales were inhabited by Celtic tribes – the British. In England, the British were overwhelmed by waves of invaders from Europe. Only in the West – in Wales and in Cornwall (known for centuries as West Wales) did the native Britons hold out. They were pressed on all sides. From the north came the Picts. From Ireland came the Scotti in their skin boats. In the east the Saxons threatened.

The structure of Britain at the end of the Dark Ages indicates the success of the Welsh resistance. England is the land of the Anglo-Saxons, fighting to hold off the next set of invaders, the Vikings. The Anglo-Saxon English had slowly forced the ancient Britons further and further west into the mountains of Wales. It was the Anglo-Saxon word "wealas", a foreigner, which gave the Welsh their new name in place of their former name of Britons. The Anglo-Saxon king of Mercia, King Offa, built a boundary

ditch from top to bottom of Wales. Offa's Dyke marked the boundary between Wales and England.

Then, in 1066, that most memorable date in history, the Normans came. They came to Wales, bit by bit, spreading westwards under the almost independent Marcher Lords. These "warlords" were given immense freedom of action by the Norman Kings of England in an effort to control the border between England and the wild Welsh.

The struggle between England and Wales continued down the centuries. Sometimes the Welsh, under a dynamic leader, seemed to be winning, but the English were always stronger in the end.

The Wars of the Roses ended, for the Welsh, in a great victory. Henry Tudor, the new King of England, was a Welshman. Far from England conquering Wales, the Welsh felt that they had at last conquered England. In 1536 the Act of Union between England and Wales became law. Henry VIII was ruler of a United Kingdom.

This brief sketch of Welsh history gives a reason to the separateness of Wales, but the feeling of being in a foreign country is due to the survival of the Welsh language. To the Englishman, Welsh is mysterious and unpronounceable, seeming to consist entirely of consonants. It is no more difficult than French or German, but few Englishmen take the trouble to learn it. Pronunciation is eased by a few simple rules, which enables you to make a stab at most place names.

"W" and "y" are vowels, usually. "W" is pronounced like "oo" in school. "Y" is not quite so easy. It is usually "ee" in words of one syllable, but in some cases it can be a short "i".

There are some strange consonants: "dd" is the same as "th" in English; "ph" is "f"; "f" is always "v"; "ch" is the same as in the Scottish "loch" or the German "Nacht".

Lastly there is "ll" which has no English equivalent. The advice of Wynford Vaughan-Thomas to aspiring Welsh speakers is straightforward and I repeat it here. "Put the tip of your tongue against your upper gums and breathe out. If you can place the tongue on the right side of the mouth so much the better. One curious statistic unearthed by the experts shows that two-thirds of the population of Wales pronounce the "ll" through the right side of the mouth."

Try "Machynlleth" and "Grwyne Fawr". If you can pronounce those, then you are in with a chance of riding green lanes in Wales!

It was to Wales that I rode to learn about riding in a group. The Bristol branch of the TRF had been going for about a year, but I had never been on one of their major outings. They had planned a weekend in mid-Wales and I was to join them for a taste of Welsh trail riding.

I had always preferred the extra challenge of riding green lanes on a road bike. My Yamaha 350 twin had toured several laps of Europe before being equipped with a trials pattern rear tyre for green lane mud. Unfortunately, all the Bristol group riders used "proper" trail bikes, and I felt obliged to copy them. A second Yamaha was added to the stable. This was a DT175 single, allegedly the best trail bike on the market at the time. It went well and went just about anywhere.

The new bike was tried on several local outings before being loaded up with camping gear and setting off for mid-Wales.

The road journey seemed long, but the sun kept

"Proper" trail bikes at the start of a green lane run. Are they called trail bikes because they travel so far on trailers?

shining and I pressed on to the campsite at Rhayader. There were quite a few riders already established on site when I arrived in the late evening. There seemed to be no site office. There was a wooden garden shed by the entrance to the site, but this was locked up. I learnt from a fellow camper that the old gentleman who collected the money would be round in the morning and that I should put my tent up where I liked.

The Rhayader Municipal Campsite is a water meadow between the main A470 road and the young River Wye. I pitched my well travelled, Black's *Good Companion* tent by the river. The tent had once been a deep orange-brown, but was much faded by Mediterranean sun to an interesting shade of beige, stained with a variety of things too numerous to mention.

On the town side of the camping ground I found a park and children's playground – swings, slide, see-saw. Beyond this, a footpath climbed into the town past one of the countless public houses. Rhayader is a market town and has need to serve the thirst of the surrounding farmers on market days. Amidst the ale houses I came upon a fish and chip shop and queued to buy my evening meal. As the evening cooled in the gathering dusk, I munched my way back to the campsite. I brewed a cup of coffee and wriggled into my sleeping bag, wondering what lay ahead of me in the morning.

Rhayader lies below the Elan valley dam, the lowest of a whole chain of dams built between 1893 and 1904, flooding the steep-sided valleys in this wild and largely uninhabited part of Wales to provide water for the West Midlands. The Elan Valley's major export is water to Birmingham. The third industry of the area, after water and sheep, is tourism. Thousands come each year to fish the lakes and rivers, to walk or ride in the lonely hills or just to sit and look.

I learned from our run organiser, Simon Northeast, that we were to ride a loop of green lanes around the Elan Valley reservoirs. After breakfast, a long line of trail bikes followed Simon westwards over the Wye and then north into the hills. There were some fifteen riders, and, as a newcomer to organised rides, I tagged along near the back so as not to be in the way.

The first lane started opposite a farm called Dderw (did you pronounce that right?) and was the ridge road to Aberystwyth, north-west of Rhayader. It also linked with an important road between the monasteries of Strata

Florida and Abbeycwmhir – the "Monks' Trod". The ridge track seemed very indistinct to me, being used to the white chalk roads of Salisbury Plain and the Great Ridgeway. Here there was barely a dip in the ground to show us the way. Simon stopped frequently to consult with his map, as we tried to pick the correct path across the open grass ridge. After much helmet scratching (You can't scratch your head while wearing a motorcycle helmet) we descended to the tarmac in just about the right place.

A couple of miles north we ignored the inviting Pont ar Elan, the bridge, and chose the wide ford across Afon Elan. You seemed to cross the river several times, each time coming out on a small, gravelly island instead of the opposite bank. The water was not deep and we all made it, at last, to the west bank.

The ford marked the start of the best green lane section of the Monks' Trod, which is arguably the most famous green lane in mid-Wales. Much of its fame among motorcyclists has been due to its use in enduro riding. For years it has formed an integral part of international cross-country motorcycle races, including the prestigious International Six Days Enduro, the top event in the enduro calendar.

The International Six Days Trial, as it used to be called, has been the ultimate test of rider and machine for decades. It began in the early days as a long distance reliability trial for teams of riders from each of the motorcycle nations of Europe. Right through to the 1950s, it continued to be contested by what were basically road-going motorcycles, only slightly modified from the standard model range offered for sale by the leading mass producers of the day. Triumph, BSA, Matchless, Norton, provided bikes for British teams in the various classes.

David Miles, a regular member of British ISDT teams in the post-war years, described the preparations for his entry in the 1949 event in mid-Wales. He used his 1947 Triumph Tiger 100 as his ride to work machine, so felt the need for quite "extensive" preparation. The engine and gearbox were stripped and rebuilt. An air filter, a crankcase guard and a shorter rear mudguard, to aid rear wheel removal in case of a puncture, were fitted. An

Green lane riding on a road bike can be great fun. The author tackles a ford on his CB125 Honda.

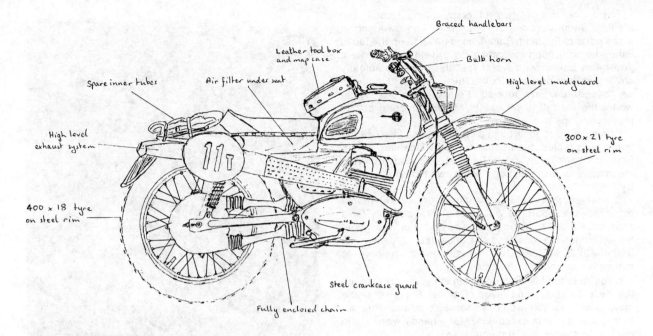

Braced handlebars

Leather tool box and map case

Bulb horn

Spare inner tubes

Air filter under seat

High level mudguard

High level exhaust system

300 x 21 tyre on steel rim

400 x 18 tyre on steel rim

Steel crankcase guard

Fully enclosed chain

1966 International Six Days Trial. This very-special-purpose MZ was used by the East German national team to win the post-war equivalent of the early reliability trial.

extra toolbox was mounted on the frame with a spare spark plug holder holding two plugs mounted on it. New tyres, chain and cables were fitted. In other words, there were lots of new parts and careful preparation, but no expensive or special competition equipment.

Captain Miles collided with another rider's fallen machine on the second of the six days, and had to repair a puncture during the final day's speed test, but still managed to collect a bronze award.

The 1950 ISDT, again held in Wales, saw the introduction of a night section and thus the need for full lighting on all machines. In this event, Captain Miles was part of an army team with BSA Gold Star machines provided by the BSA factory. In this year 32 British, one Swedish and two Dutch riders won gold medals, all mounted on British machines. Great Britain won the Trophy, the Vase and three Manufacturers' Team awards (AJS, Ariel and Triumph).

The event is now the International Six Days Enduro, not Trial. The bikes are special enduro bikes these days, though replicas can still be bought over the counter. The basic ingredients have changed little. Riders have to cover about 1200 miles of the roughest country the organising nation can obtain. That means riding two hundred miles each day, and that is not all. There are about a dozen checkpoints each day, where you must arrive at precisely the right time. If you clock in early, you lose bonus points. If you are more than three minutes late, you lose one mark for each minute late and your Gold Medal. To win a Gold Medal you must finish the six days without loss of marks and with at least 500 bonus points. In addition to the timed cross country sections, there are special tests each day. These could be a scrambles race, a speed test on a tarmac circuit, a hill climb, an acceleration test, and so on.

All in all, I was glad we were just trail riding. Perhaps, one day, I would be good enough to enter the ISDE, but it

would take an awful lot of practice in lesser enduros before I was anywhere near proficient.

Meanwhile Simon Northeast, on his ageing silver Honda XL250 Motorsport, was quietly disappearing over the horizon. He was riding steadily, not fast, but the two or three of us at the back of the line of fifteen riders seemed to be falling further and further behind. I didn't really mind. I was in no hurry. But it was hard not having time to even draw breath when Simon stopped to let us catch up. No sooner had we joined him than he was off again. He managed a five minute breather every ten minutes, while we seemed to be riding almost non-stop.

The bogs slowed everyone down. I had never ridden across a bog before I went to Wales. I had walked across many a bog, but never ridden across one.

Bog walking is easy, if you can see where you are going. Foggy bog walking is definitely not recommended and can land you literally up to your neck in trouble. On a clear day, when you can see the far side of the bog, you are usually safe on foot. Bright green marks the wettest and most treacherous bits of bog. Soft, bottomless heaps of bright green sphagnum moss hold gallons of water and will swallow you up if you stand on them. Stiff dry stalks of grey-white grass are also bad news, but not as bad as bright green moss. The grass grows in tussocks a foot or more high, surrounded by black peaty slime. If you can stride from tussock to tussock – bog hopping – then you can cross safely. The best thing is to look for heather or, better still, short, sheep-cropped grass. This provides firm safe going and can withstand even the weight of a motorcycle.

Bogs occur wherever drainage is poor and the water lacks calcium to neutralise the acids liberated by dead plants. Plants which grow in these waterlogged conditions do not decompose properly when they die, because lack of oxygen prevents bacteria from acting on them. So large quantities of dead plant material build up.

There are three types of bog: valley, raised and blanket. Small versions of valley bogs can be found in many parts of England. Raised bogs develop on the top of valley bogs through the continued growth of bog moss. The moss can grow several feet thick and completely cover a stream or a small lake. This is how quaking bogs or "quagmires" are formed. Blanket bogs are found where the rainfall is very high. A thick covering of bog moss develops everywhere.

I am sure we rode through all three types of bog during that day in Wales, but I could not tell which was which. From the back of the group I was able to study different techniques for crossing bogs, while I waited for my turn to try.

It seemed that the intertwined layers of sphagnum moss would support the weight of a bike, but only for a short time. If you rode too slowly you and your bike would break through the moss and sink knee deep into the mire. It then took at least two, usually more, helpers to extricate you and your machine.

If you rode too fast, you could smash your way through the delicate supporting layer of moss. The bike would nose dive and you would somersault through the air before landing with a squelch. Many hands were again needed to rescue you and your bike.

Ideally you should ride through at just the right speed, with a steady throttle opening, since sudden acceleration or braking could send you into the slime. Careful balance was needed to keep the weight on either wheel just right, feeling for that sinking feeling.

After a few bogs, even the novice bog riders began to realise what they were aiming for in technique, and even the experts got stuck at least once. You just cannot always be sure of what the right speed is for a particular piece of ground.

One clear message came across. Do not follow someone else's wheeltracks through bog. They have got through, but they will have weakened the bonds between the moss, and if you follow them you will surely sink.

Another message is equally clear. Bogs are tender ecological environments and can be badly damaged by over-use. They recover in a matter of weeks, but if you come across bog already churned by a previous party, perhaps it would be better to find somewhere else to ride for the day.

When the monks came through here they put down stone slabs to help them across the boggy bits. These are generally well below the present surface of the bog and not much help to modern traffic, but it shows how important the road was in the old days.

Beyond the boggiest bit of all, on Esgair Hengae, we came to a hard surfaced, dirt road. This continued westwards as the Monks' Trod, becoming tarmac by the Tefei Pools, a series of small lakes in this high, desolate spot. The Tefei Pools were stocked with fish by the monks of Strata Florida. John Leland visited the abbey in the 1530s and remarked on the landscape, treeless as far as the eye can see, consisting of frost shattered rock, moorland peat and rough pasture. He also remarked on the excellence of the trout and eels from Llyn Hir, Llyn Teifi and the other lakes of the Teifi Pools group. The Pools are still popular with modern anglers, who agree with Leland on the quality of the trout introduced by the monks.

We turned eastwards on the hard, dirt road, which

Alan Kind demonstrating that bogs can get the better of even the best riders at times. (A. Kind)

followed the northern shore of the Claerwen Reservoir. The road twisted back and forth around the flooded valleys of tributary streams for mile after mile. We wound our way, a long procession of motorcycles, between the moorland slopes above our left shoulders and the deep, black waters of the reservoir beneath our right feet.

At last we came to the dam and a tarmac road. There was just one more green lane to ride before lunch. We would take a short cut over the northern slopes of Rhosygelynen, rather than the long tarmac loop round its southern flank.

It was some shortcut!

There was a steep climb. There were bogs, of course. Then there was a long descent through a forestry plantation. The road through the forest was made of the biggest boulders I had ever seen. The lane was washed out by heavy rainfall, which had taken away the original surface. Normally, this would reveal bare rock and areas of loose scree with pockets of soil. Here, the rain must have produced an absolute torrent of a stream. The bare rock was littered, not with scree, but with large, loose rocks and with boulders bigger than bicycle wheels. And it was steep and seemed to get steeper as we went down.

Thankfully we made it to the bottom, where Simon was

holding open the gate for us to exit onto the tarmac road again. He looked tired, as if he had been holding the gate open a long time. We saw why when we realised that Simon was about ten feet away from us by the gate, but about twenty feet below us. The last little bit of the lane was a huge rock step, the whole width of the lane. Everyone was waiting and watching to see us make this last descent.

Barry, another of the back-markers, tried riding it rather timidly, toppled over and clattered to the bottom in a shower of sparks and scraped paintwork.

Keith and I, the very last two, were not a little put off by this display. Despite the audience waiting for me to perform a feat similar to Barry's, I opted to dismount and push the bike gingerly round the edge of the step and down to the safety of tarmac.

While I completed this chicken manouevre, another rider volunteered to bring Keith's bike down. He swung a leg over the saddle and, without further ado, just rode straight over the edge of the step and out to the road below. If I hadn't seen it done I would not have believed it. I was astonished. Was this the sort of skill I needed to ride green lanes? Perhaps I had best give up now.

We rode into Rhayader for lunch, glad to leave bogs and giant rock steps behind, at least for the moment. We didn't quite ride to Rhayader. We stopped just short of the high, single span bridge over the River Wye. Rhayader started on the far side of the bridge. The houses on this side of the river were in Llansantffraed-Cwmdeuddwr – a name reserved for Welsh linguists only. We reckoned we were in Rhayader, because we couldn't pronounce the name of its suburb.

The inn Simon had found for us was beautifully situated on the edge of the river. The food was said to be excellent. Unfortunately we had arrived too late to be served food, but the bar was still open. We sat outside at heavy wooden tables and supped our beer in the sunshine.

Memories of the afternoon were rather hazy. Perhaps the Welsh ale was stronger than I thought. More likely it was simply because I was at the back all the time, trying to keep up. Under these circumstances it is difficult to find time to stop and study a map, and, as the tail ender whom everyone is waiting for, it takes more nerve than I had to ask Simon to explain where we were and where we had been, while everyone else was waiting, keen to get on.

We took the "Mountain Road" from Rhayader to Devil's Bridge. This was a rigorous journey indeed in the old coaching days around 1800. Henry Skrine wrote of his state of "perpetual alarm" as he ascended the rocky road out of the town and later bemoaned the dreary, treeless expanse of open hill which he traversed in "mournful silence". The famous scientist, Michael Faraday, founder of our modern theories of electricity and magnetism, passed this way and found the road almost as depressing. Other road users who negotiated the "dreadful steep pitches and frightful precipices" were relieved to reach the single arch bridge at Blaenycm, built in 1783 by Baldwin of Bath to span the Afon Ystwyth. The Mountain Road is tarmac now, and not nearly so frightful. It must have caused the sort of alarm in nineteenth century travellers as the lane before lunch had aroused in me.

Beyond Cwmystwth, the scenery became less bleak and forbidding. Farmland replaced the peat bog and cotton grass. We threaded our way through pine

plantations to the Devil's Bridge. The Devil's Bridge is actually three bridges, one on top of the other. The first and lowest span was built by the monks of Strata Florida. To cross this involved climbing down the steep rock sides of the valley, fine for foot or hoof, but unsuitable for the wheels of later traffic. Turnpike and trunk road developments have raised the bridge and improved the access roads. You now must pay to visit the lower spans through the privately owned glen.

The Vale of Rheidol narrow gauge railway from Aberystwyth reaches its terminus at Devil's Bridge. The railway is, unusually, still run by British Rail, unlike most narrow gauge railways which are in private hands. It provides an excursion for visitors to the seaside, but is so slow, uncomfortable and smelly, when I rode it, that it could hardly be welcomed by locals as a convenient form of public transport unless they are real, dyed in the wool, steam railway enthusiasts.

We spent the afternoon getting stuck in bogs or racing endlessly along Forestry Commission tracks, trying to catch up with Simon who was trying to find the right green lane, apparently long since buried under pine trees.

After one such chase along an endless, wide dirt road, we caught up with the rest of the group. The road had just stopped. We were surrounded by trees. We learned that two riders at the head of the group had not stopped, but ridden straight on through the trees. They discovered, in a rather dramatic way, that what had been a level road contouring round the side of the tree-clad mountain had suddenly become a 1 in 5 camber covered in a deep,

This Welsh green lane runs along a stream bed filled with slippery, weed-coated rocks.

slippery layer of pine needles and packed full of trees!

One had managed to stop by jamming his bike against a tree. The other had slithered sideways down the mountain for thirty feet before finally coming to rest.

We retraced our steps and eventually found the correct old road. This ran along a stream bed, then went straight up the side of a mountain!

The stream bed was round, weed covered rocks, like smooth, football-sized pebbles. The fine, hairy weed on the rocks was incredibly slippery. Even standing up in wellington boots was difficult. We had plenty of time to study the rocks. We queued for half an hour to ride a hundred yards and climb the bank out of the stream.

The slippery stream was the easy bit. We now had to climb the mountain. It seemed to go up and up and up for ever. It was very steep and muddy and slippery. It was fine if you could keep going. If you stopped it was almost impossible to start again. The rear wheel just span round and round and pushed you nowhere.

It was a very long hill. I climbed steadily, using my feet to push the ground away. It seemed to rush up at me all the time, first from one side, then from the other. I suppose it could have been the bike falling over, rather than the ground moving. Perhaps it was the Welsh ale still playing tricks.

I passed several riders, lying, steaming by the roadside. Eventually I stopped myself, exhausted and soaked in sweat. Simon rode down, having reached the top, calling words of encouragement: "Come on, now! You're nearly halfway up!"

It was a joy to reach the top at last, to sit and rest while the remaining few struggled up the final steep section. It was too much for one chap. He gave up, a few feet from the top, threw his bike back down the mountainside and stomped off swearing loudly and colourfully. Simon, every inch the leader, calmed him down and rode his bike to the top for him, promising that the worst was now over.

He was wrong!

After a couple more bogs, we were back in the woods again. The forest plantation had destroyed the old road, which used to descend at a gentle angle down the steep slope of the mountain to the main A44 Rhayader to Aberystwyth trunk road. Close ranks of trees were planted all over the mountain, and, every two hundred yards, a deep drainage channel cut straight downhill through the road surface and at right angles to it. The road was just discernible between the trees, but crossing the drainage channels was only possible with teamwork. One rider stood in the drainage channel, the bike's wheels level with his shoulders. Two riders waited at the far side to lift up the front wheel. Two stood behind to hang on to the rear wheel. You hung on to the handlebars of your precious bike and hoped no-one would let go. There were fifteen bikes to manhandle across each drainage channel, and there were an awful lot of drainage channels.

It seemed to take hours to reach the main road. We trundled gently back to the campsite. I was very glad to see my familiar old tent again. There had been times during the day when I was convinced I would never clap eyes on civilisation again.

If this was trail riding, I had had enough.

You will gather from this that my first foray onto Welsh green lanes was not an unqualified joy!

Looking back, I can see two important contributary factors to this, apart from my own inexperience and lack of riding skill.

First, the group was too large. My day was spent chasing the other riders, rather than enjoying their company. There was never time for the back markers to catch their breath, have a chat, find out what was going on. If our leader had waited longer, the folk at the front would have spent half the day standing still, waiting for us to catch up. The solution was not to have longer stops, but to have smaller groups. Six is a good size for a group, with both the run leader and the back marker having ridden the route before.

Second, I did not know the other riders well enough. I should have tried a couple of ordinary Group Runs from Bristol before venturing to Wales. In that way I would have felt more relaxed in the company of the rest. This is an important point for anyone starting trail riding. Don't jump in at the deep end. Gain experience of your local lanes and get to know your local experts. After this, you can get far more enjoyment from the big trips away from your home base.

My next outing to Mid-Wales was in the company of several good friends. We tagged on to a date fixed by the Bristol Group, but formed our own sub-group of half a dozen for the weekend's riding.

Our party included two friends from North Devon, Mick Comber and Martin Darch. Mick was to be our Welsh expert, having been several times before. Martin was a super-reliable back marker. With Martin at the back, you were sure that no-one would be stranded alone in the Welsh desert. Roy Scrafton from Taunton had been exploring Exmoor lanes with me for some time. Like the two from North Devon, he rode the current "ultimate" trail bike, the Honda XR200, which had displaced the Yamaha DT175 as top bike. The Honda four-stroke had the advantage of less noise and better fuel economy than the DT175 two-stroke.

I too had forsaken my DT175 for a four-stroke. I had sold the Yamaha and bought another Yamaha, an XT250. This bike was to serve me long and well on green lanes throughout the country over many years.

My fellow sufferers at the back of the previous outing, Barry and Keith from Bristol, joined us. The more relaxed atmosphere of a group of friends out for a weekend, rather than an "Official Organised Group" appealed to them as it did to me.

We rode south from Rhayader on a back road which became a green lane and crossed the River Elan at Glyn Ford. Once again the smooth, rounded rocks of the stream bed were as slippery as could be, coated with a thin layer of green weed. Most Mid-Welsh stream beds seemed to be like this, unlike the clean, gritty stones of English West Country fords.

We turned off before the chapel at Llanwrthwl and rode into one of the emptiest bits of the empty centre of Wales. We climbed steadily along a good green road and then out to the open hills. The only landmarks on the map were cairns, but the track lay clear before us. Wheel ruts, etched into the soil by the centuries, were grass grown but distinct.

The feeling of space and freedom was immense. We were alone in a primaeval wilderness untainted by modern man. Our motorcycle time machines had transported us from the twentieth century to a far simpler,

Enjoying the morning scenery in the moorland heart of Wales.

Pedal cycling on green lanes is growing in popularity. The author uses a standard 10-speed racing cycle. Others prefer the purpose-built mountain bike.

less cluttered time. We all stopped to savour the morning, each with his own thoughts.

Far away behind us were the civilised fields of the Wye valley, busily growing food for a busy nation. Here there were only acres and acres of moorland grass, the feeding ground of meadow pippits and the souring skylark.

How I wished for a SILENT motorcycle. Only now, with our engines switched off, could we hear the lonely birds filling the landscape with their song. The skylark never seems to pause for breath. He flies so high that he is invisible and he produces a music without end.

We rode over virgin moorland, which had never felt the bite of the plough. We passed only one, isolated cottage, set on a high, south-facing hillside. What a place to live!

The road ran on down the valley of an infant river. Here it was civilised. There were the wheel marks of other travellers. Local farm and forestry traffic came this way regularly.

We came out on the B4358. As we rode down the main road, the only buildings seemed to be churches and chapels. An awfully religious lot, the Welsh.

We turned off above Beulah chapel, to hunt for the old road from the south to the monastery of Strata Florida. This road, known simply as the Strata Florida to its devotees down the years, uses a succession of valleys, linked by low passes to reach the isolated monastery at the heart of Welsh culture and the centre of the Great Desert of Mid-Wales.

The first half of the route is tar macadam, but still worth riding. The scenery is magnificent. The sense of being an insignificant human, crawling, ant-like across the face of a wild planet, is diminished only slightly by the smooth, waterproof road surface.

At Nant-ystalwyn, in the middle of nowhere, the Strata Florida turns green. A tarmac road continues westwards, but the main route is a dirt track following the Tywi valley north. The road runs above the valley floor for some way, then drops down to cross the river again and again. When it rains, the whole of this stretch of the road is a river. We were fortunate to tackle it in a dry spell, and managed only half a dozen fords and one deep, muddy flooded stretch of road. The wettest part was below the vast coniferous plantation of the Towy Forest. I expect the trees have altered the drainage pattern of the soil and so damaged what was a well founded, dry road.

At last we climbed out of the valley. We looked ahead for signs of our objective, but the ruins of the abbey are hidden from view until you are almost upon them, and we still had three miles to go. Our route followed the edge of the forest plantation and then we were surrounded by dark, brooding trees. Here it was important to pick out the old road from the modern forest road. Mick did a wonderful job of navigation. We emerged from the trees onto a short section of tarmac, before reaching our destination.

Strata Florida abbey is a disappointment. It is just a collection of old stones scattered about the fields. You can trace out the various buildings. They are labelled with small plaques on metal stands. But there is no life about the place. It is impossible to imagine the great seat of learning, the monks at their scrolls and books, busy with the administration of their vast sheep ranches. Perhaps the place has been exorcised. I could find not the faintest ghost of atmosphere when I was there.

North of Strata Florida, the map is a mass of green

Keith Payne from Bristol splashes along the monks' road to Strata Florida.

Roy Scrafton from Taunton takes another of the many Strata Florida fords. In wet weather, the whole road becomes a ford.

lanes. It is possible to ride all the way to Machynlleth with precious few miles of tarmac to disrupt the greenery. We tried it in the afternoon, with Mick leading the way. We found a great variety of roads from well trodden dirt tracks to featureless moorland, but we didn't reach Machynlleth.

With the help of money from the European Economic Community, a network of dirt roads is being carved out of the Welsh hinterland. In place of the faint traces of past travellers, giant scrapers are cutting and filling to make wide, smooth roads for heavyweight farm machinery. We hit one of these roads on our way to Machynlleth. We almost literally hit it. We were riding the old road over the rough grassland until we came to a bank of rock and freshly churned soil some ten feet high right across our path. The new road had joined the old road at ninety degrees and had been bulldozed on top of it, burying the

old route and making it impassable for most ordinary traffic.

We climbed the bank onto the new road and followed it for a mile or so. But we were so demoralised by the loss of what we anticipated to be a wild and exciting old road, that we turned back. We learned later that we should have continued, since the modern bulldozed road turned off the old road as abruptly as it joined it, just north of where we gave up.

One day I must go back and try this one again.

My next outing to Wales was to the south, not the centre.

South Wales is all about coal and steel and narrow mining valleys running from north to south. No more than a stone's throw from this dark industrial landscape rise the most beautiful hills in Wales. The Black Mountains and the Brecon Beacons divide the busy valleys, crammed with choirs of rugby playing coal miners and factory workers from the empty centre of Wales where only a handful of shepherds scratch a meagre living.

Saturday morning saw us all mounted on our trail bikes, setting off for two days of genuine green laning. There were no high speed heroics, and the lanes were tough enough to test any machine and to produce breathlessness in every rider.

Once again, Mick Comber from North Devon was with us as a guide, although I did most of the map reading. We were a group of friends out for enjoyment. We knew each other well enough to relax in each other's company and I was determined to set a gentle pace, so we had time to savour the land we were riding.

Mick found a nice couple of farm lanes to lead up to the big climb of the morning. The first ran from Velindre, just south of Three Cocks to Ffostill and the second took us to Rhos-fach. These were harmless enough, except for one rock step, the full width of the lane and several feet high. Even Tony Brockington, a Cornish trials riding expert, had to put his feet down to get up this, while the rest of us needed many helping hands.

We arrived at the foot of a mountain. It was a real mountain – a great, flat-topped affair, towering hundreds of feet above us. We could just make out the zig-zag path of the old road climbing up a spur to the mountain top. This was the mountain pass to the Grwynne Fawr valley. It is, in my experience, the stiffest climb in Wales, but well worth doing.

In our party were two chaps on large capacity trail bikes. Most of us chose lightweights of between 125 and 250 ccs, but these two had found that 500 ccs were quite manageable in the narrow lanes of Somerset. Roy was a giant of a fellow, with muscles hardened by years of heavy farm work. Dave was a little lightweight. Both were sure that their big, powerful four-strokes would cope with Wales. By the time they reached the Grwynne Fawr reservoir they had changed their minds.

The road is cut into the mountainside, wide enough for a full-sized wagon, but in places badly eroded by winter rain and snow. For much of the climb, the best place to ride was on the outermost lip of the road, above the eroded roadbed on one side and a breath-taking drop down the mountain on the other.

It was steep. As well as the difficulty of riding slowly along this narrow strip of ground without dropping off either side, was the problem of riding with enough power to climb the gradient.

On a hairpin bend, halfway up the Grwynne Fawr pass, riders pause to catch their breath.

The little bikes were low-geared and light. The big bikes had too high a bottom gear to enable them to go slow and were tall and heavy. Roy and Dave climbed the mountain in a series of short blasts, between sudden stops to maintain control or falling off out of control.

Dave, having strayed from the security of the narrow edge down the mountainside, put out a steadying foot on the downhill side. His foot was nearly three feet above the ground and he performed a most spectacular roll down the mountain, pursued by his bike.

Roy collapsed, red in the face and dripping with exhaustion, declaring that this was no fun, but in rather more colourful language.

We manhandled Dave and his bike back onto the road. The following week Dave bought a lightweight 250 trail bike, and has never looked back.

We had passed two walkers at the bottom of the mountain and exchanged greetings. They passed us while we were "pausing" to regain our breath.

The hairpin bend marks the halfway point of the climb. Tony, and the other more competent riders negotiated this with feet on the footrests. I dismounted and walked my Yamaha round with the engine in gear. Dave and Roy fell off and needed all our help to make it.

The hairpin was halfway and it seemed a long, long way to the top. The group became spread out as some stopped for short breathers, while others pressed on determined.

I was third to the top, and very pleased with myself. While I sat, cooling off, the walkers came by. We had just beaten them, but they looked a lot fresher than we did. I felt as if I had carried my bike up the mountain rather than the bike carrying me.

I walked back down the road to see how the others were doing. Suzie, the only lady in our party, was only a few hundred yards from the top. She was still determined

to make it, but had run out of strength to hold her bike up.

I offered to ride it up for her, climbed aboard and immediately fell off the first available rock, smashing the front brake lever. So much for chilvalry!

Modern trail bikes are designed for falling off. Vulnerable components, like indicators are flexibly mounted to reduce the risk of damage in a spill. Nevertheless many riders will remove the indicators before an arduous weekend on green lanes.

The second most likely breakage, after the indicators, is a control lever. Light alloy clutch and brake levers snap all too easily, as I had just proved. They can be replaced with plastic levers, but I find they give the wrong feel to the controls and I do not like them. A cheaper alternative is to slacken the clamping bolts securing the lever brackets to the handlebars. They should be tight enough to prevent movement during normal use, but a hefty bash in a fall will move the whole lever assembly rather than snap the lever.

Folding footrests are standard on all trail bikes today. This avoids having to carry a metre length of scaffolding pole to straighten bent footrests after every tumble. Folding gear levers are still rare as standard equipment. An accessory gear lever with a spring loaded tip that folds back on impact is a good investment.

You would have thought this would apply to rear brake levers. However, most manufacturers make these from heavy gauge mild steel sheet. This means that if they are bent in a fall they can be straightened by muscle power alone, perhaps with the aid of a tool kit spanner used for leverage.

Fortunately Suzie was equipped with a spare front brake lever, which was fitted in place of the broken stump. I bought a new lever, to replace the damage I had inflicted, at the earliest opportunity.

The ride southwards was plain sailing after the steep

climb. We cruised in line astern above the deep valley of Grwynne Fawr and past the long reservoir.

Below the reservoir we found an ice cream van and a cluster of cars. We bought ice creams all round and I went for a paddle in the rocky river, joining a gaggle of children who were armed with fishing nets.

To the car drivers, this road was a dead end. They were limited to the tarmac. Their only access to this beautiful spot was from the south. We had come in from the north and seen far more than they ever could.

It was good to rest by the water, watching the flies swarm in spirals under the trees, and the water boatmen scud over the still pools, floating on the surface skin.

The air was heavy with moisture, but warm. The clouds were high when we had set off this morning, but they seemed to be getting lower.

We found a series of tracks which ran through the forest, along the ridge above the tarmac valley road, giving an almost continuous green route from the start of the day of sixteen miles.

We turned west for Crickhowell and a bite to eat. Crickhowell is a pretty little town, which has figured in a small way in much of Welsh history, but it could not offer us food it seemed. The hill fort of Crucywel, from which the town takes its name, is two miles to the north. Owen Glyndwr's castle against the English lies in ruins in the town. The Mediaeval gateway, Porth Mawr still controls the traffic on the main routes to the west from Crickhowell.

We rode out under the gateway towards Talybont. Here we found an excellent hostelry where we were able to eat and drink at a table in the garden, overlooking the canal. There are not many canals in Wales, and this is one of the few still in regular use. It runs down the Usk valley from Brecon to the coast.

Behind Talybont, surrounded by pine forests, is the Talybont reservoir. After lunch, we climbed into the pine forests, picking out our old road from the Forestry Commission ones. Ours was the steeper one, washed out and narrowed by the weather. It was the one blocked in a couple of places by fallen trees, where we had to manhandle the bikes.

Eventually we came out of the trees onto the bare ridge. Another green road crossed ours diagonally from left to right and dived back into the pines. We were still climbing, but soon disappeared into the low cloud which had been threatening us all day.

Beware of sudden mists on mountain tops, warn all the guidebooks. No sooner had we entered the misty cloud base, than our road became faint and grass grown. We skirted a couple of bogs and pushed slowly ahead, with the visibility so poor that it was difficult to pick out the red tail light of the bike twenty yards in front.

Suddenly we were on a gravel road, with curb stones and street lights. We thought we were in the wilderness, miles from civilisation, but here were concrete lamp posts every thirty feet along our road. And it wasn't just one concrete road. There seemed to be a whole network of them.

Gingerly we edged onwards, convinced that something was horribly wrong, but not quite sure what. Had we hit upon some secret military installation not marked on the map? Had we taken a very wrong turning, misjudged our distances totally and ridden into the back streets of Merthyr Tydfil?

In the shelter of a deserted building, out of the wetness of the mist, we unfolded our maps and puzzled. Suddenly it was obvious. Right on the join between two maps, a track swung southwards from our south-westerly road. The two tracks differed in direction by little more than ten degrees, and in the mist we must have picked up the wrong one.

We had ridden along the wrong track into the middle of a quarry complex. The street lights and curb stones were to guide quarry vehicles on the night shift. There was a quarry road out to Tredegar, but we had come in by the back door, as it were, over the mountain.

We retraced our wheel tracks and spotted the point where we went wrong. It was much more obvious from this direction.

As we came down to the Pentwyn reservoir, the clouds lifted and we could see again.

We crossed to the west bank of the reservoir and turned north. We were heading for another of the classic Welsh green roads. This was the high road to Brecon – the Gap Road.

The Gap Road used to be a very busy thoroughfare. Until a few years ago, despite its untarred surface, it was

There used to be a bridge across this gulley, but it was washed away one winter. Suzie Compton makes a careful descent.

Mick Comber takes his turn to cross the gulley.

regularly used by all sorts of four-wheeled vehicles. Then a bridge over a side stream collapsed one winter, cutting the road in two. The road is now closed to vehicles except motorcycles, which are capable of crossing the awkward gully left by the collapsed bridge.

I liked the Gap Road. It was well surfaced for most of the southern half, giving the opportunity to really drink in the superb view across the enormous bowl carved out of the Brecon Beacons in the Ice Age. The U-shaped valleys radiate north and south, and minor ones go off in other directions, leaving only the thinnest ridge of rock between them. The Gap Road hops over this narow ridge from the south facing valley into the north facing valley. A panoramic view south and west over the bare valley swept clean of all but the sparsest vegetation, is suddenly replaced by a northern view, over an equally barren valley, towards the lush greenery of Brecon in the Usk Valley.

Before we reached the Gap in the ridge, we had to negotiate the collapsed bridge. This was one of Mick's nightmares. He is a very experienced rider and can cope with almost anything effortlessly, but he did not like this spot.

Mick rode a Honda XR200, a superb lightweight trail bike with a very tractable engine, but with a very short wheelbase which made the front wheel ride very lightly across the ground. A light front end is an advantage on soft ground, and for getting over fallen trees and rock steps. But on steep climbs it can be a handicap. The steep gradient tips your weight rearwards and, if the front wheel does come off the ground, it is instantly above your head, and you find yourself running behind your vertical bike, still holding the handlebars. Mick demonstrated this twice to us as he tried to climb out of the stream bed on the northern side of the fallen bridge.

Beyond the Gap, the descent to Brecon is cut into bare rock around the edge of the glaciated valley. It is easy going down, but much more exciting coming up. The best way to tackle the Gap Road is from the Brecon end, going south, but this did not fit in with our plan for the day. To

reverse our route would have meant going down the scarp slope at Grwynne Fawr, and that in no way compared with the climb up!

There is one last little lane, not to be missed, on the way to Brecon. This takes you over a collection of loose rocks and dirt to a beautiful modern bridge over the dual carriageway Brecon by-pass, then onto more loose rocks and dirt almost into Brecon town centre.

It is a great way to end the day.

After a sound night's sleep, we were ready to tackle what is potentially the longest green road in Wales – Sarn Helen. Sarn Helen is a Roman Road. If you consult a motoring map of four or five miles to the inch, you may be

Getting down is easy. It's the climb out which is hard. Mick's Honda refuses to do as it is told.

able to pick out bits of Sarn Helen. It starts on the south coast, near Neath, runs north to near Brecon, runs along the west coast by Aberystwyth and Dolgellau, and reaches the Conway valley in the north.

Sarn means a causeway. Many Roman roads in Wales are called Sarn something or other, since the Romans built their roads on a raised bank or causeway. Helen is rather more mysterious. The popular origin of the name, in Welsh history, is that Helen was the native wife of the Roman emperor Magnus Maximus and that he named the road after her. Helen of the Legions, as she is known is a strong, romantic figure in Welsh literature at the end of the Roman occupation and into the Dark Ages that followed.

Ray Easterbook at the Gap in the Gap Road, looking north to Brecon.

Ruined drovers' cottages by the well-made bridge on Sarn Helen, a road in use since Roman times.

As the name of a road, Sarn Helen is confusing, because it is the name of two roads. The west coast road is distinct from the road from Neath towards Brecon. I would love to explore the route of the west coast Sarn Helen. Some of it, I know, is green and still rideable.

Today we were riding from Brecon towards Neath on the other Sarn Helen.

Another Roman road ran along the Usk valley, and Sarn Helen climbed from this over the hills and down to the important south coast port of Nidum, modern Neath. The point of departure from the Usk valley was not Brecon, but a Roman fort guarding the river junction between the Usk and the Yscir, three miles upstream from Brecon.

The first couple of miles of the Roman road are lost beneath the ploughed lands of the valley floor. We picked Sarn Helen up on the high ground by the Mountain Centre on Mynydd Illtyd. It was a grey, uninviting morning and the Mountain Centre was closed, but the road stretched ahead of us for miles and miles, wide and green.

There are few signs of Roman use, but clearly this was a drovers road, taking sheep and cattle over the mountains to the harbour and markets at Neath during the eighteenth and early nineteenth centuries. We came upon the ruins of a drovers hut and a complex of sheep pens, beside a beautifully constructed stone bridge.

We stopped here to look around and to warm up, because the morning was cold in the mist. The hut and the pens were tumbled down ruins, but the bridge was perfect. It was made of a single neat arch of local stone, carefully dressed and faced. This must have been an important road not so very long ago to warrant such an expensively constructed bridge.

After six miles of lonely moorland we came upon a tarmac road near the head of a southward flowing valley, but Sarn Helen took the tarmac for only a couple of miles, before turning off into the forest.

When we came out of the trees, onto a smooth open stretch of road past some standing stones, Ray asked me if I would like to try his Honda XR200. After Mick's antics of the previous day I was not too sure, but was never one to look a gift horse in the mouth.

After the weight of my 250, the Honda seemed very light. The engine had a deep throaty note to it, and pulled powerfully from low revs, but the short wheelbase made the front end seem uncertain to me. I was used to my Yamaha, which was basically a road bike with a few green decorations. This Honda was something more serious.

It would take some getting used to, and I only rode it for a mile. The others were waiting for me at the far side of a fast flowing, rocky ford, with grins of anticipation on their faces and cameras in their hands. I could not fall off another borrowed bike, having dropped Suzie's yesterday. I took the stream crossing gingerly, with feet probing the water on either side for support in case the light front wheel broke away. The Honda behaved impeccably, and I began to wonder if perhaps I could grow to like it, but I

Tony Brockington warms his hands on the engine of his Yamaha DT175. Trevor Compton makes do with the bowl of his pipe. Suzie just looks cold.

The author tries a ford on a borrowed XR200 Honda. This machine acquired an enviable reputation among green lane enthusiasts during its short production life.

returned it to Ray and collected my trusty Yamaha once more.

The simple Honda XR200 with its short wheelbase and conventional twin shock swinging arm suspension, had a lamentably short production life. It was never available in large numbers and was replaced by a machine with a more complex engine and a rising rate, single shock rear suspension system. The new bike was popular, but never acquired the mystique among trail riders of the old XR200.

Beyond the ford, Sarn Helen strode through forest. Crags and streams and distant views were hidden behind the trees until we burst free and followed the forest edge with a view to the north-west over moor and bog.

Soon we had to leave Sarn Helen, because it had lost its vehicular rights for the next few miles. We turned into the forest and ran a forest road south eastwards into the valley of the River Neath.

We had to turn back. We needed to get back to the campsite to pack up and make our way home. We rode the tarmac up the valley and picked up the first part of Sarn Helen again back to the Mountain Centre, still deserted.

At the campsite, I loaded my camping gear onto the pillion seat, while the others loaded trail bikes onto trailers, and we headed off in our separate directions home.

Chapter Six
Dover to Land's End – The Long Green Lane

I knew my local lanes on Exmoor pretty well by this time, and I was getting to know about weekend trail rides. I had itchy feet. I wanted to explore more. I wanted to travel further.

When I was fortunate enough to gain promotion and a transfer to a school in Newquay, Cornwall, an ambitious trail riding plan crystalised in my brain. Once there it would not go away. I knew it was over-reaching myself, that I was not that good a rider, that my mechanical knowledge was inadequate, that I would probably crash or break down, but the idea stuck.

There is no road from Dover to Land's End.

There never has been.

To travel from end to end of Southern Britain you have always had to use a whole series of short roads.

The journey has always been difficult. There would be few useful signposts. Many of the roads, not being much used by long distance traffic, would be poorly maintained. There would be a shortage of overnight accommodation. In the days before motor transport, such a journey could take several weeks and be an adventure undertaken only by the most determined travellers.

My plan was to take the most difficult series of short roads I could find, and spend a week travelling from Dover to Land's End by motorcycle.

The whole of Britain is covered by an almost invisible

Was there a green road from the ancient fortress town of Dover, across the widest part of Britain . . .

network of hidden highways. A century ago, this spider's web of roads tangling the countryside carried waggons and drays, stage coaches and dog carts to every tiny corner of the land.

With a good map and plenty of patience, the all but vanished traces of our past transport system can be pieced together. This is an enjoyable pastime on a dark winter evening in front of a blazing log fire in an old cottage in Cornwall. I can recommend it.

Was it possible that these old green lanes could carry me all the way from Dover to Land's End? No-one had ever done it before, so how could I possibly tell? It would certainly be a great adventure to try such a ride.

There are no voyages of discovery within Britain to rival pitting yourself against the encroaching jungle of the primeval landscape of Southern Britain. Was there still safe passage, as there had been a century ago, or would the old roads now be lost beneath a dense layer of brambles, elder and blackthorn?

Throughout the country, individuals and groups of people are fighting to keep old green roads open for us to enjoy.

My plan was to enjoy as many green roads as possible in a week's journey into the unknown – Dover to Land's End – the long green lane.

I was confident that my bike was right for such a journey.

Yamaha designed their XT250 for those wanting a bike for tarmac roads and green lanes, but with the emphasis placed on tarmac riding. Compared with the competition, it was very mild mannered, under-tuned and over-silenced. Even the paintwork was slightly less loud than

. . . to the wild rocks of Land's End in Cornwall?

the products of Honda, Suzuki or Kawasaki. Despite these apparent disadvantages, it has proved to be a very suitable green lane bike. It is well liked by all who have ridden it, and has proved both reliable and economical.

All too many trail bikes seem to lose their sparkle after a couple of thousand miles, and are then traded in for the next year's model. While this may be an excellent sales strategy for the manufacturers, it does not meet my expectations of a consumer durable. Trail bikes should not be designed so that they are worn out after four thousand miles riding.

The XT250 fitted neatly into the Yamaha marketing package of the early 1980s, being the logical step up between the immensely popular two-stroke DT175, still many people's ideal trail bike, and the four-stroke XT500, too much of a handful for all but the most skilful trail rider but an enviably reliable road bike. The XT250 had the agility and light weight of the 175 combined with the four-stroke reliability and some of the slogging power of the 500. It suited me just right.

On the tarmac it would cruise at anything between fifty and sixty miles per hour all day, without losing speed up hills as a two-stroke powered bike would. It has a top speed of over seventy miles per hour, which gives a safe margin of acceleration for riding out of trouble at cruising speeds in the fifties. The engine has a gear-driven balancer shaft rotating in front of the flywheel. Single cylinder engines are prone to vibration from primary out of balance forces. The gear driven balancer shaft is Yamaha's sophisticated answer to this problem, and it works. The motor is smooth and the bike is comfortable to ride for long distances because of the lack of vibration.

The other great virtue of the XT on the tarmac is its fuel economy. Each new generation of Japanese motorcycles offers better and better high speed performance and faster and faster acceleration, but with poorer and poorer fuel economy. The XT goes against this trend. A fuel consumption of ninety-five miles per gallon at a cruising speed of fifty-five miles per hour is normal for this model. The smaller DT175 Yamaha consumes almost twice as much fuel at the same cruising speed. The XT's economy, combined with its larger fuel tank, makes it a far more acceptable road machine than the DT175, although the smaller bike may have the edge on handling on green lanes.

In early spring I planned a weekend excursion to test out my bike and to explore a little more of my long distance route. I had mapped out a series of lanes linking Exmoor to Dartmoor via Fingle Bridge, but I had yet to ride it. The Easter holiday gave me the chance to try out this new section and I took the opportunity to invite some old friends from Devon and Somerset along.

There are advantages to having relatives living at strategic points. My parents had retired to Burnham on Sea in North Somerset, which would make a good stopping off place on Day Three of the Ride. My father-in-law lived in Exeter, an ideal base for exploring the fringes of Dartmoor. I drove my wife and son to Exeter, with the Yamaha on the trailer, planning to stay two nights and fit in one day's trail riding.

Unfortunately, things did not work out quite as planned. I was struck down by a fearsome twenty-four hour virus the night I arrived in Exeter. I had to phone my friends and ask them to carry on without me. I heard later that they had a most enjoyable day's ride, while I lay and fought off the bug. However, I was determined to ride the lanes myself, and set off, solo, on the day after their ride, from Exeter.

The exploration proved most fruitful. I discovered some of the lanes I had planned to use were unsuitable. One did not exist, blocked off by barbed wire and invisible on the ground. Two were tarmac, pretty, but hardly worth a detour to ride, if you are journeying from Dover. One was overgrown. I found one new one I had not thought to include which made an excellent alternative to the two tarmac ones. The lanes on the eastern edge of Dartmoor proved superb. They were real moorland tracks, challenging going with spendid views across the tors. I was worried by threats from Devon County Council to close many of the green lanes within Dartmoor National Park, but was reassured that TRF man Gwynn Thomas had the situation in hand.

It was time to return to base in Cornwall and consider the question of luggage.

I have long been an advocate of panniers to carry luggage. They load the bike where a pillion passenger would sit, so the frame and suspension should be designed for them. However, the high level exhaust and the basic solo nature of trail bikes ruled out panniers. I had fitted a grab rail to the rear of the Yamaha. This allowed me to strap on my lightweight tent and sleeping bag, but gave room for little else. My thoughts turned towards a tank top bag, something I had never used in many years of long distance touring. I journeyed to Truro to see what the bike shop could offer me. Among the many colured bags on show, some big enough to take a fully clothed rider and pillion passenger, was a rather small and dusty, black bag. The shopkeeper offered it to me at such a low price compared with the gaily coloured and oversized alternatives on display that I could not resist.

Clutching my treasure, I hurried home and tried it for size. It was small enough to fit on the Yamaha's petrol tank without getting in the way of my knees or the handlebars, but would I ever get all my camping gear into it?

The Yamaha XT250, fitted with a tank bag to carry all the little necessaries of a week's camping. The map board proved invaluable, speeding navigational decisions at every crossroads. (M. Thompson)

The purchase of the tank bag forced me to become a lightweight camper. It was simple. Anything that would not fit in the bag could not be taken. Out went spare jumpers and reserve supplies of waterproofs. A change of footwear was discarded. Spare riding gloves were left behind. My faithful Camping Gaz stove was replaced by a much smaller back-packer's alternative with a tiny, detachable gas cylinder. The back-packing stove fitted into its own tiny saucepan, so I could discard the stacking set of pans from years earlier.

I would take emergency supplies of dried food – instant soups and freeze-dried vegetable meals, but planned to buy the ingredients for my evening meal each evening when I camped. Lunch would be sandwiches and these would travel in the ex-army rucksack on my back with the set of maps.

Water is a problem. No-one markets a water bottle designed to be mounted on a motorcycle frame. I tried various types and sizes, eventually settling for a flattish plastic bottle holding one litre, which could be strapped on the grab rail, wedged between the sleeping bag and the tent.

I even found a lightweight alternative for my airbed. I cannot sleep on the ground. It is too hard, too cold, and by three in the morning has developed bumps in all the most uncomfortable places. I had to have an airbed, but my rubberised canvas one, although a "lightweight" was too heavy and too bulky to fit on the bike. An inflatable pvc sunbed, with pictures of dolphins and seagulls all over it, folded up to almost nothing and weighed very little. It was very narrow when inflated, but was better than cold Mother Earth.

Riding gear had been pretty well sorted out over the years. I had found a waxed cotton suit to be the most versatile. It was not as waterproof as some plastic alternatives, but it was breathable and therefore more comfortable on a long ride. This turned out to be an excellent choice for the trail riding part of the journey, but the waxed cotton was not really windproof enough for the long tarmac ride to the start. I had to keep stopping to warm up.

I carefully sewed up the many small tears and holes worn in jacket and trousers over the years. More wax-proofing was rubbed into the entire suit and persuaded to soak into the fabric with the aid of my wife's hairdryer to melt the wax. I also sewed up the seams in my unlined gloves, which were always in need of mending. I cleaned my wellington boots and polished my goggles.

I sent precise details of my first day's ride to Ian Roscow in Kent. I received the most marvellous reply produced on Ian's computer. He commented on all my proposed lanes, warning of potential problems, fallen trees, and road blocks and so on. The most awkward bits he drew out on the computer, giving precise directions about which gate to go through and so on. Trees and streams were drawn in and the whole thing looked clear and easy to understand.

With just one week to go, I made a final revision of the first day's route and telephoned Ian to check the modifications. He confirmed that these were clear.

I was ready.

High pressure would produce a stable, westerly airflow over Southern Britain for much of Whit week, according to the Meteorological Office. This would give me a

Riding suit is waxed cotton thornproof. To body belt, wellington boots, helmet and goggles, socks and gloves are added an extra coat and pair of gloves for warmth and a dayglow vest for road riding.

following wind for the ride from Newquay to Dover on Saturday, and a headwind for the rest of the week on the way back. The high pressure promised dry weather with the possibility of showers. I hoped that this would hold for a week, but was not going to wait for the British weather. I was off.

Daisy was loaded up on Friday night. Everything was crammed into the tank bag and my rucksack, except the road map and route directions for the road ride, which were mounted on the map board fixed to the cross-brace on the handlebars. The bicycle pump was also strapped onto the cross-brace with two elastic bands cut from an old inner tube. Another elastic band secured the instant tyre weld bottle between the headlamp and the speedometer and rev. counter console. My riding gear was put out ready for the morning.

I was up at five o'clock. I managed some breakfast, telling myself to eat well as I was to live on sandwiches and cold water till I reached Dover. I wrapped my towel round my neck to double as a scarf, pulled on my waxed cotton suit over my quilted anorak. Thick socks, wellies, dayglow safety bib were put on. My wife gave me a sleepy kiss. I promised to see her on Thursday.

Out in the cold fresh dawn, I donned my helmet and gloves, kicked the bike into life and was away.

At long last the adventure had started.

I rode through fog on Bodmin Moor, but it was being broken up by the westerly breeze. The following wind made sixty miles an hour cruising an effortless affair on the empty, early morning roads. I pulled off near Exeter to warm up and have a bite to eat, thinking that it would soon be proper breakfast time. I was to get used to rising at five o'clock as the week progressed.

The A30 took me round the Honiton by-pass. I remember sitting in Whitsun holiday queues here as a child, while my father watched the car's temperature gauge rise and newspaper and ice-cream sellers walked past the stationary lines of cars. No such queues today. There were still very few vehicles on the roads.

I stopped for petrol before Andover. The cashier was fascinated by my map board, mounted on the handlebars. She asked where I had bought it and how much it had cost. When I explained that it was a spare piece of hardboard held on by two heavy duty elastic bands, and that I cobbled it together myself, she was rather taken aback. Perhaps I should smarten the idea up a bit and market it. It is a very simple idea and performed perfectly throughtout my week's ride, enabling me to route find as I rode along, without the need to stop and unfold a map to see where I was going.

I stopped for lunch high on a chalky hill, in a draughty lay-by with the traffic howling past on the dual carriageway. It was a short lunch break.

On and on and on I rode, determined to reach my

My campsite at Dover. Unfortunately I did not take a picture of my fellow camper, who had ridden overland from Japan on the first part of a round the world tour.

campsite as soon as possible and then to relax and prepare for the real journey tomorrow. It was a long way to Dover and very boring. At the speed I was travelling I saw very little. As you go faster a sort of tunnel vision occurs. You look further and further ahead to anticipate potential hazards on the road and so you see less and less on either side. I flashed past villages and by-passed towns, looking only at the vehicles ahead to see if they would slow me down.

At last I reached Eastbourne and turned along the coast road for Dover. I stopped on the outskirts of Dover and took a photograph of bike and "Dover" sign, just to prove I had made it to the start. I didn't want anyone thinking I had cheated and not ridden the whole way.

The campsite was tucked away in Martin Mill village, just north of Dover. It was a very welcome sight after three hundred and fifty miles riding. The worst thing about long distance riding is being cold. I started at six o'clock and reached Martin Mill about three, and I was chilled through and through. I kept stopping to warm up every hour or so, but after a while this was not enough. I suppose I was suffering from the beginnings of hypothermia – numb fingers, cold face, tiredness, lethargy. I should have worn warmer riding gear, but I had nowhere to stow it for the trail ride home.

The sun shone at the campsite and I busied myself unpacking and putting up the tent. I had a little paddock to myself, surrounded by hawthorns and apple blossom, set aside for motorcyclists. The paddock was right next to the shop, which was handy, and the campsite manager's house, which would ensure I had an undisturbed night's sleep.

It was really nice, so quiet after the noise of travelling. The grass had been freshly mown and smelled delicious in the warm sun. The birds were singing their spring songs. On the embankment behind the paddock, express trains thundered past every fifteen minutes. Well, you can't have everything.

I popped into the shop and bought supplies for my evening meal. When I returned, another motorcyclist had set up camp in my paddock. A chat to him put my little jaunt into perspective. This chap had just ridden his Honda XL250 trail bike twenty-one thousand kilometres from Japan in ten weeks! He had travelled through India, Pakistan, Iran, Turkey, Greece and then across Europe. He planned to drop in on a friend in Wales the following day. Perhaps he would look at London as he passed.

"Were there any problems on the way?" I asked.

"Yes. Plenty," he replied. "Especially with tyres and with chains breaking."

I noticed that he had a spare tyre strapped to the top of the vast mountain of luggage on the rear of his bike.

"Oil was a problem in India," he continued. "Very poor quality and very expensive. But petrol was very cheap in Iran."

"Wasn't Iran rather dangerous? There is a war going on at the moment."

"Yes', there were lots of men with guns, but I kept clear of the war zone in the south. It was as well I was Japanese. A white man would be assumed to be an American and would not have been popular. Being unpopular with men with guns was not a healthy thing."

"Where next?" I asked.

"Back through France and into Spain, the Sahara desert and some of Africa. Then if money allows and the bike is still working, I go to America. I will ride across America and home to Japan."

Wow!

I retired, thoughtfully, to my tent. All I was doing was riding for a week on green lanes. What an adventure my Japanese friend was upon. If only I had the time and the money, I might do the same. I wonder how much of each country he would see. I wanted to see the south of England at close quarters. He was seeking an overview of the whole World. Both our journeys had merit in their different ways. But I still envied him.

Ravioli, vegetable soup, Bovril sandwiches, a large tin of peaches, coffee and ginger biscuits were devoured for supper. The Japanese biker put on a pair of orange earphones and tuned in his transistor radio to a pop music station so loud that I could hear his headphones from the far side of our paddock.

I was in bed by half past nine and asleep very shortly afterwards.

Sunday
Kent – The Pilgrims' Way

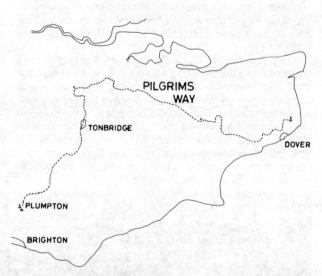

Sketch map of Sunday's route from Dover to Plumpton.

I was up at five o'clock. The sky was clear and the birds were shouting their morning chorus all around me. I breakfasted on crunchie cereal, bread and honey, and a cup of coffee. After washing and cleaning my teeth in the clean and totally deserted toilet block, I loaded my camping gear on the bike and set off for the first green lane which would take me from Dover to Land's End.

I would start in style. The first green lane was to be part of the Roman Road from Sandwich to Dover. Roman roads rarely look like Roman roads should except on a map where they run straighter than any other roads. On the ground they are all too often just ordinary farm tracks. This one started with a cul-de-sac sign and a fingerpost saying "To church". The lane went past the church, through the farmyard and was a very ordinary farm track. It was disappointing, but at least no-one was shouting at me and the way was clear and unambiguous.

My confidence grew as I crossed the tarmac to the next bit of "Roman" road which ran through open fields of bright yellow and smelly oilseed rape. Hedges of hawthorn and tall white parsley appeared on either side as the lane continued straight ahead . . . and then stopped.

The Roman Road to Dover is a very ordinary green lane.

It had been chopped through by the newly re-routed A2, which now by-passed Dover to drop its high speed charges straight into the ferries at the ferry terminal for France. A stile let pedestrian Romans continue on their road, but chariots had to turn left and run parallel with the new road for a quarter of a mile on a grassy, wooden fenced diversion, cross over the A2 on a motor bridge and then, it seemed, follow a similar grassy, wooden fenced diversion back to the true route of the Roman road. Unfortunately when I took this diversion, it left me a field of green wheat away from the true route of the Roman road.

It was seven o'clock and the sun was shining. I had to leave my Roman road and take a tarmac, medieval route for the last mile from my campsite to Dover.

After circling Dover's one way system several times I found myself on the new A2 road passing the stiles at the end of the Roman road again. Confused, I stopped at the next roundabout to reassure myself of my route. I was right, if surprised, and made my way to Chilton farm. I gave the farmer "Good day", as I chuffed past his outbuildings. His jacket, flat cap, trousers, wellies, even his bucket seemed the same shade of greeny-brown working-on-the-land colour. He raised a hand and a smile, and I rode up the hill and into the woods.

It was while negotiating the muddiest, wettest, most hoof-churned bit in the woods that I met the first dog walker of the day, dressed in orange cagoule in case it should rain. His broad Kentish accent stretched vowels beyond belief.

"Naauuow!" he replied, "Never dries out 'ere. S'always muddy." My mind's ear, accustomed to countrymen with a West Country drawl, was startled by this London sounding voice. But it was not a London accent. It was Kent. Local accents survive the worst that television can do in its attempts to bring us all down to the same level. It was a pleasure to listen to him.

I left him to walk his dog as tens of thousands of other dog walkers were doing throughout Britain and continued on my adventure into the unknown and unexplored morning.

The next green lane and the next little adventure lay ahead. The lane started innocently enough. There were two well established hawthorn hedges pointing the way along a track well muddied by horses' hooves. Off I went, growing in confidence all the time, to be confronted by a freshly ploughed field. There were no hedges, no grassy ruts, no flowers. A hundred years of natural growth had been wiped out in a day by one man and a tractor.

I aimed my bike straight ahead across the furrows until a gate came into view on my horizon. Riding across soft, freshly ploughed earth is not easy. It has to be tackled with determination or both wheels will sink in and lose direction and you will fall off. I crossed without mishap. Beyond the gate, the green lane continued as if nothing had happened.

Ploughing of public rights of way is a major problem which restricts public access to the countryside. The Countryside Commission published a report on ploughing of footpaths and bridleways in 1985. It concluded that very many paths are ploughed out and not properly reinstated, but that the law which is intended to prevent this happening is not enforced. Public carriageways – the old green roads – CANNOT be ploughed, so the Countryside Commission did not consider them in its report, despite the fact that, as I had just discovered, old green roads are disappearing under the plough at an ever increasing rate.

The farmer, running a commerical enterprise, has always been encouraged to maximise his profits by cultivating the maximum possible acreage. But the farmer's profits and the nations's food surplus must be balanced against the increasing use of the countryside by the general public for recreation. Walking across a ploughed field does not compare with walking along a grassy, hedged green lane, lined with wild flowers, undisturbed for over a hundred years. At last, the recreational value of the countryside to the spiritual needs of the public is beginning to gain against the commercial demands of agriculture. Unfortunately, the change in attitude has come too late to save this lane from illegal ploughing.

I paused to photograph my first oast house of the trip. These were once THE buildings of Kent, where the stilt walkers of the hop fields, having harvested their crop from the ten feet tall plants, would dry the hops ready for use in brewing for the vast thirst of London and the surrounding country.

Tucked up in his Mini sat a CB radio operator. He was manning a checkpoint on a forty kilometre sponsored run organised to raise money for the local military cadets. He seemed content enough, but declared that he was fed up with waiting for the runners. They should have begun to reach him a quarter of an hour ago, but his radio contact at headquarters told him that they had not yet left the start. He was marshalling another sponsored run this afternoon to raise money for aid to Africa. He must enjoy helping in this way, despite his claims of discontent.

Behind his Mini lay my next lane, running through a wood carpeted with bluebells, then dropping down over tree roots and loose flints to the valley floor. I was enjoying myself. The lanes were good and the weather was splendid. I climbed the chalk ridge behind Folkestone and looked down an almost vertical slope to the huge level landscape which stretched away to Romney Marsh and Dungeness.

On Etching Hill I met another CB radio operator sitting in his car. He seemed happier, but told me the runners had still not started their forty kilometre trot. My lane ran from behind his parking place, across a downland field of sheep and then dropped into Lyminge, the first town or village I had entered since Dover.

Folk were collecting their Sunday papers as I rode through.

The next green lane should lead me to Stowting. The lane dived downhill, steep and muddy. It was the sort of lane you prayed would not be blocked. You knew that if you had to turn back you would never be able to ride up the steep muddy start. Riding solo is fine, but if this lane were obstructed I would welcome another pair of hands to push the bike up that wheel spinning incline.

My luck held. The lane was clear.

Then I was on part of the North Downs Way. This was the first of many sections of Long Distance Footpath I was to use. Most Long Distance Footpaths follow ancient routeways. But of course most ancient routeways have always carried vehicles. This means they have carriageway rights. This could make their designation as Long Distance FOOTPATH confusing for the unwary walker. I was pleased that everyone I met on a Long Distance Footpath accepted my right to drive along it without question. The publicity given to these routes produces much higher useage than on others which are less well advertised. I was pleased that the publicity had stressed that these were ancient roads not just footpaths.

The real advantage of Long Distance Path status to all is the increased maintenance it affords. Signposting is a priority and is usually to a very high standard. Gates are well maintained and the road is usually clear of undergrowth to an acceptable width.

My next road ran up by Fishponds Farm, through a nature reserve. The man in shorts in his front garden looked up from his motor mower as I passed. He must have caught a glimpse of me out of the corner of his eye as I wound my way along the track through the trees. He could not have heard me above the noise of his motor mower. Modern motorcycles are much better silenced than most horticultural and agricultural machinery. The noisiest device in the countryside is the chain saw. They are frightful. They disturb the peace for miles around.

Horses churn up soft ground much more than wheeled traffic. They are much heavier than motorcycles and their hooves sink into the ground far more than do low pressure tyres. On the level, they produce a randomly churned area which varies in rideability depending how wet it is. The wetter it is, the more difficult it is to ride. When they climb hills, horses step in the hoofprints of other horses and produce sort of sunken steps between a

I would love to tackle a long distance ride on horseback.

I had to stop on Crundale Downs. It must be the prettiest lane in Kent. The roadside was awash with blue and pink and yellow flowers.

foot and eighteen inches apart. The steeper the hill, the closer the steps. The climb through the nature reserve had horse steps with a spacing and depth which would shake the fillings out of your teeth if you tried to ride them sitting down. Standing up to ride them resulted in eyeballs loosening in sockets, but was otherwise satisfactory.

Horse riders have a perfect right to use these green lanes, and I do not criticise them for doing so. Horses have been ridden over these hills for several thousand years and long may they continue to do so. I merely comment on the entertaining effect of their use on the progress of our more modern and more "sophisticated" forms of transport.

On Crundale Downs I had to stop. The morning was just too good to rush. The road ran along a wooded ridge packed to bursting with the flowers of early summer. The ground was a mass of blue and white and magenta. The trees wore their brightest and freshest shade of green. The sun shone clear of any clouds. The trees sheltered me from the chill of the westerly wind. I sat among the flowers on the edge of a clearing and ate a chocolate bar as I basked in the warmth and soaked up the sights around me.

Mr Toad was right about this sort of journey. His description of its joys in Kenneth Grahame's "Wind in the Willows" fitted my mood exactly:

"The open road, the dusty highway, the heath, the common, the hedgerows, the rolling downs! Camps, villages, towns, cities! Here today, up and off somewhere else tomorrow! Travel, change, excitement! The whole world before you, and a horizon that is always changing!" That was just how it was on that Sunday morning.

I hoped that I would not go the way of poor toad and be seduced by the newest and fastest mechanical marvel on the road, so that I would miss out on the pleasure of a journey at leisure for the dubious and less satisfying thrill of speed for its own sake.

A motorcycle came into view round a bend in the road. (R. Marston)

Mr. Toad had the right idea about the joys of the open road. Gypsies are still an occasional sight on green lanes in the South of England.

Modern travel is all about speed. Getting there is the sole concern. Our aircraft and our trains go ever faster. Countless millions of pounds are spent on designing them to insulate and isolate the traveller from the world through which he is travelling. He emerges from the terminus at the end of his journey without having so much as breathed the air through which he has passed in his high speed dash to reach his destination.

Road travel aims for the same destination. Ever better sound proofed cars and coaches with "in car enterainment" being an increasingly important selling feature. Our motorways, a water meadow wide, hurl us through the countryside at such a pace that we get no more than the briefest glimpse of the most beautiful scenery in the world. "Was that Kent?" they ask vaguely, glancing through the tinted glass.

I am sitting on Kent, surrounded by Kent, breathing the real air of Kent here, in the wood on this ancient green road. I am journeying. The cars on the motorway are merely passing through.

A motorcycle came into view round a bend in the road. The rider stopped for a chat. He was a local lad just out to enjoy the morning. He often came up here, by himself or with a friend. It was really good round here, he told me. Plenty of lanes to ride and no problems. He used to live near Dover where things were not so wonderful. The misbehaviour of some local riders — riding where they should not and making too much noise, and the aggressive attitude of some farmers to anyone trying to use the old green roads, made the scene around Dover most unpleasant. It is a shame how a few can spoil it for the many.

A wide dirt road brought me from the chalk hill tops to the picturesque village of Wye by the River Stour. Here is what must be the most attractively located college of London University. The main building is an elegant old structure next door to the flint-walled, 13th century church, surrounded by blossoming shrubs and trees. This must be a quite idyllic place to study.

I crossed the River Stour on an ancient five-arched bridge, which bore the names of the six workmen who repaired it in 1683.

Near Westwell I picked up the Pilgrims' Way at last. This was to take me on my journey for most of the rest of the day.

I had started my day with a Roman Road which linked two major Roman ports at Dover and at Rochester, next to Sandwich. This was obviously an important road in its time, but it could never rival the route I was about to take.

The Pilgrims' Way is as old as man's occupation of Britain, and probably even older! Studies of prehistoric plant and animal distribution suggest that many of our oldest routeways were mapped out by animals, not by man. Following the last ice age there is evidence of large herds of wild cattle moving across Britain in the way that herds of wildebeeste in Africa and herds of caribou in North America still do. Picture thousands of highland cattle, with shaggy red coats and long horns. In Britain they would have followed the upland routes and ridgeways, avoiding the marshy lowlands. The Pilgrims' Way may well have begun as a migratory animal route along the North Downs ridge about 8000 BC.

Migrating cattle do not move in single file, creating a narrow trackway, but in a scattered body spread over a wide area. They would keep their routeway clear of encroaching vegetation for a width of two or three miles by continued use and grazing on the hoof. So the early Pilgrims' Way was not a trackway, but a broad routeway, much wider than any modern motorway. This was how it was used by its first human travellers.

Migrating animals would join or leave the major route at many points, producing a complex network of communications. When the earliest humans arrived in the British Isles about 5000 BC they would have used the existing animal routes to follow and find their food as nomadic hunters. Man hunted wild cattle for food long before he learned to domesticate them.

Eventually, man became a farmer as well as a hunter. Settlements grew up at strategic points on the route, especially where rivers were forded. He traded the tools he needed for farming and hunting. The Pilgrims' Way was used by "churt traders" who dealt in beautifully shaped stone arrow heads, axes and other implements. Samples of their wares have been found all along the Way.

In Neolithic times, the Pilgrims' Way was a "main road" between Wessex and Kent carrying all manner of trade. Again archeologists have found evidence of this from items discovered along the route.

The name Pilgrims' Way derives from its use in medieval times by pilgrims travelling to the shrine of Saint Thomas at Canterbury. The name was not adopted until comparatively recently, perhaps the eighteenth century, long after its use for pilgrimages. Before then it was simply the "Old Road", a very old road indeed.

Like most ancient roads in Britain, the Pilgrims' Way keeps to the higher ground above the natural water table.

There is little water available along the route. For this reason, settlements tended to grow up a mile or two off the road, where a spring or a stream could provide a reliable supply of water. I think this is why there is almost no documentary evidence of the precise route of the Way in ancient travelogues. The Way must have been the route taken by Henry II in July 1174, when he landed at Southampton and rode eastwards to make his penance at Canterbury. The journey is recorded, but place names are very few, because the Pilgrims' Way passes through so few places. King Edward I, on his pilgrimage to the shrines of saints in 1289-90, must surely have used the Way to travel west from Canterbury to Hollingbourne and the manor of Leeds.

For three hundred and fifty years, pilgrims followed in the footsteps of kings to travel to Canterbury along the Way. It became more of a holiday than a pilgrimage. This is clear from the most famous description of all by Geoffrey Chaucer. His *Canterbury Tales* was the first great literary work to be printed in English. Chaucer's stories have provided us with a fascinating picture of social life in the fourteenth century through the words of the travellers on their pilgrimage along the Pilgrims' Way. This great book symbolises the birth of the "Revival of Learning" which produced a more enlightened civilisation out of the Dark Ages.

My first encounter with the Pilgrims' Way was not from Geoffrey Chaucer, but from a motorcycle magazine. I remember an article from the early 1970's, one of the first tests of "trail bikes" in this country. The article compared a 250 Triumph Trail Blazer, a lovable lump with an exhaust system that disintegrated faster than any made before or since, a Suzuki TC90 Trail Cat with an eight-speed gearbox, very short wheelbase and bouncy suspension, and a Greeves Pathfinder which had an Austrian Puch 125 engine in a genuine trials frame and was described as "too good" for just trail riding. Armed with an Ordnance Survey map, the trio of journalists were able to follow much of the ancient route of the Pilgrims' Way, now reduced to a narrow track from its broad prehistoric beginnings.

None of the bikes in that road test are on the market today, but the Pilgrims' Way is still there, almost exactly as they described it. It is not easy to imagine today's mixture of high speed trunk road, quiet tarmac lanes and

The Pilgrims' Way survives, as a mixture of high speed trunk roads, quiet tarmac lanes and narrow green lanes. (R. Marston)

narrow green lanes as the great trading route it has been over thousands of years. But here, only thirty miles from central London, is the most ancient history of our island written into the hillside.

In my ride along the Pilgrims' Way I found the modern surface varied. There was little mud this year, which can often cause problems in the South East. The route was everywhere well signposted. In places the Way was wide enough for two vehicles to pass, but in general it was reduced to the width of my handlebars. Usually there were tall, straggling hawthorn hedges on either side. In places the hedge was sparse, and all too often had been taken right out and replaced by barbed wire fencing.

A single track was trampled out by many feet and a considerable number of motorcycle and pedal cycle wheels. I have tramped many miles of ancient path in my time. From experience I know how much more enjoyable company is on a long walk when you walk alongside each other, instead of talking to the back of the rucksack in front of you as you are forced to walk in Indian file by the width of the path. I am surprised that most of the Pilgrims' Way has been allowed to narrow down to this extent, reducing everyone's pleasure for the sake of a little hedge trimming.

Perhaps this single file marching accounted for the stony look with which my greeting was received by one pair of ramblers. They did look hot and tired in thick woolly socks and knee breeches. The next group I met were a much more cheerful bunch. Clad in white shirts which told me they were going to "Run The World" for charity. They were on a sponsored walk to raise money for food for Africa. They were taken aback when I told them how far I planned to ride. They appreciated what a great adventure I was upon, and wished me luck. I rode on with my wheels several feet above the ground, happy to be alive.

Only once in twenty-four miles of the Pilgrims' Way that I rode did I cross open meadowland. Here, just before the huge war memorial cross, cut into the soil above Lenham, I stopped for lunch. I enjoyed my picnic in the sun, but the wind remained cool and did not encourage me to linger long.

In a few places the ancient road has all but completely disappeared, where land hungry farmers "need" every last foot of soil to increase the height of the Common Market grain mountain. If they were growing food for Africa, rather than for profitable subsidies, perhaps we would not object so much. It is not pleasant to ride surrounded by nothing but wheat, growing so close you can scarcely squeeze along the road. Much better is the protective bank and old hedge which had kept me company for most of the Way, even if the hedge does restrict the view and harbour a million pedestrian-eating flies.

At Hollingbourne I came upon the Pilgrims' Rest Inn, built right on the Way. Its sign showed the archetypical medieval pilgrim, his feet in a bucket thoroughly enjoying a well-earned rest. That sign must have brought many a smile to the face of modern walkers, trudging the route.

The pilgrim of the middle ages wore a well-established "uniform", which served to show others that he was on a holy mission and so afforded him special treatment. At least, that was the idea. But as pilgrimages became more and more the medieval equivalent of a package holiday, the holiness and special treatment declined.

Pilgrims wore a broad-brimmed hat and russet gown, drawn in at the waist with a belt or a rope. Sewn onto the gown were cloth crosses, intended to emphasise the religious purpose of the pilgrimage. Typically a pilgrim carried a leather satchel to contain all the necessities for his journey and a stout stick to help him on his way.

The Pilgrims' Way was tarmac where it edged round the northern rim of Maidstone. Just beyond Boxley, I came across a "Road Closed" notice, blocking the tarmac route ahead. I thought those sort of signs were reserved for old films, where the good guys are diverted from the proper road into a trap laid by the bad guys. I wasn't falling into any such trap today. Armed with the evidence of my map and the advice of the local TRF rights of way expert, I headed straight on past the "Road Closed" sign. The road was fine. There was no need for the sign.

The tarmac dived off left towards Maidstone, and the Pilgrims' Way was wide and green ahead of me. After wrestling with a few muddy patches I came out on a garage forecourt beside a busy trunk road. The Pilgrims' Way was forced to leave the dry escarpment and cross the Medway valley. Its route was lost, buried in lowland development. I opted to cross the River Medway on the M20 motorway and rejoin the Pilgrims' Way on the far side of the valley.

I had some difficulty with the Snodland by-pass. New roads were definitely causing me more problems than the ancient ones today. First there was the complicated system in Dover, now Snodland had been by-passed. Eventually I found the green road past the cemetery, which took me up to the now familiar Way, once again squeezed between the wooded upper slopes and the ploughed, gentler, lower slopes of the chalk escarpment.

On and on I rode, stopping every so often to remove branches placed across my path. These no doubt made the ride more interesting if you were on a horse, but were rather a chore on foot or on a bike. I put them to one side. Whoever was training their pony for the next show jumping Olympics could put them back if they so desired, but I wished they would not leave them in the road after they had finished with them.

The Pilgrims' Way disappeared beneath the combined weight of the M20 motorway and the A20 trunk road at Wrotham. These two roads ploughed a huge canyon through the chalk ridge, wide enough to bury the entire village of Wrotham. A concrete sign told me that the Pilgrims' Way was reduced to a tarmac footpath. Vehicular rights had been destroyed by the two autoroutes.

Beyond the village, I picked up my last little section of the Pilgrims' Way, but it was beginning to be swallowed up by the commuter suburbs of the Big City and it was time for me to turn southwards.

That old motorcycle magazine article mentioned one more lane that I could not miss out after the Pilgrims' Way. They had included it simply to finish off the day, expecting little special, but they found it to be the cherry on the cake. They described a narrow uphill gully containing a huge rock, which even the Greeves Pathfinder trials bike could not climb. They manhandled their three bikes past this obstacle and then proceeded to enjoy rocks, slopes, mud and leaf mould for a mile or more. It sounded like just the lane to ride before heading for the campsite.

Oldbury Lane is a medieval highway now under the protection of the National Trust.

I found a National Trust signboard at the start which told me this was a medieval highway – Oldbury Lane. It ran along the edge of ancient woodland which was filled with antiquities. The area was well-used by people interested in history as well as those just out for air and exercise. It was somewhere I would like to come back to and explore more fully on foot. Today, time was going on and I wanted to tackle that huge rock in the gully they had spoken of.

The lane climbed steeply up the side of the hill under the beech trees. The ground was covered with fallen leaves, rotting down to mud. Beneath the leaves was bare rock. It was steep and with an awkward camber in places, but I managed to paddle my way past. At least I hadn't needed to get off and push as the journalists had needed to. The climb continued over rocks and tree roots buried in deep layers of leaves. Then the lane levelled out and opened out into the woodland on top of Oldbury Hill. The light in beech woods is something special. It gives an air of space even at this late hour of the day. Fir trees are so claustrophobic. The descent from the hilltop was even more demanding than the ascent. It was steeper and muddier and rockier. Or perhaps I just enjoy going up more than going down.

After this lane, I decided to take a break. I needed a rest before riding the long tarmac section to my campsite.

I went to look at Igtham Mote. It was well worth looking at. Tucked away between the hills, as the best old manor houses often are, this had been the home of the Selby family for over three hundred years. Now it was run by the National Trust and open to the public. The public were queueing up to get in when I arrived. The house was partly timber and partly small red bricks in construction, surrounded by a moat with swans and ducks, and reached across a little bridge. The surrounding gardens were full of flowers and people. The air was pierced periodically by the harsh shreik of a peacock. There was another newer house, Tudor I think, facing the moated manor across a terraced lawn. The whole place was beautiful and buzzed with folk enjoying it.

After half an hour I left. Here was another place to come back to and explore more fully.

The road south took me through Tunbridge Wells and the great heathland of Ashdown Forest to Plumpton Green. I was to camp at Plumpton Racecourse, which was turned over to campers when not being used for horse racing. The campsite manager had some difficulty deciding what rate to charge for a motorcycle. He was used to cars, pedal cycles, walkers, but not motorcycles. Eventually he decided I was the same as a pedal cycle. We agreed a price for the night and he led me to my pitch. We went past rows of frame tents parked by the stable blocks where the horse boxes would pull up on race days. We went through white gates towards the grand-stand, and stopped by the winner's enclosure. He pointed to the rich grass under an oak tree at the centre of the winner's enclosure, and asked if that would suit me. It would suit me just perfectly, I said, thinking that perhaps the winner's enclosure was a little presumptious after only one day of my long distance ride.

I unloaded and set up camp. The tent was still wet from the early morning start. The dew had not dried before I packed up to go. It soon dried out in the evening sun, while I washed and prepared a meal. There was no food available on the site, so I tried some of the instant dried food I had carried with me. A cup of vegetable soup was followed by soya bean "feast" with prawns and rice. It was pretty tasteless but filling. After coffee, cheese and biscuits, I determined to relax. I had travelled 134 miles since breakfast. I took a stroll round the race track – barefoot. I had no room for spare shoes and my wellies were resting in the tent.

Walking barefoot is an exciting sensation to feet brought up in shoes. The unknown textures of different grasses are discovered with each new step. Coarse, tough marsh grass; soft, springy moorland grass; lush, damp meadow grass; the prickle of twigs; the stab of a sharp stone; the softness of bare, sandy soil; the cool ground shaded by trees; the hot grass in the open sun. I felt all these surfaces as if for the first time as I ambled across the acres of Plumpton racecourse in the fading day.

My feet looked soft and white from years of shoes and socks. Watch how the toes spread out, gripping the ground! My foot goes down flat, not booted heel first, to spread the load and lessen the effect of unseen sharp objects. The whole shape of my walking changed without shoes. Each step felt the undergrowth. Each pace was a new sensation.

It was nearly night. The sun had set. The afterglow turned the north western sky to pale gold. Overhead the air was French blue. The Earth shone not in the sun's light but in the sky's light. A trail of high cloud drifted south west. A small cotton wool cloud hung very white to the north.

I wriggled into my sleeping bag and slept.

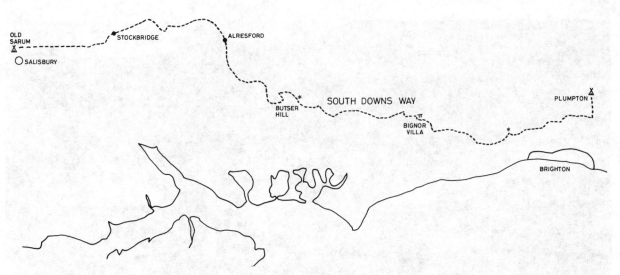

Sketch map of the route from Sussex to Old Sarum.

Monday
South Downs Way – Sussex to Old Sarum

I woke at a quarter to five to the birds singing and the sun shining. Breakfast; wash; tent down and equipment packed. I was away by seven. It looked like the start of another tremendous day.

The signposting of rights of way has long been a contentious subject, especially for carriage roads. Land-owners do not always want to encourage folk to cross their land by "advertising" the presence of a right of way. There is a problem occasionally where people use a green lane with a vehicle without being fully prepared for potential difficulties. An ordinary saloon car can be driven along a green lane quite legally, but may not always be able to cope with the condition that the lane is in. A car filled with stranded picnickers blocking the green lane to his field is not the farmer's delight in his busy summer season. Instead of using his tractor to tow loads of hay, he has to use it to tow cars out of the mud.

I like "Unsuitable for Motors" signs. They let the user know what he is likely to encounter and deter those with less athletic vehicles from getting into difficulty. The West

Sussex indicate their green lanes with blank wooden fingerposts. The author's Honda roadster is clearly overloaded and handled poorly on loose surfaces.

"Unsuitable for Motors" sign on a county-maintainable green road is usually a pointer to a lane worth exploring.

Country counties have opted for "Unsuitable for Motors" signs on their green county roads and it is a system that seems to work.

Sussex, I discovered, have a different policy. My first lane of the day carried a wooden finger post at its start. It looked the part – a suitably rural sign in a natural material, rather than a loud, retro-reflective road sign. I was puzzled by the fact that the finger on the finger post was completely blank. It took a little experience of more of the Sussex signs to uncover the secret of their system. Fingerposts were used for all categories of rights of way. Footpaths were signed "Footpath", bridleways were signed "Bridleway" and Roads Used as Public Paths (RUPPs) were given blank signs.

This made casual use of green lanes by strangers to the area difficult. What did a blank signpost tell them? But

Gareth Richards checks the route ahead. The South Downs Way can be seen sweeping round to the right in the middle distance.

it meant that, once you had cracked the code and knew the meaning of a blank sign, you were guided on your route most effectively. The blank signposts were reassuring company for the whole of my morning's journey across Sussex.

The first fingerpost pointed the way across No Man's Land on a white chalk track into scudding grey clouds. This was very different to yesterday's close hedged lane at the foot of the steep scarp of the North Downs. Today I rode high on the downs, on a wide, well used, well signed track. It was dry underfoot and I felt I was flying.

Through Findon to the next blank fingerpost, which would take me onto the South Downs Way. I rode miles and miles of fast dry chalk. Fourth gear much of the way and on occasion touching twenty-five miles an hour! That is really fast on green lanes. I had no wish to go any faster, because if I did I wouldn't be able to see anything.

The South Downs has been a sheep farming area all through the centuries. There were sheep grazing these high ridges and steep slopes when the Romans ruled here, and there were still sheep here when I was at school. Now I rode past acres of wheat. The thin chalky soil has at last succumbed to the plough.

My route took me off the South Downs Way as I came towards the crossing of the River Arun near Amberley. The South Downs Way has bridleway status for a short stretch. A blank sign pointed me slightly further south for a while.

What a difference to the road once it ceases to be a Long Distance Path! The road surface changed from bare chalk to rich grass, rich in different species of grass, not the planted monoculture of many "meadows". The grass sparkled with dew and the way was lined with cowslips.

I wandered along country lanes below the downs to Bignor. Here I had to stop to investigate the Roman villa. It was too good to miss.

The Roman who had his villa sited at Bignor, in the lee of Bignor Hill, facing south, had a good eye for a pleasant situation. The modern presentation of the excavated site is really quite charming. The ruins are housed in a series of thatched wooden huts. I paid my entry fee and wandered round, reading the notes about each room as I entered.

The villa was discovered in 1811. The mosaic floors are its great feature and must make it one of the most famous villas of Roman Britain. It was built in the middle of the fourth century AD and has six mosaics. Some of these are mainly geometric designs, but there is also "Ganymede being carried off by an eagle which is Zeus in disguise", Venus, and Medusa. All the mosaics were really big and beautifully preserved. In its prime the villa must have been quite a place – a real stately home of Roman Britain.

From the courtyard of the villa, now the car park, you can look south to the tangled slopes of the South Downs. The villa lies close to the main Roman road from London to Chichester, called the Stane Street. It is quite amazing that the exact line between London Bridge and Chichester was established by the Roman road builders and was actually followed by the road as far as Ewell in Surrey. Then the road turned to pass through the Mole Gap at Dorking. The A3 and A24 roads via Tooting and Merton still follow the original Roman alignment.

Beyond Dorking much of the A29 marks the original road. Beyond Pulborough, the A29 wanders off course in the Arun valley, but Stane Street turns after crossing the river and heads straight past Bignor villa to climb along a spur just north of Bignor Hill onto the South Downs. Across the summit of the escarpment, the road remains as a massive bank up to thirty feet wide running across the downs towards Chichester.

No-one knows how the Roman engineers achieved such accurate alignments of roads over such large distances as from London to Chichester, but it was a common feature of their major roads nearly two thousand years ago.

My next green lane was something very different to the arrow – straight military Stane Street. Dog Kennel Lane wriggles over a chalk spur to link the village of Sutton to Dog Kennel Cottages on the A285. The A285, after its own climb up the South Downs escarpment, picks up the last stretch of Stane Street for its final run into Chichester.

Dog Kennel Lane is surfaced with chalk and huge flints surrounded by gulleys deep in wet beech leaves. It is a climb worth concentration and gives a sense of satisfaction if done well. After the tricky bit, I pottered gently through the level section of the beech woods. Beyond the woods, the lane has been opened up to make a wide, smooth farm track, which emerges to the howl of traffic on the A285 trunk road.

I rejoined the South Downs Way Long Distance Path. This is a route at least as old as the Pilgrims' Way of yesterday's ride. It begins at Beachy Head and runs along the northern edge of the South Downs for miles, descending to cross the River Cuckmore at Alfriston, the Ouse at Lewes, the Adur at Steyning and the Arun, just behind me at Amberley. I was to follow it for a further seventeen miles to where the Long Distance Path ends near Petersfield.

The main claim to it being ancient is that it passes through an area so rich in antiquities that the road itself must have been important in ancient times. Modern afforestation and farming, as well as modern road developments, has removed much of the evidence, but old aerial photographs show the downlands covered in tracks and roads of all periods running in every direction. The South Downs Way is almost certainly prehistoric but it is not an isolated prehistoric "motorway". It is only a part, and a very small part, of an immensely complex pattern of roads and paths, most of which are as old as the South Downs Way itself.

My next section started by a quarry and climbed onto the downs as a good dry track, wide and well trodden. Then there seemed to be miles of muddy going through the woods and plenty of long distance walkers.

It was ten o'clock. I met a troop of scouts. "Skip" told me they were walking to Eastbourne. We agreed that it was a long way, but they looked keen and fit, and I had no doubt that they would make it. Real Scouts are great people, with a love of the countryside and an enjoyment of life which is a treat to share. These were real Scouts. They left no mess behind them, went quietly on there way and with their eyes open and their ears listening. "Skip" had trained them well.

The sky was full of cloud, now, so low that it almost touched the hill tops over which I rode. The wind was brisk and cool, blowing straight towards me. I did not

A dry stretch through the woods. Afforestation affects the drainage even of a ridgeway route like the South Downs Way and can make much of it muddy.

expect rain yet, but I put on my quilted anorak underneath my waxed cotton jacket to keep the wind at bay. It was a measure of the easy going as well as the penetrating power of the wind, that an extra coat was necessary. On many green lanes it is such hard work to ride over the broken surface that, even in mid-winter, you are too hot for comfort, not too cold.

I climbed the hill beyond the Cocking gap, still on the South Downs Way. It was here that a previous attempt to ride from Dover to Land's End had ended, when the entire electrical system of my Honda 125 had stopped working. The newer and better maintained Yamaha continued without any sign of faltering.

I looked back from the top of the climb at the sort of view that inspires me to ride green lanes. Stretching behind me across the valley and over the far ridge, as far as the eye could see, was a thin ribbon of white. It ran back into the cloudy distance of the past and stretched ahead of me, over the brow of the hill, into the future.

I rode on.

The next person I met was a Canadian lady. I had passed several walkers in the last few miles, trudging singly or in pairs, but something about this woman made me want to stop and find out a little about her. The others looked as if the walking was hard. They plodded along in heavy boots, more often then not under the weight of a vast pack. Even those with a tiny daypack, big enough for a flask and some sandwiches, seemed to find the walk an ordeal. This lady positively flew along, her feet as light as could be in red sneakers. Her rucksack was too big for a daypack and yet was clearly too lightly loaded to contain the mountain of gear that the other walkers needed for a long distance walk. And when I spotted the Canadian red maple leaf on the pack my curiosity could not be contained. I had to stop and talk.

I apologised for interrupting a walk she was clearly enjoying, but explained that the Canadian flag had impelled me to disturb her. I thought afterwards, what would have been the reaction of a solitary woman, walking alone along a tarmac road, when a strange, grubbily clad motorcyclist stopped alongside her for a casual chat. It would certainly not have been the friendly response I received today. The unusual setting and the singular nature of our reasons for being there, made such a meeting, not merely socially acceptable, but inevitable. It would have been bad manners to have ridden past without a word.

She told me she had flown over from Canada for a short holiday. She had devoted the last eleven years of her life to raising her children, and felt that at last she deserved a treat. This holiday was her reward for eleven years of hard work. She had bought a guide book in Canada and planned a walk along the South Downs Way. which would take her eight days. Now she was here and thoroughly enjoying herself. I asked her about her rucksack which seemed to be too small for such a trek. She replied that she wanted to walk with pleasure not with an enormous burden on her shoulders. She had no wish to camp out at night, especially when her guidebook listed excellent overnight accommodation all along her route. Since she didn't have a heavy pack, she didn't need heavy boots to protect her feet. She could walk in comfort and make the most of the holiday she had been promising herself for so long.

We parted, wishing each other good luck on our respective marathons.

The Royal Oak Inn was a sorry sight, at the end of this section. Tucked into the valley, a quarter of a mile before the South Downs Way joined the main road, it could not pick up any passing trade apart from the likes of myself and the Canadian. Neither of us was likely to stop at such a tired looking inn. The paintwork was scruffy, the windows were dirty, the yard was full of rusting machinery and nondescript heaps of tarpaulin. There was no sign of life. Yet it was a large, quite imposing, building and must have enjoyed some prosperity in the not too distant past. It made a sorry comparison with the cheerful Pilgrims' Rest Inn of yesterday.

I zipped along the main road for about three miles, and rejoined the green South Downs Way for its final stretch to Buriton near Petersfield. At the start, I met a doctor taking her poodle for a walk. The little dog yapped and snapped at my wheels, even after I had stopped to allow it to calm down. I cannot abide noisy, silly dogs. The doctor was nice though.

Next I met a middle-aged couple pushing their bicycles up the hill towards me. These were the first pedal cyclists I had met, though I had seen a number of tyre tracks along the way. Their bicycles looked rather special. They told me they were ATCs – All Terrain Cycles. They were fitted with big knobbly tyres, extra low gear ratios and especially strong but light frames. They were kitted out with neat pannier sets and everything looked brand new. The husband told me that he and his wife had just bought them and thought they would give them a try along the South Downs Way. They had spent much time pushing them up hills despite the low gearing, and had fallen off a couple of times in the mud, but were quite enjoying themselves even if they were exhausted!

They warned me of muddy patches ahead.

They were right. I encountered the muddiest stretch so far. Deep puddles which you bumped into and bumped out of were mixed with slippery, chalky mud. The mud went on for quite a while under the trees. Then the South Downs Way became tarmac.

I was not quite sure where I was. Had I passed Sunwood Farm or not? Was this the edge of Ditcham

Cyclists warned me of muddy going ahead. In such conditions, All Terrain Cycles may prove an advantage.

Woods or Queen Elizabeth Forest? I had been bouncing along all morning, relying on blank signposts and South Downs Way signs. I had become disorientated. I was lost.

I followed the tarmac road, trying to identify features. I rode off the chalk ridge. Did that mean I was on the final stretch into Buriton or was I crossing a minor valley? The tarmac road went round a sharp left hand bend. Straight ahead, through a gate was the muddy track, signed "Cart Road to Buriton". That couldn't possibly be the South Downs Way. I followed the tarmac road which climbed up a hill and then down to another valley. This made no sense at all with my reading of the map.

Ahead I saw a minibus, loading up with teenage boys. It looked like a school camp of some sort, or a field trip. I stopped and asked one of the boys if there was someone in charge. A scruffy chap in an ancient sweater and grubby jeans appeared from the depths of the minibus.

"I'm sorry to trouble you," I began, "but I am lost. I have been following the South Downs Way all morning, and am trying to get to Buriton."

"Oh, no!" was the immediate reply. "You can't come down here. This just goes to the farm."

This was not much help, I thought. My bike could go just about anywhere. Perhaps he didn't think I could cope with the sort of bumpy farm track that seemed to be beyond the minibus. But which farm was he talking about. Was it Sunwood Farm, that I seemed to have mislaid earlier?

A second, rather less untidy teacher, in the same field trip uniform of sweater and jeans, came out of their camping field. He was clearly the Geography teacher, because he had a much better idea of where we were and where I was trying to go.

"You might be able to get through, ahead," he admitted, "but you ought really to follow the tarmac road back to where you came from."

"I've come from Dover," I pointed out, "and can't face the thought of going all that way back. I've been using green roads for most of the way and there should be a green road into Buriton."

The penny seemed to drop. "Try that track signed "Cart Road" just back down the road, then," he replied,

The classic green road in Cornwall rides the ridge to Helman Tor, lined with bluebells.

In early summer green roads are alive with light and colour.

The start of a trail ride in Taunton. Riders are sorted into groups of 6 before setting off in different directions to explore.

Motorcyclists act as marshals for the annual Quantock Horse Ride organised by West Somerset Bridleways Association.

This lane was ploughed the previous autumn. I cannot imagine why. By mid-summer it will be grassy again.

A snowbound lane on the edge of Exmoor calls for a team effort.

The lane runs through a flooded quarry where stone was extracted 100 years ago to build the nearby farm.

By late summer many southern lanes are real jungles.

Fords can be deceptive! This one was shallow the last time I used it.

On open moorland you need a good sense of direction to make sure you follow the right track.

On the white cliffs above Folkestone, looking for a green road from Dover to Land's End.

The Roman road to Old Sarum (Salisbury).

Splashing through a gentle ford in the depths of the countryside.

A rainbow over Minehead after a shower on the Quantocks.

Porchester's Post in the heart of Exmoor.

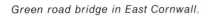

Green road bridge in East Cornwall.

Nearly at Land's End. This is Mulfra Quoit.

One of my North Country guides – Gordon Thackray from Otley.

Riding into the unknown. Mist in the Dales.

Sunshine in the Peaks.

A classic northern lane, lined with dry stone walls.

Fighting the gradient on the Chapel Gate road out of Edale.

Giant rock steps. I was glad to be going down, not up.

A centuries old lane in West Derbyshire.

The author, fully loaded with camping gear for a week, finds yet another green road to explore.

"but you'd enjoy it much more if you were walking."

"I would love to walk, but I'd never make it to Land's End by Friday. The Cart Road to Buriton is just what I was looking for, but I lost my sense of direction. Thanks very much for your help! Sorry to have disturbed you!"

He shook his head at my folly and was clearly still prejudiced against bikes in the countryside. I left, embarassed at having to ask the way, when I had just ridden past such an obvious and inviting sign bearing the name of my destination. How could I convince him that trail riders were not all morons when I had just lost my way in such an idiotic fashion.

The blue and white minor road sign "Cart Road to Buriton" beckoned me down a steep muddy holloway. The bike slithered through soft, gritty mud and decaying leaves, almost under control, in first gear, with me trying to keep my feet on the footrests to maintain my balance but generally failing and paddling wildly about with my legs trying to find something firm to push against to keep myself upright. There followed a slightly less muddy climb, then a gentle farm track into the village.

"It wasn't really that difficult," I told myself. " I am sure it wasn't. It was just the reaction to getting lost which had upset my concentration and machine control."

I would stop in the village to collect my wits.

I pulled up in the large, untarred car park next to the church . The church stood on a little rise, tucked into the corner of the village, overlookng a pond. It was the pond that dominated the village, not the church. The pond was huge, surrounded by wide, sloping grass banks, and with a single, large willow tree right in the middle of the water. It was the sort of pond that should have a ducking stool.

I could imagine it being used three hundred or so years ago to try some lonely old lady for witchcraft. The villagers would line the edge of the pond to see the proceedings as the poor woman was brought before her accusers. She would be thrown into the water, and whether she sank or swam would decide her innocence or guilt. If she floated, she was a witch and would be pulled from the water to meet her punishment. She would be burned on a giant bonfire, just as we burn dummies of Guy Fawkes each November the Fifth. It was a slow, painful, horrifying way to die. If she sank, then of course she was not a witch. She would drown – dead but innocent. It was a "no win situation", the ultimate Catch 22.

Today, all was tranquility. The village green was quite deserted. I strolled round the pond, talked to the ducks and generally relaxed.

Feeling spiritually refreshed, I realised that the bike was in need of liquid refreshment. It was Bank Holiday Monday, so the village petrol pump was closed. I headed for the nearest town, Petersfield, in search of fuel. The main road was jammed with cars, crawling into town. Each car was packed with pent up families overflowing with anticipation and frustration. I filtered carefully past on the outside – motorbikes are handy in traffic jams. I found a filling station at the first roundabout and quenched the Yamaha's thirst. The queue of traffic seemed to stretch for miles. I could see no obvious attraction in Petersfield. There were no hoardings advertising something special. I beetled back the way I had come to rejoin my green road.

Terry Jolley had advised me against trying the climb from Twentyways Farm onto the Butser ridge. His local Trail Riders Fellowship group only tackled it after a long dry spell, because it was so steep. He warned me not to try it alone. This seemed rather timid, but, knowing Terry, I was prepared to accept his advice. I took the next turning off the tarmac and climbed from Lethe House onto Butser ridge. After a muddy start, I rose over the chalk scarp and looked down on the other, the not recommended route. It was vertical!! Terrry's group must go riding with a crane to haul their bikes up there!

I climbed higher, passing through a series of earth ramparts and into a thick white mist as I reached the cloud base. It was in this sort of mist that time travellers in novels always changed centuries. Was I about to enter a time warp? Would I come out of the mist into an iron age village behind these protective banks? I looked out for hairy men with spears and blue, woad-stained faces and came upon a Morris Minor, on the tarmac at the top of the ridge, ambling towards the radio mast, just visible as a grey outline. A Morris Minor didn't really qualify as a time warp, even though it is a rather antique car. Mist plays funny tricks on your brain. Hairy iron-age men indeed!

I rode a green, chalky track along the ridge to Hyden Hill and came down a muddy incline to HMS Mercury. Even on dry land, the navy pretend they are really at sea by giving their shore bases the names of ships. HMS Mercury was a collection of brick and corrugated iron buildings with lots of signs warning of the poor road sense of the navy – "Slow! Troops crossing", "Beware of troops on the road" and so on. I suppose, if they were pretending to be on board ship, they really wouldn't expect passing motorcycles. Just astern of the quarter deck, abaft the mizzen mast, the green road headed north across Wether Down.

Wether is an old name for sheep, but there were no wethers on the down today. The smooth gravel and flint track led to cattle sheds not sheep pens. The farmer used the track only as far as his cow sheds, and so was concerned about maintaining it only that far. After this the track became muddy, but with tyre prints giving evidence of recent use by trail riders' motorcycles.

The lane crossed a tarmac lane at Coombe Cross. You can often spot the position of an old green road by names ending in Cross. A name like Fourways Cross with only three roads leading from it is an obvious clue to a lost road. A couple of houses marked Coombe Cross, on the ridge half a mile above Coombe Farm.

The ground seemed to be drying out at last. Oh no! I had spoken too soon. Here were more mudholes and slippery chalk. I was tired. It was twelve-thirty and time for lunch in the woods. A steady westerly wind had blown the low cloud away, but made the air chill. I sheltered from the wind on the lee side of the wood. I sat with my back against an ancient beech tree, with my legs splayed out in front of me, and tucked into freshly made sandwiches, spread thick with pate with my penknife. Peanuts, sultanas and several large digestive biscuits provided dessert. A generous drink of water and I was ready for the afternoon.

More mud lay before me. I followed the skids and slides of earlier trail bikes which had used the lane over the weekend. The lane ended with a flight of bungalows and a sign saying "Halnaker Lane". I wonder how that name originated.

From East Meon to West Meon and then to Warnford was tarmac. The green lane from Warnford ran through a

"Conservation Area", or so the sign at the start informed me. The lane was lined with a ribbon of old trees and their acompanying undergrowth of wild flowers. I spotted a huge orange fungus protruding from the roots of one tree. The whole way was lined with bluebells.

Past Blackhouse Farm and south of Hinton Ampner House, the lanes were at last showing real signs of drying out. I had had my fill of mud for one day. I rode a grassy track enclosed by barbed wire across the parkland of Hinton Ampner House and turned north at the source of the River Itchen. All this mud and water must be flowing into the Itchen, I thought.

A mixture of green roads and tarmac lanes took me past Alresford. Local pronunciation varies. Some say "Awlsfd" and some say "Arlsfd". It was once Aldersford – the ford of the alders. One chap had tried to make use of all the wet I had been complaining of. In the twelfth century, Bishop de Lucy, the Bishop of Winchester, dammed up several streams at Old Alresford to provide water to make the Itchen deep enough for shipping. The trade he hoped to encourage came up the river as far as Winchester. Alresford did not develop as a trading centre. The episcopal reservoir has now dwindled to a pond, rich in wildfowl. The road from Old Alresford to New Alresford still runs along the top of the Bishop's original embankment. The rector's wife at Old Alresford, Mrs Sumner was the founder of the Mothers' Union.

"New" Alresford is older than the Bishop's dam. It was already well established in the twelfth century.

Both Alresfords suffered from frequent fires throughout their long history. After the battle of Cheriton, fought on the dry ground surrounding the green road from Bramdean, the defeated Royalists tried to raze the villages in their retreat, but the Parliamentary troops seem to have got the fires under control before too much damage was done.

Parked cars and strollers lined the green road out of the Itchen valley. As the gradient increased, I left the walkers behind and followed a smooth grassy track over dry chalk. I met two riders from Winchester. An experienced green laner on a Kawasaki 175 two-stoke was showing his novice friend on a Suzuki SP370 what trail riding was all about. The novice was definitely hooked despite several tumbles during the morning. Both were riding sensibly on well silenced machines. We chatted about the local scene, which we agreed was really good.

There were miles of green lanes open to riders to enjoy. It was just a question of knowing where they were. The novice was particularly impressed that I had been able to follow a largely green lane route all day, although he found the idea of green lane riding to Land's End rather daunting. I showed them the last few lanes I had used on my map and gave them membership details of the TRF. Clearly they needed to join up if they were to get full benefit from their local network. The alternative was to talk to the County Council Rights of Way Officer, but he would be less geared up to the needs of trail riders than the local experts in the TRF. In the United States of America, most states have teams of trail riding experts working for them, planning and maintaining long distance trails for the public to use. There it would be the best plan to approach the state or county authorities for advice. In Britain we are years behind the Americans' enlightened approach.

Novice and expert enjoying a Hampshire lane. (D. Giles)

My two new friends were able to give me several useful tips about the lanes which lay ahead. All were in fine condition, they said. They had ridden most of them that morning. They were able to point out one or two potential navigational difficulties, and I warned them of the mud ahead of them in a few lanes time.

I joined the Lun Way, yet another very ancient long distance route. After passing Lunway's Inn, the Lun Way becomes a splendidly wide green road. I imagine it owes this great width to its use in the last century as a drove road. I whizzed along, but not as fast as the twelve year old girl in a pink sweater and riding wellies on her white pony. They were really flying over the turf. After half a mile she pulled up to check for nuts and bolts which might have worked loose at such high speed, or is it girths you have to check on horses?

"Lower Road" ran parallel to the Lun Way, but a mile south of it. It was equally wide, but had lost much of its grass to reveal the underlying chalk as it drove past the back gardens of a smart new housing estate. I crossed the dual carriageway A34 on a concrete bridge and rode over Worthy Down on dried mud, worn smooth by the footsteps of many walkers. This stretch did not seem to see too many horses. It ended by an oil well. Stockbridge Number One was run from Texas by Texaco, who had found oil beneath the rolling Hampshire chalk.

Through a gate by the side of the main road, I picked up the green lane over Crowley Down. This was another wide, well-used chalky road. Where it entered the woods it resembled a "ride" through the grounds of a great estate more than an ancient public highway. By this I mean that it looked too attractive to be a road for us peasants. It looked as if it had been planned by some landscape artist for a rich landowner. Perhaps the opposite was true. Perhaps the landscape artists saw how this old road had developed and decided to copy it. We are so used to seeing copies that we fail to recognise an original.

I turned right from the "ride" along a grassy track. This took me past a hidden campsite, buried in Crawley Forest, and brought me to the A30 Roman road to Stockbridge.

I stopped in Stockbridge to buy a new film for my camera and an ice lolly. The weather had warmed up considerably. The sun was hot in the shelter of the houses. Stockbridge, as the name implies, grew to importance as an overnight stop on the long cattle drive from Wales to the great fairs and markets at Farnham and Maidstone in the pre-railway age. The railways took away this use of the roads as well as most of the passenger traffic in the reign of Queen Victoria. The railways put the drovers out of work as well as ending the golden age of stage coaching.

One private house near the actual bridge in Stockbridge used to be an inn. I am told that it still bears the announcement: "Gwair Tymherus, Porfa Flasus, Cwrw Da, A Cwal Cysurus" (Worthwhile grass, pleasant pasture, good beer, and a comfortable shelter) which was a message to the passing Welsh drovers assuring them of a welcome in their own tongue. I am afraid I couldn't find the house, which was disappointing.

I found the Roman road to the west out of Stockbridge, which goes straight over Meon Hill while the stagecoach road takes an easier gradient on what is now a dual carriageway. The Roman road is a quiet, grassy track between hawthorn hedges. The modern road rejoins it over the brow of the hill. It is quite spectacular to see the green lane becoming the modern trunk road, running straight ahead, far straighter than most of our modern motorways, as far as the eye can see.

I turned off the Roman road at Houghton Down Farm, where three men and a dog were playing cricket. The dog, of course, fielded far better than a full cricket team. Nothing could get past him. A boundary was out of the question, even in the front garden.

I rejoined the tarmac on a back road in Broughton, where I was faced with an enticing sign – "Deep Ford". I like fords, and this looked well worth investigating. A second warning sign marked the ford itself, where tarmac gave way to water, flowing fast and perhaps four yards across. I plunged in, using first gear to be prepared for slippery rocks. I splashed out on the far side without difficulty. The water was no more than a foot deep.

A car had followed me along the tarmac to the ford. I parked the bike and went back to watch him cross the stream. I tried not to put him off, but, after much consideration, he reversed back along the lane to find a drier route to Broughton.

A great, hairy-hoofed horse came along the road, his harness jingling and his cart fit for a show. His driver halted him for a chat and to allow me to take his photo. To such a vehicle a foot deep presented no problems. It was hardly something to notice. It is the timorous motor car which has replaced our fords with bridges, not the horse and wagon.

"Clarendon Way" said a new wooden fingerpost, which took me past Broughton village fete. The fete was well under way. The maypole had been plaited and unplaited by the dancing school children, and the vicar was announcing the winners of the raffle through a loud hailer. As I took the lane between tall hedges, a lone Spitfire droned overhead – a relic of the Second World War brought back to life to lift the eyes of the fete goers and make them remember their fathers and grandfathers who had fought and died so that such village festivals might continue.

I joined the Roman road from Winchester to Salisbury; more precisely, to Old Sarum, since Salisbury did not exist in Roman times. I always think of Roman roads as

Early summer growth makes this lane rather too green.

being raised on a causeway above the surrounding land, but this one had sunk two feet or more below the fields. The centuries of use since the Romans left Britain had worn it down, while the surrounding agriculture had raised the fields up to their present levels. The Roman road took a turn at Middle Winterslow in a concave holloway in a beech wood. It was easy to follow to Dunstable Farm.

The crossroads had become slightly displaced in the intervening two thousand years and the road now ran between barbed wire fences. There was a long stretch as wide as a field which ran behind some houses. Then it narrowed to a single track and all but disappeared in the beech wood. And then I saw the causeway stretching before me. This was what Roman roads should be like! It had been cleared of encroaching scrub and undergrowth recently and stood straight and grassy. My thanks are extended to those who saved this stretch for me over the centuries and who cleared it so recently for me to enjoy.

I met a family out walking and stopped to talk. They were French, and were more astounded than I at finding such a road. The two children collected grass and sticks, while the mother, in perfect English, and grandmother, in beautifully clear French, explained to me that in France even the footpaths which grandmother had known as a girl had disappeared. They said this was the story all over France. No-one was fighting for access to the countryside. The country roads and paths were being swallowed up without protest. This was their story and we agreed that it was a sad one. How lucky we were in Britain that nameless thousands of country lovers had fought hard and worked long to save such treasures as this grassy Roman bank for future generations to enjoy.

We parted thoughtfully. I followed the green bank to the trunk road to modern Salisbury. The Roman road crosses over, still aiming for the great hill of Old Sarum and I followed its now tarmac surface to the very foot of the hill. My campsite was a few yards away in Hudson's Field, and I chuffed wearily but happily towards the warden's portakabin.

The campsite was a fenced part of a huge meadow, used as a recreation ground by this end of the city. The meadow was lined with horse boxes when I arrived. There had been a gymkhana. The crowds had gone and the last horses were being encouraged into their trailers. The hot dog seller's van was selling his last dog to a

A well-laid hedge is a very rare sight these days. This one is the result of a hedging competition.

hungry young jockey. The loudspeakers were being enticed into the back of an estate car.

I threaded my way through the melee, parked and entered the warden's office to book in for the night. Before putting up my tent, I rode towards Salisbury in search of food. It was nearly six o'clock and most shops would have closed by now.

I was in luck. Just down the road from the campsite was a local supermarket which was still open. Having purchased the ingredients for supper, breakfast and lunch tomorrow, I continued into Salisbury to explore.

The original Salisbury was on the commanding hilltop at Old Sarum. This is a prehistoric site, later an Iron Age hill fort. The Romans built a town here at an important crossroads and called it Sorviodunum. It was a saxon settlement in the Dark ages, known as Sarobyrig. Saxon jewellery has been found on the site. The Norman conquerors took over the hill and built a castle and a cathedral on it. Osmund, a relative of King William the Conqueror, was the first bishop and lord of the castle. Over the years, disputes developed between cathedral and castle. The growing population of the town around the hilltop suffered from a shortage of water. They began to drift to the water meadows in the valley below. Things came to a head between church and military in 1220, when Bishop Richard le Poore moved his seat two miles downhill to establish New Sarum, the modern Salisbury. The old cathedral was demolished and a new one was built, on rather doubtful foundations, close to the river. A new town was mapped out by the bishop, each building plot paying him a ground rent of twelve pence a year. The castle survived as a military establishment until the fourteenth century, but the town of Old Sarum died and the town of New Sarum grew and prospered.

The beauties of Salisbury have been increased over the centuries by a rich variety of buildings. The original gridiron street plan of Bishop Richard remains, with the cathedral close the richest treasury of achitecture. The open water courses along many of the streets have long been a matter of debate.

In 1635, Lieutenant Hammond, in his "Short Survey of the Western Counties" approved, "Every street is here supplied with pleasant little rivoletts which are knee deep gliding sweetly through her bowells, to wash and cleanse them." Daniel Defoe, however, thought "it keeps the streets always dirty, full of wet and filth, and weeds, even in the middle of summer." Celia Fiennes, visiting the city fifty years after Lieutenant Hammond, said it had "pretty large town streetes broad but through the midst of them runs a little rivulet of water which makes the streetes not so clean or so easye to passe in."

My impression was not so much of water as of traffic. Juggernauts tiptoed through the narrow streets on eighteen giant wheels, growling through their gearboxes and spitting fumes from cavernous exhausts. Monsters, snared in the medieval maze of the town, they were desperate to escape to their natural habitat — dual carriageway and motorway, where their turbochargers could howl joyfuly as they gobbled up the kilometres. Here, their brakes hissed, their tyres squealed, as they squeezed past pedestrians and pushchairs. Their hot breath coughed at the old houses as if, like the big bad wolf, they would blow the houses down.

It was a relief to get back to the quiet campsite. I found a corner to myself and pitched the tent. I took a hot shower in the sports centre block which adjoins the campsite, then snuggled into my tent for a tasty supper. Rissotto, yoghurt, crunchie cereal, coffee. I was still hungry. I lay in my sleeping bag, listening to the rain spattering on the flysheet, waiting for the water to heat for a cup of powdered soup. Instant soup in cup sized packages is the salvation of the weary lightweight camper.

A more serious bit of lane maintenance. A team of volunteers tackles a fallen tree on a steep lane south of Bristol. (D. Giles)

I reflected on what had happened and what lay ahead.

A day's ride in a friendly group on well-explored tracks is very different to day. after day of solitary trekking into the unknown. Plucking up courage to tackle yet another lane. Will it be ploughed out? overgrown? end in a front garden? Will there be angry voices and loud abuse?

The sight of a tyre track gives you moral support. Someone else has used the lane recently. The second time through is so much easier, but loses the excitement of the new and unexplored.

A rope is attached to take the weight of the tree and stop the chain saw being jammed. (D. Giles)

Breakthrough! (D. Giles)

Once you've cleared the lane, you will want to ride it! Richard Tallon's antics indicate the steepness of the lane which is not really apparent in this shot. (D. Giles)

Those eloquently blank signposts in Sussex were a great reassurance, after a day of painstaking map-reading across Kent where only the long distance paths were signed.

Riding home is definitely the way to go. As you become more tired each day, as the aches spread to more and more parts of your body, as the mud and damp penetrate further into your once clean clothes, the thought of ever more familiar tracks is a great comfort.

Most of tomorrow's lanes I had ridden before.

Tuesday
Turnpikes and Mud – Into the West Country

Sketch map showing the way into the West Country.

I woke to strong winds and a sky filled with grey clouds. Most of the night had been dry. The tent was dry. But it looked like it would rain soon.

The now familiar breakfast of crunchie cereal, bread and honey was washed down with a cup of coffee. That was the last of the honey, which was sad, but I only packed a tiny plastic container and did not expect it to last long.

My wash was rather hurried, as I watched the clouds thickening. I just got the tent down before the rain started. Taking down a wet tent is not too bad, but putting up a wet tent at the end of the day, especially if it has rained all day, is no fun at all. The tent and everything else was wrapped up in polythene bags for the day's ride to try to keep the wet out.

The northern ring road took me round Salisbury to Wilton. I passed under the railway bridge and on to the turnpike road over Grovelly Hill. I hoped that this road, with a few diversions to avoid tarmac where possible, would take me from the heart of Wiltshire across the border to Somerset.

The first turnpike appeared over three hundred years ago. In 1663, the Houses of Parliament passed an Act which enabled the justices of the peace for Hertfordshire, Cambridgeshire and Huntingdonshire to levy tolls on travellers for the repair of the Great North Road where it passed through those counties. The first toll gate or turnpike was established at Wadesmill in Hertfordshire. A new era of road development was dawning. After twenty-one years this first toll system was dismantled, but its advantages were recognised as a way to pay for the maintenance of roads.

By 1700, seven Acts of Parliament authorising Turnpike Trusts had been passed. In the next fifty years, several hundred Trusts were set up. The last decade of the eighteenth century saw an average of fifty Acts of Parliament setting up Turnpike Trusts each year.

These Acts gave permission to local people, who were prepared to raise money by public loans to build or repair roads, to levy tolls for the use of the road and so to repay the loan. Travellers on foot were exempt from tolls, as were soldiers in uniform and Royal Mail coaches, but all other users were charged a toll based on the size of the

carriage or waggon and the number of horses pulling it, or in the case of stock, the number and type of animals in the drove or flock. Specially high rates were charged for wagons and carts having wheel rims less than three inches wide. It was thought that wider wheels would help to roll the road surface smooth.

The establishment of thousands of miles of turnpike roads led to a huge increase in traffic which eventually threatened the very system itself. In the early eighteenth century they made travel smoother and faster for all. But as the century advanced, traffic multiplied and complaints about the state of the turnpikes increased. Arthur Young, travelling in the 1760s, described some turnpikes as terrible, infamous and execrable. The turnpike system became simply overloaded with traffic. Daniel Defoe described many roads as "exceedingly throng'd with a vast number of carriages" carrying agricultural produce of all sorts, with "infinite droves of black cattle, hogs and sheep" as well as pack horses, mail coaches and ordinary travellers on horseback.

I wondered what my turnpike would be like. Would it be "exceedingly throng'd" or would it be worn out by all that eighteenth century traffic? The drizzle stopped as I rode through a great avenue of beeches and came out in the open on a chalk track over rolling downland. The road was a series of swoops and bumps, with the occasional puddle. I passed a milestone standing two feet tall at the side of the road. It told me I was "V MILES FROM SARUM" and was dated 1750. It was erected when the road was given its turnpike charter by Parliament.

Between this milestone and the next, I passed a brace of partridge and two hares. To say I passed them is not exact. As I approached to within twenty feet, they took off across the surrounding fields. I was surprised how much bigger Jack Hare was than his cousin, Peter Rabbit. Hares are a rare sight these days, especially in the close countryside of my home in Cornwall.

I stopped at the sixth mile stone. I took its photograph and paced out the road width at this point. It was about seventy feet wide. My motorcycle looked lost in the middle of such a road. Most turnpikes seem to have been even wider, typically a hundred feet wide to allow for droves of animals to graze as they walked. Perhaps this

"VI Miles from SARUM" declares the turnpike milestone, dated 1750.

along the Great North Road in 1708. The earliest milestones were the result of private enterprise. They would make the way easier to follow and thus more attractive to paying customers at the toll gates. In 1773 an Act of Parliament ordered all Turnpike Trusts to provide both guide-posts and milestones on their roads.

The view to the south over the Nadder valley was huge. Carved into the chalk hillside in the distance was a great, white map of Australia. Maps, flags and badges were cut into the hillsides by troops stationed in the area during the War. A homesick Australian regiment had been billetted near here.

I followed miles of splendid going, up and down over the grassy undulations of the ridge. When I first rode this lane, ten years before, I became lost in a network of paths at the edge of Grovelly Wood. I could not get lost today, because too many motorcycle tyre prints marked out the correct way.

The only vehicle I met on the turnpike was an ancient Renault van with an even more ancient driver in a flat cap. We exchanged nods and touched a finger to our respective peaks, but you can't stop to chat to someone in a closed vehicle very easily.

Past Manor Farm, the road was wider still, and then narrowed to a single track between well-spaced, but overgrown hedges. I passed through a gate into a huge open sheep pasture. There was no sign of the turnpike road! I looked at the map. I looked back the way I had come. All seemed correct. I left the bike and walked around a bit, searching for landmarks. There was a wood which seemed to be in the right place compared with the map. The turnpike should go straight before me over the brow of the hill. I took a compass bearing, started the engine and chuffed ahead. A compass is all too often essential on green lanes. All was well. Over the crest I found the A303 hurtling past. I joined it for a little while before picking up the green turnpike at Gosney Cottage.

To avoid the next tarmac stretch, I had plotted a detour slightly further south for a few miles. I searched for my detour across Two Mile Down, with the drizzle blowing hard in my face. I found the gate, but there was no road beyond it. Sheep grazed in a field with not a trace of a lane. There was no sign as far as the eye could see of a green lane. There was not even a bump in the ground, not the trace of a wheel rut. At least, in this driving drizzle I could find nothing. I gave up and found a way round my planned route.

one had lost some of its former width to the farmer's plough. Its edges were marked with barbed wire fences — all too easy to take down and re-erect a few feet closer together. It has happened in some parts of Wiltshire, I know.

Milestones appeared on our roads in the reign of Charles II. The Romans, of course, knew all about them, but no-one afterwards used them until the Dover Road was marked out with them in 1663. Stones were set up

The road was seventy feet wide at the VIth milestone. My motorcycle looked lost in such an empty width, which would have been "exceedingly throng'd with a vast number of carriages" in the turnpike's heyday.

I took a tarmac road through Hindon, and picked up a wide, hedged track which, for two miles, paralleled the tarmac turnpike to the north. I ran out of alternatives and had to take the trunk road to Charnage Down. Here, the turnpike was green again, and there was another milestone. It informed me that I was now twenty miles from Sarum and ninety-eight miles from London. The milestone bore the same date as the others I had passed, 1750. I was still on the same wide green route I had picked up just outside Salisbury.

While looking at the milestone and the sweeping view to the south, a herd of young cows came across the field behind me. As I rode on, they followed me on their side of the fence. It shows how fast I ride, because they could easily keep up with me. Sheep run away from you as you approach because they are scared, but cattle run towards you because they are curious.

After crossing the B3095, we have a dual carriageway green lane! It is eighty feet wide, with two quite distinct and very well used tracks. "XXII Miles FROM SARUM 1750" said the milestone and, carved on the back, RB 1919. Was this early twentieth century graffitti? Was RB the father of Kilroy?

Whitesheet Hill marked the end of the Wiltshire chalk downland. The Hill carried many marks of ancient habitation. There was a causewayed enclosure from the New Stone Age about 3000 BC, Bronze Age burial mounds from between 1800 and 800 BC, an Iron Age hill fort from 600 BC to 0 BC. The surrounding hills bore the marks of medieval strip farming. It seemed to me that my turnpike from the great hilltop castle at Old Sarum had been a route to Whitesheet Hill long before the Turnpike Trusts, in fact long, long before the Mother of Parliaments passed its very first Act.

I swooped from the high chalk into the green holloway of Long Lane, lined with bluebells and tall, white parsley sparkling in the sun. On the horizon stood Alfred's Tower, which marked the Somerset border. Alfred's Tower stands on Kingsettle Hill in the grounds of Stourhead House, though two miles from the house itself. The triangular tower is one hundred and sixty feet tall, built of brick in 1772 to mark the place where King Alfred the Great raised his standard before marching to victory over the Danes in 879.

Between Wiltshire and Somerset there is a natural county boundary, which is uncommon in England. Here it is not so much a boundary line as a boundary zone. The ancient tracks and roads, visible for miles over the ocean swell of the chalk downs of Wiltshire, dive into a labyrinth of hills, streams and forests, and are immediately lost. One road survives as far as Bruton — my turnpike from Salisbury, which became Long Lane and is now called the Hardway, but this too disappears before penetrating far into Somerset.

The boundary zone is the primeval Forest of Selwood, which once clothed the countryside in a huge arc from the neighbourhood of Bath southwards to Dorset. It had width as well as length, extending well into Wiltshire around Warminster, where the woods of Longleat are its vestiges. The name "Selwood" means "the Wood of Sallows" and tells of the waterlogged nature of the terrain in ancient times.

This natural frontier protected the Britons of the decayed Roman Empire from the invading Saxons. The legendary King Arthur and his Knights of the Round Table are at least partly based on historical fact. His castle of Camelot in the Sixth Century may well have been Cadbury Castle. This would make Camelot's role obvious. It would command the eastern gateway, south of Selwood, into the heart of Arthur's kingdom.

The same natural frontier of Selwood helped King Alfred the Great hold off the Danes from his western strongholds while he regrouped and prepared to counter-attack.

The change in landscape also marks a change in building materials. Houses were almost all stone now, not brick. I noticed the mainly brick houses all over the chalk lands of the south-east. Through West Wiltshire, I passed few buildings. The farms I did see were brick. Now, in Somerset, even the garden walls are stone. Wooden fences in Selwood Forest are rare, because stone is so readily available.

As I came round a bend, I saw two cars parked at the side of the road with orange hazard lights flashing. There had been an accident. I was the fourth vehicle on the scene. Someone had been despatched to Bruton to phone for the emergency services — police, ambulance and fire brigade.

The crashed car was lying on its side. Its bonnet was jammed between a tree and a high stone wall. The tree had smashed the windscreen.

The first people there, seeing the injuries were not too serious, had managed to help the two occupants of the car to climb out. This had been anything but easy. It entailed climbing onto the side of the car and lifting open the passenger door, then helping the two inside up and lowering them to the ground. The driver of the crashed car had broken his hand and blood was dripping from a gash in his forearm.

As I approached, the two men from the crashed car were walking down the road away from me. The passenger was supporting the injured driver, who was clutching his wounded forearm.

The little knot of rescuers looked on.

"They shouldn't walk about like that," said one. "They should sit down."

As we watched, the behaviour of the two men became ever more odd.

"They've climbed into the field!"

Perhaps this was a lavatory visit?

"No! Look! They're running off!"

Sure enough, the two were scampering across the fields as fast as their injuries would allow them. They were in a great haste to get away before the police arrived on the scene.

"They are joy riders!"

"They must have stolen the car."

"It stinks of booze. They're afraid of the breathaliser."

They were gone and that was for sure.

I talked to the two men who had rescued them from the crash. They had learned the "post-accident" drill and put it into practice. They had parked their cars to "protect the accident scene" with hazard warning lights flashing; noted injuries and sent for the emergency services. On reflection, they thought they should have left the two men in the car then they could not have run off. But they were lying on top of each other in a tangled heap in the overturned car and the driver, underneath, was suffering. They had done well to get them out of the door five feet in the air.

One of the rescuers was stained with blood on his shirt and his trousers. The thanks for his help was to see the two accident "victims" run off before the police arrived and to have his day out with his family ruined by the bloodstains on his clothes.

"I can't go in dressed like this!" he complained.

"Of course you can," replied his wife. "When you explain why you are spattered with blood, they will give you the best table in the restaurant. You deserve it!"

It would be nice to think that she was right.

A red car drew up and a young woman alighted. She had phoned the police and the ambulance. They would be along shortly. Three cars were now parked by the scene of the accident awaiting the arrival of the police. I felt superfluous. It was time for me to go. I had seen nothing of the accident itself and could give the police no real help. At least I had been willing to help, but there had been nothing for me to do.

I kicked the engine back to life once more and looked for the next green lane, where I could escape the all too real "carnage on our roads" which we were told about in the road safety campaigns. I thought, if I had been ten minutes earlier along that road, that drunken joy rider could have taken me with him between the tree and the wall. I hastened back to the solitude and safety of a quiet byway.

As I climbed out of Pitcombe on a dry, well-used dirt road, I tried to forget the tangled mess I had just seen. At a quiet crossroads of two green lanes I stopped, found a spot sheltered from the wind, and settled down for a rest and lunch.

Up to now, most of my green lane journey had been along major green lane routes – the Pilgrims' Way, the South Downs Way, Roman roads, the Salisbury turnpike. From now on, I was to follow country lanes which had never, as far as I could sort out, formed much of a long distance route.

The first part of the green lane past Grove Farm had been attacked by a hedge slashing machine. The second part was a climb in a deep holloway between "mature" hedges thirty feet high, containing a tremendous variety of trees. I understand that the greater the variety of hedgerow trees, the older the hedgerow. This one was certainly old. A grey squirrel scuttered across a fallen sapling above my head. I stopped to look at a badger's set. Brock's excavations had produced a spoil heap which half blocked the lane.

After Castle Cary I was on the first part of the Somerset Levels, the flat rich wetland that surrounds the River Brue on its tortuous journey from Bruton to Burnham on Sea. The green lane to Boulter's Bridge was lined not with hedges but with drainage ditches called rhynes (pronounced "reens") which lowered the water level to a foot or more below that of the surrounding farmland. The Levels provide very rich soil, traditionally used for dairy farming. I passed through a field of dairy cows, surrounded by an electric fence.

Boulter's Bridge itself was a narrow, hump-backed affair. It was no more than five feet wide and had no parapet. I parked the bike on its side stand and walked forward to open the wooden farm gate into the fields beyond the bridge. I heard a dull crunch behind me, and turned to see my trusty Yamaha lying on its side. It had been unstable on the sloping bridge and had rolled off its stand. It lay with the handlebars over the edge of the

bridge, five feet above the water surface. The water looked deep. I had come very close to losing my bike in the murky, brown depths of the River Alham.

It was the devil of a job to pick Daisy up again. I could not get underneath to lift, because she was too near the edge. I dragged her sideways and finally heaved her upright on my knees beneath her.

On we went across more dairy grassland. I had to stop to remove an electric fence across my path. I turned round, and the bike was lying on its side again! Surely it could not have fallen off its stand again? The ground was flat. No, this time the stand had simply sunk completely into the ground. It had broken through the thin, hard crust of dry earth and buried itself in the soft mud beneath. This time Daisy had sustained some damage. The speedometer mounting, plastic for lightness, had taken the weight of the bike as it toppled awkwardly over. An elastic "bandage" repaired the injury. I carried one or two strips cut from an old inner tube to strap on anything which came loose during the trip. One of these would act as a temporary repair as far as journey's end.

I must be more careful parking in future.

I trundled south-westwards along the Roman Fosse Way, now the A37 trunk road and turned off at the Cross Keys Inn on the crossroads. The green lane ran out of the rear of the pub car park. It was VERY muddy, churned up by cows sinking to their knees in dark goo. Beyond the railway bridge it was a green, grassy track between trim hawthorn hedges and then it was REALLY muddy. Heavy brown putty, churned and pock holed by cattle stretched before me for nearly a mile.

The best way to tackle mud is with speed. If you go at it

Mud is a problem when riding solo. It cannot be taken too fast for fear of an accident. Colin Patient takes it steady on his Suzuki four-stroke.

Dave Barnet finds a muddy pothole to wash his Kawasaki. (D. Giles)

quickly, you can skim over the surface before it has a chance to suck your wheels in and clog everything up. But this lane was narrow and I was alone. Too much speed could see me upside down in the hedge, and I would have to wait a very long time for rescue. I went as fast as I dared, standing on the footrests and trying to aim between the worst of the mud and the encroaching hedge. I got very hot with the effort and concentration needed for this sort of riding.

Once again I was reminded of the extra difficulties of riding solo. In company I could have relaxed more and gone faster, knowing that if I took a tumble there would be helping hands to pick up the bike and to share a laugh at my expense. Solo riding was more serious.

The next lane was an improvement. A single track had been cleared between sparse hedges and a ditch. Someone had worked hard clearing this. The Somerset Levels are very fertile, which is good for agriculture but means that keeping green lanes open can be a constant battle against encroaching vegetation.

I took in a little cross of green lanes near Charlton Mackrell, which were a pleasant rest after the mud.

Then I dropped down over the last outpost of Selwood Forest to Compton Dundon. The lane ran through the trees, down the side of a steep, wooded coombe, then

into a stream. The whole wood showed signs of being used for trials riding practice by motorcycles. I knew that this was with the consent of the landowner, and tried to stick to the public road amidst the maze of other tracks. I jammed the bike in one section of the stream. The water had washed such a deep gully through the gritty soil that, although the spring-loaded footrests flipped back out of the way as they were designed to, the engine itself became stuck. The gully was too narrow for the engine to get through.

I paused to consider the problem. Brute force was the answer I decided. A mighty heave on the handlebars and a powerful burp on the throttle, and we were clear.

From the ridge above Street I could see Brent Knoll, twenty miles away as the crow flies, which marked the end of the day's ride at Burnham on Sea. I skirted Glastonbury and set out across the main expanse of the Somerset Levels on Godney and Westhay Moors. By some strange quirk of geography, the Levels south of the River Brue are called something Heath, while those north of the Brue are called something Moor. The land is the same both north and south – miles and miles of dark, flat peat. It is as flat as the Fenland of Cambridgeshire, and I have never seen anywhere flatter than that. The flatness can be devastating in its monotony when walking or cycling. You never seem to reach the far side, and a headwind can turn level going into the longest hill in the world. It is not so bad on a motor vehicle. You feel you can conquer it with the aid of internal combustion. The local farmers seem to feel the same. For centuries they wrestled with this wet, windswept landscape. Only the tractor, replacing horsepower, has made it possible to grow crops here. Dairy cattle and willows grown for basket making used to be the only harvests. Now the main crop is the soil itself. Mechanical excavators dig up the peat for sale to gardeners throughout the country. Sedge peat is the boom industry of the Levels.

I rode six parallel green roads across the Moors. They all cross the North Drain, one of the main drainage channels of the Levels, on steep, hump-backed bridges. I know one or two people living locally who have used these to see how far their bikes can fly! I had no wish to copy them. You approach each bridge totally blind to what is on the far side, since the bridges tower some ten feet above the surrounding ground. To rush at such a hurdle with sufficient speed to take off, not knowing what lies beyond, is recklessness beyond the bounds of the basic rules of trail riding.

The lanes became steadily easier as I progressed westwards. The first two were deep in peat, black and bottomless where it was wet, brown and passable where it was dry. The more westerly tracks were given hardcore surfaces of broken brick and other building rubble. All around the farmers were busy digging up and selling their land by the bagful.

I climbed the steep ridge which joins Wells to Wedmore, an island in the midst of the wetlands. Mill Lane at Latcham was a green lane I remembered well. It was here that I had burnt out the clutch on my 350 Yamaha road bike. Two of us had tackled this lane, not knowing what to expect. It started innocently enough, but then turned into the heaviest, stickiest mud I know. Bostik is a lubricant next to this stuff. The standard road tyres of my standard road-going Yamaha 350 nearly doubled in diameter, the mud jammed between wheels and mud-

Farm vehicle ruts, sunk deep into soft mud, should be tackled with circumspection. Notice the half-buried branch, which would throw off an incautious rider.

guards and stopped the wheels turning. It pulled off our wellington boots, which weighed a stone with all the mud stuck on them. Within twenty yards of the end of the lane, the engine ceased to drive the back wheel. The smell of a cooked clutch is something unique. It must be smelt to be appreciated. Once smelt it is not easily forgotten. I can smell that Yamaha clutch now, and the mud. We towed it home and I finally admitted that trail riding in Somerset in January required a trail bike, not a road bike. I kept the 350 for summer use for several more years, but bought a "real" trail bike for the winter mud.

Mill Lane revealed none of this history of my trail riding "career" today. It was dry and gentle, and I could relax and enjoy the view to the north across Wedmore Moor to Cheddar Gorge and the Mendip Hills which mark the northern boundary of the Levels.

I wanted to find a fitting lane to end the day, and chose Madwoman's Lane, Wedmore. I had never ridden it. It had always been totally overgrown when I lived in Somerset. But I knew that the local Trail Riders group had cleared it recently and its name made it irresistible. It turned out to be impossible. On reflection, I would have been able to come down it in company, but there was absolutely no way I could ride up it solo. I made about a hundred yards progress, but was completely stopped by a series of natural steps which would have made a good observed section in a competitive trial, except the lane was too narrow for anyone to observe. The first giant step

The extra grab handle, made from a redundant seat strap, is useful for hauling the bike out of really deep potholes in the mud.

was earth, the second was a great slab of rock and the third was a narrow rock gully, similar to the one I had jammed in at Compton Dundon, except this one was rock not earth and I was trying to go up not down. And the smell of the lane was awful. Somewhere nearby must be a cowshed whose effluent flowed away along Madwoman's Lane.

I turned back. The last lane of the day had defeated me, but I had done enough. I turned towards the coast and a bed for the night. Burnham on Sea has more than its fair share of campsites. I even knew of one or two good ones. But Burnham on Sea was also my parents' retirement home and I had arranged to spend a night with them on my journey. They thought the whole expedition quite hare-brained and pointless. Perhaps they were right. I felt I was having the most tremendous adventure, but could not persuade them of this.

I dined well. Mum's cooking takes some beating. I listened to all the local news and slept indoors. It was good to relax and turn my mind to other things than green lanes for a while. But I would keep thinking about tomorrow.

My mind would keep coming back to trail riding and the road ahead. What was the weather forecast? Sunshine and showers – which sounded just right to me. Tomorrow I would cross Exmoor, the best trail riding country in the South of England.

I had leisure enough to consider bike maintenance. Tried and trusted old Daisy had needed very little on this trip. I filled up the chain oiler with the spare oil carried in an old shampoo bottle each evening. I adjusted the chain only twice throughout the entire trip. I checked the engine oil level through the sight glass in the gearbox, but the level did not alter all week. Maintenance was complete.

What a far cry was this modern motorcycle from the early machines which struggled along our pre-tarmac

Routine maintenance involves checking the chain tension and refilling the oiler, seen here just above the chainguard. Note the spring-loaded roller chain tensioner fitted to the lower chain run.

roads. Even the machines of my youth required a major service, spread over several evenings, before undertaking a long run to, say, London. Spare parts would fill every available pocket. The addresses of bike shops on the way would be noted. Parents would be warned of my estimated time of return, and would be on standby with car and towrope. Such things were part of my youthful motorcycling for any journey of more than fifty miles.

I turned in for the night, confident that Daisy would cope with the next day's challenging green lanes without missing a beat. Would I be able to ride her up the steep hills and through the fords and over the open moor of Exmoor? Tomorrow would prove my ability to ride. Daisy would not let me down.

Map of Route across Exmoor.

Wednesday
Exmoor

I had warned my parents that I would be away early and we had said our goodbyes before going to sleep. I was on the road just after six. Not having to pack up the tent speeded my early start.

I knew I had a long day ahead of me. Exmoor and the surrounding country contains so many good lanes, that I was hard pressed to decide which ones to leave out. The area could occupy a week's trail riding by itself, and a separate book to describe what there is to see.

I missed out the network of good lanes between Bridgwater and the Quantock Hills and headed for Hawkridge reservoir. There were a couple of fishermen there even at this early hour in the middle of the week.

The sun breaks up early morning mist on the Quantocks.

Parson's Lane took me above Aisholt on my favourite approach to the Quantocks. You climb through the woods, which start to thin out and give glimpses of a view opening out on either side. The tarmac ends and a dirt road bears off right leading to a car park and viewing point. Straight ahead is a well used dirt track, littered with large stones, which beckons you onwards. You follow the edge of the forest, slowly climbing the side of a great combe which stretches away on the left. Exmoor ponies, turned loose to graze on the hills, can often be seen here amongst the bracken.

As I mounted steadily towards the main ridge, I came up to a herd of red deer. It was too early in the morning for them to smell danger. They looked up, puzzled but not alarmed by my passing within a hundred yards of them. Stag hunting remains a favourite local sport, both on the Quantocks and on Exmoor. Although I do not condone the cruelty of chasing an animal to its death, I am sure from my knowledge of the local farming community that, but for the Hunt, the red deer would disappear from the Quantock Hills. They would be poached out of existence to make room for more sheep and ponies to be grazed.

I joined the Ridgeway, which runs the length of the Quantocks, from the south-east near Taunton, north-west to the coast at West Quantoxhead. The dense pine forest dogged my right hand as far as Triscombe Stone. This is the Somerset rival to the Blarney Stone, but kissing the Triscombe Stone brings good luck rather than the "gift of the gab". Parked by the Stone, which can be reached on a tarmac road from Bridgwater, was a gaily painted old bus, converted to a mobile home for hippies. The Peace Campers were sleeping peacefully as I passed.

I followed the prehistoric ridge route, wide between its towering beech tree boundaries, for another two miles. The beeches are superb. They may once have been planted as a hedge and windbreak when this was a drove road, but now they are mature and majestic, looking down at me on my little mechanical beetle scuttling along amongst their roots.

After the road crossing above Crowcombe Park, the beech trees are left behind and the wide dirt track follows the bare ridge for a further three miles to Bicknoller Post. I passed a second herd of red deer on this section. These were rather more skittish, perhaps because it was now later in the morning. Perhaps the rain squall which hit me shortly afterwards was the cause.

I could see the rain approaching from Dunkery Hill on Exmoor fifteen miles away. It came along the north flank of the Brendon Hills as a black shadow in the bright morning and tried hard to soak me for ten minutes before driving on along the coast towards Bridgwater. After the rain there was a rainbow which arched out of the fields towards Minehead's white houses gleaming below the wooded cliff of North Hill in the distance. Across the Bristol Channel ahead of me, the coast of South Wales was obscured by cloud as it all too often is. I watched the

The Blue Ball Inn nestles below the steep climb to Triscombe Stone.

rain squall's progress past the great concrete monoliths of the Hinckley Point nuclear power station. I could see along the English coast, around the vast sweep of Bridgwater Bay to the solitary, unnaturally round hilltop of Brent Knoll and beyond, to the distinct mauve outline of the Mendip Hills which divide Somerset from the modern county of Avon.

They say that Bicknoller Post, near the northern tip of the ridge, was a staging post where horses were changed on coaches climbing the Quantocks from east to west on the main road to the West Country via Bridgwater. The Old Coach Road shows up clearly on early nineteenth century maps, before the new turnpike was cut into the foot of the hills around Quantoxhead. Perhaps there was a stable block up here, but I have never found any remains buried in the heather.

I sat back in the saddle and trundled peacefully round Beacon Hill towards Staple Plain. I have never been able to rush this bit, the view is just too good to hurry. Below is one of the deepest and steepest of the many deep and steep Quantock coombes. Its sides are covered in tall bracken, capable of hiding a whole herd of red deer from

all but the most careful observer. From the foot of the coombe stretch mile after mile of patchwork green fields. Beyond rise the hills; first the Brendons, green and patched with dark woodland; then the great heather humps of Exmoor, rising to a point at the stone cairn surmounting Dunkery Hill, the highest point in Somerset.

The last few hundred yards to Staple Plain are covered in stone cricket balls. The gritty sandstone provides grip, as long as you keep your balance. I once fell off within feet of the car park on Staple Plain and was most embarrassed. It amused the massed picnickers in the car park no end.

Today the car park was deserted and I passed no dog walkers as I descended the tarmac track to Staple village. I had hoped to bump into the Quantock Warden, who is often up and about early patrolling the hills on horseback. Later in the day he takes out the Land Rover, but the early morning round is usually tackled on his hunter. It was the Warden, Rik Stokes, who pioneered the use of motorcyclists to patrol the Quantocks. He approached the local Trail Riders group and asked for help. "Set a thief to catch a thief" was his principle, and his team of poachers turned gamekeepers went a long way to restoring tranquility to the heather topped hills and bracken clad valleys. Noisy, thoughtless bikers had so disturbed the area that the entire network of green roads on the Quantocks was under threat of closure. Voluntary wardens on motorcycles helped manage the problem, and showed that there were quiet, thoughtful motorcyclists around who cared for their countryside and wanted to share in protecting it.

The smooth farm track to Lower Weacombe is covered in golf ball size stones. The soil on the Quantocks and all points west is red. Yesterday the soil was black, the day before it was white.

The pretty little track above the Donniford Stream at Woolston was recovering from a stiff haircut from a tractor-mounted barber of the old ex-army school of hairdressing. A "short back and sides" was the order of the day. The first part had been cleaned out to its full width, with very bald hedges. The greenery was beginning to return to normal as the lane went on.

The old coach road over the Quantock Hills.

Growth in the summer can be quite phenomenal. A lane which is wide and clear in the spring can become a green sea of nettles and parsley six feet deep in the summer, and an impenetrable mass of hanging brambles by autumn. To keep green lanes clear they must be used. If they are not used they are in danger of disappearing completely under a jungle of vegetation.

There is a super system of lanes which links Roadwater to Dunster. It swoops and dives and climbs through all the steep little valleys below the Brendon ridge. The first of these lanes climbs past Woodadvent Farm above an idyllic valley, snuggled in away from the wind and apparently beyond the reach of the hurly burly of town life.

Along the foot of the valley used to run the mineral railway from Watchet harbour to the foot of the Brendons. An incline linked this low level railway with a second railway running along the top of the Brendons, where the Brendon Hill miners lived in a remote little community. They mined iron ore, which was carried along the top of the hill on the high level railway. A full truck was lowered down the incline's rails on the end of a cable. The cable passed round a large wheel at the top of the incline and was attached to an empty truck at the bottom of the incline. The full truck going down would pull an empty truck up to the top. The full trucks were then taken along the low level track to the coast, where the ore would be loaded into ships to be taken across the Channel to the steel works of South Wales.

It was a hard life on the lonely, windswept Brendons. The mine owners were strict Methodists and would allow no alcohol near their workers. To get to the nearest inn at Raleigh's Cross, the miners had to sneak past the strategically placed Methodist chapel on Brendon Hill.

The mines became too expensive to compete after the turn of the century. The railways have gone and so have the mine buildings. The chapel is still there and the Raleigh's Cross Inn does a flourishing business in the holiday season. The incline can be picked out on the hillside and the lower level railway is now used as a farm track.

I relaxed too much while admiring the familiar view, in the morning sunlight, after the rain had washed the air clear. On this easy track, my front wheel stepped out of line and caught a tussock of grass. I was taken off balance, over-corrected and tumbled into the bank.

I laughed.

How silly, I thought, to ride hundreds of miles of unknown lanes and to fall off on one of the easiest of the most familiar tracks on Exmoor, which I had been riding for years.

The front mudguard seemed to have bent right back on itself. It is an excellent design – one of the few modifications I made to my Yamaha shortly after I bought it. The standard mudguard is full of holes to let the air (and mud) through to the air-cooled engine. This may be a good idea in hot, dry California, but in muddy England you need a mudguard that guards both bike and rider from the mud. The Centurion mudguards I fitted to both front and rear wheels did just that. They did not get full marks for style, but they certainly worked as mudguards. They are made of unbreakable white plastic. When I heaved the bike off my left leg and the bank I saw that the unbreakable white plastic had broken. The front eight inches or so of the front mudguard was still embedded in

A tumble near Roadwater broke my "unbreakable" front mudguard.

the bank.

Oh . . . Bother! I thought.

I began to wonder if the bike would survive to Land's End.

I scrubbed the mud from the bank off the mudguard with a handful or two of grass. Everything was wet after the showers of rain earlier in the day. I dried the mudguard as well as I could with a cloth from my toolkit. The broken piece was placed over the stump of mudguard and bound in place with super sticky duct tape. The duct tape had been a gift from Exmoor Group organiser John Gibbs when he had visited me in Cornwall. I knew it would come in handy, but I had not expected to use it on my unbreakable mudguard. Many thanks for the tape, John!

On closer inspection I saw that the whole top surface of the front mudguard was crazed. I guessed that the effect of several years of sunlight, mud, water and vibration had weakened the chemical bonding of the plastic. The mudguard had aged and become brittle. It had been good while it lasted. I wondered if I could buy a new one at the end of my journey. Good designs in motorcycle parts seem to disappear from the market place as soon as you discover how good they are. Like the large tyre lever with a loop in the handle which I could bolt to my silencer to double as a heat shield to protect my leg. I found this one tyre lever, but had never been able to buy a second one. It was the best lever I have ever used on tyres as well as being easy to fix on the bike.

At the end of the lane you turn right and right again on a green lane which has been tarmaced. It is still worth riding. It descends steeply to the valley floor and passes under a bridge beneath the old low level mineral railway, then climbs to the Methodist chapel at Leighland. The tarmac then takes you round a hill to Leigh Barton farm. After passing through the farmyard it is important to take the top gate climbing up the valley side. I long to take the lower gate into the woods and ride round the valley to the waterfall and the old incline, but this is a bridleway. Perhaps I could get one of those All Terrain cycles. Pedal cycles are allowed on bridleways.

The farm gates were new, painted with red oxide primer, not galvanized with zinc. Red paint is cheaper than galvanising, but the gates will rust. Is this a carefully planned economic decision on the part of the farmer, or is he being short-sighted and failing to see the long term cost of several red gates compared with one, long-lasting galvanised gate?

I climbed up the valley side, looking to my left for the waterfall on the far side, but the trees were too well fledged. The greenery hid the great spout of water. After another red gate, the lane was deep in leaf mould and loose rocks in a narrow holloway. Here was a real Exmoor lane at last! I bounced and slithered my way to the top, enjoying the challenging going.

A tarmac lane took me to the bottom of the next coombe. Here the green lane has been taken into the concrete farmyard. I went through two sets of gates and climbed what was usually a dry, rocky holloway. But the farmer had moved most of his cattle to new sheds on top of the hill. Mud, churned by a hundred hooves, filled the holloway. The rock steps poked through the mire, slippery and treacherous. I had to dismount and push for part of the way.

Green lane runs through the concrete farmyard. Don't forget to close the gates.

The old green fields at the top were fine. The sunken route of the road could be picked out, even though the hedge which bounded one side of it had been grubbed out some years ago to make the field a few feet wider.

I trundled down a rough, concrete, forestry track to the floor of Druid's Combe. The next few lanes were well known to me. The climb to Croyden Hall; the easy green track past the gibbet tree at Felon's Oak; the track across the open common of Withycombe Hill. Even the loose rocks which filled Hill Lane seemed friendly and familiar as I dropped towards Carhampton. A green lane took me round the back of Dunster deer park so that I approached Dunster village from the south-west rather than the east. Dunster is rightly one of the most popular villages with

The view of Exmoor from the green lane over Withy-combe Hill.

visitors to Exmoor. The Castle dominates the wide main street and is well worth a visit. It has beautiful gardens. At the top of the main street, outside the Luttrell Arms Hotel is the Yarn Market, an octagonal open-sided building, which must be the most photographed place on Exmoor. Tucked behind the church is the quaintest vicarage garden and a splendid dovecote. The packhorse bridge has the neatest and most flower bedecked row of cottages leading to it, and is no more than a stone's throw from the working water mill, where you can see the flour being ground and buy some to take home.

Dunster is well worth a visit, but I have visited it many times before, and took the back road to Minehead, avoiding the bottlenecks at either end of the main street. At Alcombe I stopped for petrol and could not resist the chalk-board sign outside the butcher's shop opposite, advertising home-cured ham. I bought a couple of slices for lunch later on.

Minehead is sheltered from the prevailing westerly winds by North Hill and from the winds from the south by a ridge of hills collectively referred to as Grabbist. The green lane over Grabbist was once the main road to Bampton. Its start can be traced through the modern housing on the outskirts of Minehead to where the aptly named Bampton Street leaves the old market square. I climbed into the woods on Grabbist Hill, bearing right by the sign which says "No vehicles beyond this point". This sign has been very carefully positioned. It can be argued that it only refers to the footpath straight, ahead, but it certainly deters strangers from following the perfectly legal vehicular route of the Bampton road. The descent on the south of Grabbist Hill starts with two tight stony hairpin bends and then swooping stone-covered curves take you to the bottom. I am always wary here, because this side of the hill is heavily used by the local riding stables.

The green road crosses this tumbling stream on a cobbled bridge.

Almost at the end of the lane I met a whole herd of horse riders. I stopped and switched off the engine to let them pass in the narrow lane. Their leader reined in for a chat. We discussed the legal situation of the lanes on the Grabbist ridge. I know many of them have been used by vehicles over the centuries, but would not press for modern vehicular usage because the area is too heavily utilised by other recreational groups, such as walkers, picnickers and the like. He said that he had always wanted to learn more about trail riding but had never been able to find the right person to contact. I fished in my bag and hooked out a membership application form. I wondered if he would persuade the rest of his twelve-strong party to swap four legs for two wheels.

At Timberscombe, the modern main road wriggles and twists its way for mile after mile along the tortuous valley bottom to Bampton. The old road crosses the valley and climbs the far side, then sails serenely as a seagull over the hilltops on a parallel but infinitely easier route. The old route is now a quiet tarmac lane.

I followed the valley floor road for a couple of miles to Pitt Bridge, which marks the start of one of Exmoor's most famous green lanes. Today it was magnificent. The farm gate had gone from the start and the initial climb over hub deep leaf mould and tree roots had been destroyed by heavy forestry machinery. There still remained a steep, rocky climb preceding a single rocky groove in the sandstone surface, filled with mud – wet, slidy mud all the way. It was not clinging and gluey like yesterday's mud. It offered some grip, but let go just enough to make both back and front wheels wander from side to side, requiring concentration to stay in the groove and to avoid the high, flower covered banks on either side. It was superb! On the final muddy grass stretch across more open going I saw the first buzzard of the day rise from the top of an oak tree bordering the lane.

You cannot ride Pitt Bridge without also tackling Kersham Lane. The Pitt Bridge lane brings you up from the valley bottom road, to the ridge road to Bampton. Kersham Lane takes you back again. The first half of the lane is tarmac, covered in grit and gravel and soil washed out of the high banks by spring rain.

I saw a fox! Bright orange-red, he trotted across the lane twenty feet ahead of me and into an old barn by the roadside. Buzzards are common on Exmoor, but I had never seen a fox here while trail riding. I was very proud of myself. My mental "I-spy" book of Exmoor had another tick in it.

I dare say foxes have been here as long as I have been riding past. It is one of the disadvantages of trail riding that you ride past so much. I would have liked to stop here for a day and really explore this valley. Perhaps then I could have found that fox's den in the woods. Perhaps there was an owl in the old barn. Certainly I had no right to feel proud of having seen the fox. It had required no effort on my part. I had just been lucky to be passing as he crossed the road.

At last I reached the bottom of the hidden valley between the high ridge and the main valley road. Here, through a shallow ford, the green lane started. It climbs over great, rounded, bare rock steps which are slimed with algae growing in a constant trickle of water. The steps are not even, but are set at all sorts of angles and spacing. In company, I try to ride it clean, without taking my feet from the footrests. Solo, I took it slowly, with feet used to steady my progress, aware that a fall on this unforgiving surface could be disastrous.

I crossed the main road at Wheddon Cross. I climbed towards Dunkery Beacon then took the green route back down the hill to Luckwell Bridge. The green lane out of Luckwell Bridge was in prime condition, full of lovely, slithery mud. I took the ancient Ison Lane from Oldrey to Winsford. Motor vehicles have been using this track in its present form since the motor vehicle was invented. Its surface of solid bedrock, thinly covered in places by grass, has never needed a waterproof coating of tarmacadam.

I stopped short of Winsford village and turned north to ride Kemps Lane and then the terrific climb over a huge rock staircase onto Exford Common. After this I decided it had to be lunchtime. I found shelter from the wind behind a bank and beech hedge on the boundary between the enclosed fields of Exford and the open heather moorland

The road to Luccombe village, in the heart of Exmoor.

of the Common and tucked into sandwiches filled with delicious home-cured ham.

I took the road to Exford, but, as at Winsford, I stopped short of the village, and headed up the Exe valley. I knew of a splendid, short but very steep lane which was too good to miss. I turned off the tarmac to ford the River Exe at the start of my lane, but was stopped in my tracks by the sight of a bright red Post Office van parked in the middle of the ford.

The postman was in the water alongside the van in his shirt sleeves and wellingtons. He was using a long-handled floor brush to give his van a clean. It transpired that this was his usual way of keeping his transport sparkling. After discussing the difference between "trail" bikes and competition "trials" bikes, he told me of his own passion for marathon running. He was fifty-six years old, born and raised on Exmoor. He trained over the local moorland through places which sounded so familiar to me – Elsworthy, the Chains, Simonsbath, Landacre Bridge. He completed the London Marathon this year. I wish that I can be as fit as him when I am fifty-six.

Did he know Colin, I asked. Why yes, of course he did. Colin and he shared the Exmoor postal round. I explained that Colin had been one of my regular riding companions for several years until he suddenly disappeared from the scene. Oh, yes, Colin was still very much around, he told me. He had taken a passionate interest in fishing. That was the thing about Colin; he always put his heart and soul into whatever he did. He worked and saved for months to buy his trail bike, I recalled, and thoroughly enjoyed every ride we had. It was a shame to lose him to fishing. The green lanes have more need of his

enthusiasm than the fish have need of his hooks.

The two of them had an enviable round. Postman Pat in the children's story may be very happy in his fictional North Country dale, but I am sure he would be equally content with his lot in the heart of Exmoor. Winters were hard but the summers were glorious. Winter on Exmoor could mean the red van was unusable in the deep snow. Land Rover, a trail bike or walking boots were the only way to get the mail through. Often the mail took second place to helping with animals in difficulty, or perhaps a fire alarm on the summer moorland.

I climbed my steep climb and rode out across the open moor from the Simonsbath road to Withypool. There are few open moorland tracks on Exmoor. Most of the best tracks are the steep climbs up the sides of the deep valleys. The open moorland track into Withypool is almost as good as the open moorland track out of Withypool on the far side. The view from the top of this second is perhaps the best on Exmoor, which is certainly saying something. If you stop by Porchester's Post you can look in all directions and see nothing but heather covered hills. Not just heather on the hills of course, but a rich mixture of heathers, bracken and different grasses. The scene is in its best colours in the autumn, when the bracken is bright rust, the heather green and purple, and the grasses a patchwork of green and ochres. It makes me want to go back there again, just thinking about it.

The plunge through the trees to the river at Tarr Steps is strewn with loose rocks. The cafe proprietor at Tarr Steps could recall vehicles using this steep, rocky track before the road via Hawkbridge Church was tarmaced and took away the traffic. Both roads involve steep

The famous ford by the clapper bridge at Tarr Steps. The bridge is said to have been built by the Devil.

climbs, but the untarmaced one is much shorter. The wide ford at Tarr Steps is best tackled with steady determination. The water is quite deep and the rocks can be slippery. There is usually an audience of day trippers. Today was no exception and I did not stop. The main attraction is the clapper bridge across the River Barle alongside the ford. The bridge is made of unshaped slabs of moor stone six or eight feet long set on pillars of rough rocks. The clapper bridge is just wide enough for two walkers to pass. Horses and vehicles take the ford. No-one knows just how old the bridge is, but locals say it was built by the devil who sunbathes in the middle of it.

I climbed out of the Barle valley on a narrow moorland track which took me to the Exe valley at Winsford. The Barle and the Exe are the two great south-flowing rivers which rise on Exmoor. A number of short, fast flowing streams flow north to enter the Bristol Channel, but just these two wind south. The Barle joins the Exe just north of Exebridge, and the Exe winds right across Devon before entering the sea south of Exeter at Exmouth.

Winsford is a picture postcard of a West Country village, thatched cottages and the inn on the green by a hump-backed bridge and a ford. I usually stop for petrol or an ice cream at the garage, but this time I had to press on. This was the longest riding day, with the most challenging lanes, and I wanted to fit in as much as I could.

Climbing Edbrooke Hill on steep, bare rock hairpins, I joined the ridge road to Dulverton. The first half of the ridge road is tarmac, but the second half is green and pleasant. I arrived high above Dulverton town, outside the school gates, level with the top of the church. Dulverton is the capital of Exmoor. It still manages to be more of a country town serving the farming community than a holiday town serving the tourists, despite being the administrative headquarters of the Exmoor National Park.

The steep climb out of the Exe valley on a spur of rock in Barlynch Wood can be a frightening experience on your own. My thoughts were on the best climb of all which lay just ahead. I trundled down the track opposite the deer sanctuary to Bury and nosed through the ford in the middle of the village. I had been looking forward to the climb out of Bury all week. The road is steep, sunk below the surface of the surrounding fields by centuries of use and water erosion. It is partly filled with fallen leaves and

mud, but the high spot of the climb is the vast, sloping, sandstone slab about halfway up. There are other, lesser rock slabs after this and more mud and leaves before the top is reached, on the border of Somerset and Devon. Then there is a comparatively easy descent over leaf covered loose rocks, still in a holloway onto the tarmac Morebath road.

I had looked forward to tackling this great climb, but was to be sadly disappointed. Within a hundred yards of the start, a landslip had brought down the stump of a dead elm tree and a mass of earth in such a way that I could not ride over it or round it. I had to turn back. I was miserable. I was fed up. I was frustrated. I was angry. It was not fair. I would contact the local authority when I finished my ride and make sure they cleared my favourite lane. I may have missed out on it, but others would be trying to meet its challenge throughout the coming months. The lane was difficult enough without having to climb over tree stumps.

I felt too dejected to tackle the string of little lanes which join Bury to Bampton. I took the tarmac road and rejoined my green lane route south of the town. I left the main road at Cove, humped over the Exe in front of a very pink, thatched toy of a cottage, and rode four familiar lanes at Carscombe, Quoit-at-Cross, Iron Mill Stream and Coleford Bottom, after which I felt much better.

It was a long ride from Exmoor to Dartmoor and the day

Fording the river near Winsford.

A successful climb of the bare rock slabs at Bury produces the broadest of grins.

was drawing to a close. I pushed on south over Witheridge Moor. I had not used the road to Chapple Farm before. The farm was up for auction, but the farmer still had to milk his cows. Gates were across the road. The dairy herd waited patiently, penned in the road, for their turn to be milked. I walked into the milking parlour. The cowman in rust brown coat and tired wellies amidst his six milking stalls gave a start as I called a cheerful "Good afternoon!" I don't suppose many folk came along the road that day, but he quickly saw my reason for disturbing him. I was covered from head to toe in clues — muddy wellies, muddy overtrousers, muddy motorcycle jacket, white helmet. It did not take much to realise I was a trail rider bent on riding down the green road through his farm.

The cows were in two groups. We drove the ones that had been milked into the cow shed so that they did not mix up with those still waiting to be milked. We manouevred a network of steel gates tied up with orange twine to redesign the pen, and then with much arm waving and the traditional cow herding cry of "Goo-arn! Goo arn then!" we shifted the rest of the herd clear of the road.

"'Tas bin a beaudiful day!" he called, as I rode through. "Leave the gates. I'll do un!" With a wave, I was on my way again.

A splendidly steep, loose rock descent brought me, bumping and slithering, to a narrow ditch of a stream, which I dropped into and bounced out of again. A steep, muddy climb took me to the tarmac and to Puddington.

Sharp left in Puddington, past Smynacott and there was a sharp, steep, rocky descent to splash through

Thatched Devon cottage guards the hump-backed bridge at Cove.

Binneford Water and climb out over another steep gradient. The green lanes here were short, but good fun.

I rode through Woolfardisworthy. There is a name to try to pronounce! Surely five syllables are too many for a West Country name. How many syllables should you swallow? Though perhaps the slow, South Devon accent might well savour each delicious sound. Then I found a clue to pronunciation. The water mill at the foot of the hill was named "Woolferry Mill" – only three syllables.

I remember my pronunciation of Exford being corrected by a youngster brought up on Exmoor. Outsiders say "Exf'd" with all the stress on the "Ex", but, she explained, it should be "Exe Ford", the ford across the Exe, which was logical, and the correct local pronunciation.

I passed through Crediton and splashed through a ford below Oldridge. A long stony lane led to Oldridge Farm. A quarter of a mile from the farm, I came across three sheep with three large lambs. I gently shepherded them towards the farm. You cannot pass sheep in a narrow lane. They just run faster and faster in front of you. If you do manage to overtake, they dive head first at the hedge in a blind panic to force their way through. So you don't try to pass. You just follow them back until you find the place where they escaped from their field.

Round the corner, a tractor was parked across the lane just beyond an open gate into a meadow. The lad from the tractor, in blue overalls and orange ear protectors, was pleased to see his missing sheep trot into the meadow. He closed the gate behind them and moved his tractor barricade, now that the whole flock was where it belonged. I reckoned he needed a sheep dog – or, perhaps, a trail bike!

A tiny, muddy lane past Heath Barton led me to a wide, modern bridge over the A30 dual carriageway. Cars and caravans rushed below me as I crossed the bridge. They were oblivious to the land around them. At the speed they were travelling, they had time to see nothing but the speedometer and a gap to overtake the car in front, while they tuned in to local radio to hear of traffic jams ahead.

I cantered on amid the Devon dumpling hills. My younger brother was called a Devon Dumpling, being fortunate enough to be born in the county, at Brixham. Other counties have similar pet names for their offspring. I don't know whether dumpling was the right word to describe my brother, but it definitely fitted the round humps of green hills which float on the rich red soil of Devon.

My next green lane started as a tarmac lane rushing down the side of one dumpling hill, becoming ever steeper until it became a series of desperate hairpin bends over battered, gravelly tarmac, finally splashing into a cobbled ford with an inch or two of water flowing past. These sort of fords are always followed by a "Try Your Brakes" sign. I suppose the sign has meaning to a pedal cyclist with rim brakes which would be wet, but it is a joke for a motorcycle.

My last lane was signed to East Down and West Down. West Down turned off right, East Down turned off left and the green lane went straight ahead, wide enough for a car from bank to bank with the lushest, greenest grass. It soon narrowed to a single track where the banks had grown in, and became muddy through inefficient drainage. A gate led into the woods, where the lane regained its full width and was carpeted with fallen leaves. Another gate led out of the wood and I was on the tarmac road again, lined with a profusion of white and red campion.

Clifford Bridge campsite was less than a mile away. it was spread across the water meadows of the River Teign, between the massive, wooded hillsides which formed the narrow river valley. As I arrived, the sun was dipping below the hilltops. The camp shop had closed, so after pitching the tent and washing I sampled the bar snacks in the tiny campsite bar.

The owner/manager/barman who had shown me to my pitch and now served my hot snack told me a little about the campsite and I told him a little of my journey. He and his partner had sunk their life savings into the site three years ago. They did not expect to make a profit for a further seven years at least, all the money they made being put back to improve the site amenities, which were largely worn out at the moment I had to agree. Since they purchased, they had seen their property's value rise and rise. How could it do otherwise? A campsite in a deep valley on the very edge of Dartmoor just had to be a wise investment.

When I told of my journey, he asked if I had found the "hunting lane" just down the road. After some discussions, we agreed that it was the last lane I had ridden. He told me of the landowner's attempts to have the lane closed completely in recent years and how the local people had fought successfully to keep it open.

I went out to walk round the campsite and climb the surrounding hillside before the light faded completely. I climbed up through the woods and caught up with the sun. I sat on a tree stump in a clearing and looked north across the valley. It had been quite a day and this peaceful spot was an ideal place to finish. I looked forward to staying at this campsite again in a few years time, when the facilities matched the prices.

There ought to be deer on the hillside opposite, but it was still not dusk. June days were long, and the deer would stay hidden until they were safe from threatening eyes. Perhaps I would get up early and try to catch a glimpse of them in the morning.

I trudged down the hill to my tent, cool in the heavy shadows cast by the wood across the meadow grass. The horse and the goats in the paddock had been shut up for the night. The swimming pool was covered over to keep off twigs and leaves. I wriggled into my sleeping bag to keep warm and brewed some coffee. I was a long way from Dover. I was still a long way short of Land's End. I was very tired.

Thursday
Devon and Cornwall

Fingle Bridge was only a mile or two from my campsite. The tarmac stops just beyond the bridge, then the road climbs up and up, round hairpin after hairpin, from the bottom of one of the deepest valleys in Devon to the start of the high plateau of Dartmoor. I counted six hairpins, all covered in loose stones. What a way to enter the moor! It is no wonder that this road has been used to test the reliability of cars and motorcycles for so many years. It is an observed section in the annual Exeter Trial, first organised by the Motor Cycle Club in 1910. The sign at

DARTMOOR

✕ FINGLE
BRIDGE

TAVISTOCK

⌂
ST. COLUMB
MINOR

LOSTWITHIEL

H.19601

Sketch map of route through Devon and Cornwall.

the tops says "Unsuitable for Motors" and has a large dent in it.

Back roads carried me round Moretonhampstead. Three tarmac sleeping policeman guarded the green lane to Langdon Farm. Here was a new type of countryside. The lane was lined with huge granite blocks, big enough to build a cathedral. The blocks formed banks topped with windswept blackthorn and hawthorn. The granite was made of large sparkling crystals. It was very old but very hard, showing scant signs of smoothing by the centuries. Rocks were still as rough textured as when they were first dragged here by Iron Age farmers clearing this windswept landscape to make their small fields.

The scenery of Dartmoor is unique. The green moorland hills rise to points topped by spikes of rock, which stick out of the ground like giant warts. I was surrounded by tor-topped hills, where volcanoes once smoked across a very different landscape. The tors are the remains of the core of the ancient volcanoes. Much harder than the surrounding rocks, they have weathered to their present weird shapes and acquired a rich variety of descriptive names.

My next lane climbed over huge granite slabs, as wide as the lane, strewn with loose rocks, past Honeybag Tor, Chinkwell Tor and Bell Tor. Hound Tor and Hollow Tor and a dozen nameless outcrops, studded the horizon. This was the landscape seen by Sir Arthur Conan Doyle, when he planned the great adventure of his hero, Sherlock Holmes, tracking down the fiendish Hound of the Baskervilles. To be afoot among these soulless rocks, when the wind whips the mist into strange patterns and howls through gaps in the crags, must be one of the most unnerving experiences. Local folk talk of people being "mazed", meaning that the experience of being lost on the mist-shrouded moor had loosened the grip of sanity upon their imagination. Mazed people had staggered, screaming, into the safety of a farm, after "seeing" horrendous monsters loom up through the swirling fog.

After six hairpins, this is the top of the Fingle Bridge road.

Bell Tor, but no sign of the Hound of the Baskervilles.

The tiny village of Widecombe in the Moor is where Uncle Tom Cobleigh and his chums were aiming on that poor, grey mare, when they disappeared. Do their ghosts really haunt the tor tops? The village, made famous by the ballad of their tragic journey, seemed to boast more trinket shops than houses. I climbed from this tourist trap, past a ''no through road'' sign, through a gate, onto open moorland. The track was just visible ahead of me as two faint wheel ruts in the close-cropped grass. On the ridge, I could see no trace of a track. I was thankful that there was not one of those sudden mists for which the moor is notorious. In the distance, I could just make out a track climbing northwards along a line of tors. I identified this on my map and knew that it could not be my route. I had to bear slightly to the left. I eased the bike forward a few yards. I saw a dry stone wall ahead. Keeping this on my left, I edged downhill until I saw a gate, and, yes, a walled lane. I had made it to the exact spot where my road left the moor without a sign of a track under my wheels. It was there as clear as could be on the map, but there was nothing on the ground.

Beyond the gate, I began to wonder if this ever had been a lane fit for walking along, let alone riding along. At some stage in the past, the surface must have been better. The path was full of loose rocks and rock steps. It was all I could do to keep the motorcycle pointing downhill, using my feet to fend off approaching rocks as I tacked from wall to wall.

Huge granite slabs have fallen into this Dartmoor lane, making the going very hard.

Somehow, such lanes are always more fun going up. I think it has something to do with momentum and gravity, but I can never quite explain it. Going uphill the bike responds to the throttle. Careful balance and sensible throttle control are all that seem necessary. Going downhill, the brakes are at least as important as the throttle, and balance is at a premium. On the downhill, either front or back wheel can start to slide away all too easily if the controls are over-used. Once a slide starts, loss of balance means you fall off. It takes great skill to ride down a steep, rock-strewn lane.

I wondered how any machinery could withstand the punishment being received by my motorcycle? Surely no man-made device was designed for this? Tyres trounced by rocks. Sharp stones and thorns vying to stab punctures. Springs pounding in uneven and unpredictable rhythms, soothed by damping oil seething hot. The engine bounced and bashed on its brackets, exploding three thousand times every minute. What a primitive but exhilarating way to travel! How long can it last? All the way to Land's End?

I slithered to the end in a shower of stones and flying legs. The route to Cornwall was now tarmac. I could find no green route to follow across the heart of Dartmoor. The only road I could use was the one across the moor, to Two Bridges and past Dartmoor Prison at Princetown. The moor road was bleak and the wind blew cold, directly against me. It was not a pleasant ride, but I was in Tavistock in half an hour and Dartmoor was behind me.

I steered for the Cornish border at Gunnislake. There were still some Devon hills to climb. Lumburn Bridge was followed by a long and very steep hill. The old road went straight up, according to the First Edition of the Ordnance Survey Map of 1807. The modern road climbs the hill in two great sweeping bends, first to the south and then to the north, to ease the incline. This has made the lower half of the old road too dangerous to use. Where the modern road sweeps from south to north across the older climb, the exit from the old road is made so steep by the modern embankment that no room is left to stop and look for fast moving traffic. It would not take much on the part of the county engineers to make the exit safe. Why have they not done so?

The upper half of the old road is usable and well worth riding. It ends in a corner of a large car park for a public house. Surely this was an old staging post, where extra horses needed to haul carriages up the hill would be unhitched, while the passengers recovered from their walk. They would not have ridden in the carriage up such a hill. Even ten horse power would not have pulled a coach and its passengers up! Both horses and passengers deserved a rest and a drink after the climb. The pub did a brisk trade in those days.

New Bridge at Gunnislake joins Cornwall to Devon across the River Tamar. The Tamar stretches from Plymouth nearly to the north coast and makes Cornwall almost an island. The ''New Bridge'' was built about 1520 by Sir Piers Edgecumbe who lived in the beautiful old manor of Cotehele just down the river. New Bridge was the lowest crossing of the Tamar for four and a half centuries, until the post-war Saltash to Plymouth bridge was opened. It must have brought prosperity to Gunnislake and the adjoining villages, but they show little sign of it.

New Bridge crosses the river on six granite arches,

This is not a green road, but a granite railway, below the distant pinnacle of Haytor.

over thirty feet above the water. The river is about eight feet deep here, being just beyond the reach of the tide from the English Channel. In flood, the water can rise to twenty feet, which explains the height of the arches.

The bridge played an important part in the English Civil War. Sir Richard Grenville defended it against Lord Essex on 20th July 1644, but after a hot encounter, Essex took the bridge with the loss of some forty men killed. The defending Royalists lost two hundred dead or taken prisoner. A month later, Charles I pursued Essex into Cornwall, defeated him at Lostwithiel and left Cornwall "safe and sound" by New Bridge on 5th September 1644.

When I was planning my ride from Dover to Land's End, I had hunted for a ford across the Tamar. Upstream from New Bridge is Horsebridge (built 1430!). Between the two bridges is a long stretch of water in a deep valley, apparently too wide and deep to cross. But a county road runs past Lamerhoe and stops on the river bank. On the Cornish bank opposite is a county road which climbs the valley side some three miles north of Gunnislake. Was this a ford? I scoured my old maps until I found it. Yes. This was Latchley Ford. In fact it was still marked as such on a cycling map of the 1930s.

I wrote to a trail riding friend who lived in Gunnislake and asked him to investigate. His reply brought mixed blessings. He confirmed that it was indeed a ford, but that it was about waist deep in high summer – in a very long, dry summer. He did not recommend it as a crossing point in June after a very wet spring.

The only other likely ford was many miles to the north, near Tamartown and the old, dried up, Tamar canal. However this northerly ford made nonsense of all attempts to link it to a long distance green lane route. I was forced to admit that the only sensible way to cross the Tamar into Cornwall was on a bridge. If this was to be so, then I was happy to follow in the hoofprints of King Charles across New Bridge.

Running out of road! A tarmac road slowly returns to its natural state.

I stopped in the hamlet of St Ann's Chapel. This was a sad little place. A string of terraces along the main road, whose reason to exist was taken away by the modern bridge at Saltash. Saltash prospers, but St Ann's Chapel has died. A little general store served the peeling painted terraces. I climbed its stone steps, opened one of the narrow, glazed double doors to the sound of a bell on a large curved spring. They sold everything from cheese to moustraps. I picked out a Mars bar and a packet of crisps and sat outside in the wind, trying to warm up. The sun was shining but the ridge road through St Ann's Chapel would catch the draught from almost any point of the compass. The view south was nice and went some way to compensate for the dreary houses.

Six miles further south brought me to a very different lifestyle. I rode through the bright plastic entrance of Mellion Golf Course and Country Club. "All were welcome" according to the signs, but perhaps I was not dressed correctly. The golf links flowed smoothly down the hillside on each side of what had once been a green farm track. The track was now tarmac as far as you could drive a golf cart. Where the gradient became steeper, the old track fell some ten feet below the surrounding ground level. The golf greens were cut into the steep hillside on either side in tiers like rice paddy fields in the Far East. The terracing of the golf course had been achieved with giant mechanical diggers and scrapers, unlike the paddy fields which were created by countless hours of human toil with pick and shovel. The machinery used to create the golf course seemed to have dumped any surplus rubble into the old track. The track was smothered in smashed rocks, broken bricks and the like. The earth movers had shoved this into heaps. Each heap spanned the full width of the lane. Riding over these was somewhere between bouncing over giant sleeping policemen and riding a roller coaster. Perhaps they have plans to smooth the heaps down and return the lane to something like the condition it has enjoyed for the last couple of thousand years, before golf was invented.

This part of Cornwall is very much like the southern half of Devon. There are rolling hills and deep valleys. No sooner do you climb one hill than you must go into another valley. I stopped on top of the next hill, in Crendle Wood, for cheese and biscuits. A Marbled White butterfly fluttered by under the oak trees. Somewhere in the wood I could hear a cuckoo. The "hedge" that divided the wood and the green lane from the surrounding fields was a real Cornish "hedge". A bank of boulders and smaller rocks stood nearly six feet high, made of the surface litter

A Cornish lane, lined with ferns and flowers.

cleared from the fields when they were first cultivated. The rocks were now covered with soil in which all manner of things grew. From where I sat munching my cheese, I could spot six different sorts of ferns, several large fungi, a spattering of yellow, white and red flowers amongst the foliage, and a badger's set. The bank was topped by an unkempt, tall and dense growth of beech, hawthorn, blackthorn, elder, oak, hazel and ash, all of which I identified. Twining round these were dog roses, blackberry and honeysuckle. There were more plants than I could name in the short stretch I could see from where I sat. All this could be replaced by a barbed wire fence in the interests of agricultural efficiency. I hoped the farmer realised what a treasure house of nature was growing on the edge of his fields and that he would be able to resist the financial incentive to destroy what had taken centuries to grow here.

In the centre and south of England, hedges were the result of the enclosure of the feudal open fields. The feudal system gave each peasant a number of strips in three large fields surrounding his village. This strip farming gave the peasant enough crops to live on, while his cattle grazed on common grassland and his pigs foraged in the surrounding woods. Villages, as well as their open fields, were swept away by powerful landowners two centuries ago to be replaced by sheep pastures, enclosed by quick set hedges.

The hedgerows planted at this time have become a "natural" part of the countryside. Changes in farming created them and now changes in farming threaten to destroy them. Mechanised farming cannot operate efficiently in very small fields. The bigger and more powerful the machinery, the more space it needs to operate efficiently. Every year two thousand miles of hedge are grubbed up and their ditches levelled to give elbow room to ever more massive machines.

The ecological consequences of grain growing on this scale are becoming better appreciated. The value of windbreaks on soils which are light and likely to be blown away, and the effects of hedges on wildlife are obvious to anyone who stops to think. The hedgerow is vital to birds, small mammals and many plants. I do mean quite literally vital. They cannot live without it.

There are still some six hundred thousand miles of hedges in Britain. If they average only two feet wide, they cover an area greater than all the officially designated nature reserves.

Again, I admit that hedges occupy potentially productive land, but without hedges the countryside becomes most strange and bleak. The open fields of the medieval peasants had no hedges, but they were surrounded by great woodlands, which we have since destoyed. For us it is the hedgerows which give the appearance of luxuriant growth to the country of most of southern England. The English landscape without the hedge would not be the English landscape.

My next few lanes fitted Celia Fiennes' description in the account she has left us of her journey to Cornwall in 1698. "The road contracts and the lanes are exceeding narrow, and so cover'd up you can see little about. An army might be marching undiscover'd by anybody (along such lanes)". "All along on the road where the lanes are a little broader, you ride by rowes of trees on each side, set and kept exactly even and cut, the tops being for shade and beauty . . . as if a grove to some house. At first

I thought it was neer some house, til the frequency and length proved the contrary, for there are very few if any houses near the road, unless the little villages you passe through; this country being almost full of stone, the streetes and roades too have a natural sort of paveing''.

It is clear that the enclosures in Cornwall are even older than those further east. The countryside of East Cornwall has changed little in the last three hundred years. With the exception of her amazing spelling, Celia Fiennes' seventeenth century description fitted twentieth century observation exactly.

Hidden deep in the Seaton valley is Lydcott Wood. In the heart of the wood, a stone bridge crosses the River Seaton and a green road climbs the valley side. This is Cornwall's answer to Devon's Fingle Bridge road. It is on a smaller scale, but just as good. There are three hairpins, steep and covered in rocks before the hill top is reached.

River after river flows south across the landscape, cutting deep grooves in the hills. I was riding at right angles to the rivers, down and up and down again, mainly on green hedge-bordered lanes.

I had passed only one walker, clad in blue denims, since entering Cornwall. The holiday makers know all about the Cornish coastline and flock there in their tens of thousands every summer, but few ever try to explore the hidden landscape behind the cliffs and the beaches.

Crooksball farmhouse had been burnt out, I guessed about five years ago. The fields around were still grazed, but the house was being reclaimed by the landscape. Brambles invaded the living room. Thistles hid the paving in the yard. The grass grew long in the little garden, strangling a few remaining potato plants. The apple tree still stood, but no-one would harvest the russet red crop this autumn.

I reached Lerryn, and rode under the woods along the bank of the flooded valley of the Lerryn River. The tide was out and the pretty yachts and dinghies lay rather forlornly on the mud, like the toys of spoilt children, forgotten and left out in the rain.

My road to Lostwithiel was signed ''Impracticable for Cars''. This was not an expression I had come across before. The sign had been cast in the foundry of W. Vissick and Sons Ltd at Devoran and must have been at least thirty years on this spot. The lane descended a gentle valley and I could see nothing ''impracticable''. There was a little ford and then the lane narrowed and became quite definitely ''impracticable for cars''. Not impracticable for motorbikes, though, I told myself, until I came to a series of natural rock steps, each about half a metre high, where the topsoil had been washed away over the years. With a little help from full throttle in first gear, I more or less carried the bike over each step in turn. The steps were just too high for me to ride over. I would get the front wheel up, but then the engine would rest on the rock and lift the back wheel clear of the ground, so that the wheel span uselessly in the air providing no force to push me upwards. The lane was so narrow at this point, where the banks had fallen in, that I could scarcely stand alongside the bike. I found the only successful technique was to put Daisy as close to the bank as possible so that it could half climb and half be lifted round the end of each rock step.

I stopped at the top, exhausted. The sun had come out. The lane was sheltered from the wind. I was soaked in

The sign said the lane was ''Impracticable for Cars'' but it was not impracticable for motorcycles. (M. Thompson)

sweat. I peeled off my jacket, gloves and helmet and collapsed against the bank.

A group of ramblers hove into view, striding purposefully towards me. Father, mother and two strapping youngsters looking so brim full of vitality that I wilted even further into the flower covered bank. They wore stout boots and thick sweaters, and were armed with sticks and rucksacks. They looked ready to tackle the Matterhorn, stomping to the top while singing ''Eidelweiss'' in strident harmony. They had chosen to assault my little lane, perhaps because it was nearer than the Matterhorn.

They were so properly turned out in such typically sensible rambling gear that they seemed too much to be true. They were acting the part of great walkers. Real walkers are never so smartly equipped. Real walkers choose comfortable, well broken in clothing. Perhaps these were in a film. Was there a camera round the corner? After all, they were walking DOWN the lane, whereas I had just exhausted myself riding UP it.

I pulled myself to my feet to greet them. We discussed the nature of the ''impracticability'' of the lane for cars. I agreed that it had been fairly difficult to ride up on the motorcycle. I was not prepared to admit just how difficult to such an efficient looking group. The British art of understatement has its virtue at times like this.

I chose my words with care, and sparingly. We parted on friendly terms, wishing each other well on our respective journeys. I did not hear them break into song as they marched down the hill. Perhaps ''Eidelweiss'' isn't really a marching song after all.

I trundled into Lostwithiel, avoiding the by-pass, to savour the narrow 15th century bridge across the River Fowey into the heart of the town. Lostwithiel is a maze of

The typical Cornish green lane, with Helman Tor in the background. (M. Thompson)

stand on the footrests of your bike, you can see over the walls and across the rolling farmland – a mass of small fields – on either side. Part of the road is unfenced, giving a wider view north east to the distant purple of Rough Tor on Bodmin Moor twenty miles away. Here the road has enormous blocks of granite, piled up higgledy piggledy alongside by a modern earthmover, clearing some of the high meadowland for ploughing and planting with grain.

I have never seen rising butt farm gates outside Cornwall. On Exmoor they use two gates on one gateway, so that if the wind blows one open it must blow the other closed. On this road they use a sort of double hinge on a single gate, so that whichever way you open the gate it falls closed under its own weight.

Nearer to Helman Tor, there is a stretch of lane lined with bluebells and brown bracken, with a view north east to Bodmin on one side, a view over a strange, impenetrable marshland and scrub as far as Criggan Moor and Goss Moor on the other side. Over your left shoulder can be seen the white mountains of the spoil heaps of the china clay workings above St Austell – Cornwall's little Switzerland. (Was this where those ramblers were heading?) Ahead rises the weird jumble of giant pebbles that form Helman Torr.

You have to stop and walk over the rocks of Helman Torr to begin to understand its fascination. I feel it is like coming home to an old friend after the cold, lifeless tors

alleys, lined with houses, shops and warehouses from the days when it was a port, small but important, at the head of the uppermost reach of the tide.

The town lies downstream of the imposing but isolated Restormel Castle. The massive, stone, circular keep of Restormel Castle was built by the Norman conquerors in the 12th century on a spur of land high above the River Fowey. The town which you might have expected to serve such an impressive fort was never built. For some reason traders did not use the bridge across the Fowey at the foot of the castle mound, but chose to cross at Lostwithiel. Only farm vehicles use the bridge by the castle today. Lostwithiel grew up one and a half miles away and the castle, despite its splendid defensive position, never prospered.

I have been asked in the past to explain, at the drop of a hat, what trail riding is all about. Just what is a green lane? If I had to choose one lane in Cornwall to be held up as an example of a typical green lane, to initiate a newcomer to the special joy of riding green lanes, to convince the unbelieving of the existence of such things, to illustrate the continuing, ever changing use of roads over the centuries, then I would choose the road from Lanlivery to Lanivet by Helman Tor.

There is nothing demanding or challenging about riding the Helman Tor road. Riding it is a pure pleasure for more subtle reasons than the joy of conquest at the end of a difficult lane. It runs along a narrow ridge of hills which mark the most south westerly outcrop of the hard granite of Bodmin Moor. Much of its length is between granite walls, partly smothered in summer flowers. If you

You have to stop and explore the rocks of Helman Tor. (M. Thompson)

of Dartmoor. They are dead, but Helman Torr is alive with magic. The giant, smooth granite rocks have been piled up by some distant hand to form a jumble of narrow passageways and tiny caves in which you can lose yourself for half a day, while all the time being able to see the countryside spread out for miles around. The natural rock outcrop has been surmounted by what I believe to be a complex collection of burial mounds, whose soil covering and whose buried contents have long ago disappeared.

The Tor is a weird jumble of giant pebbles ... and quite fascinating. (M. Thompson)

There is a sense of being watched by nameless hidden eyes, which I have never experienced in such an exposed place before. It is so clearly deserted, yet the presence of ancient humanity haunts the place. It has the air of a hermitage rather than a temple. It is not the place of great ceremonies, but of solitude and contemplation. Crowds have never gathered here to celebrate the changing of the year at the solstices or the equinoxes which have been absorbed into our modern religions. I have a feeling, not of peace, but of exhilaration on Helman Torr. The green lane stretches behind you to the horizon. On all sides all around you there are countless miles of countryside waiting to be explored. It is a place of inspiration and renewal. Such a place can not really be captured in words. Go there on a bright, clear day in early June and see if you can feel the magic for yourself.

After the euphoria of Helman Torr, the green lanes thin out. There are no more than half a dozen in the twenty miles between the Tor and Newquay. I would ride four of these, all fairly short and ordinary, before reaching my home at St Columb Minor in the evening. Some parts of Cornwall are rich in green lanes. I do not know why this area should have so few, although there must be an explanation.

Beyond Lanivet I followed narrow, tarmac lanes, buried deep below high banks past a series of farms. The farms had grown neighbouring houses over the years and now formed little communities, too small to be called hamlets. Each farm was the nucleus for a small collection of cottages and bungalows, tucked away in a sheltered corner of the landscape.

A green farm track took me to Withielgoose. The next lane ran through a farmyard. I interrupted a tea party on the lawn in front of the farmhouse. The farmer's wife

rushed ahead of me in her summer frock to move a tractor from my path. I assured her it was not necessary, and rode carefully round the tractor. She was as flustered as a mother hen, disturbed from her eggs. I hurried through the gate, so that she could return to her guests. This lane has three fords. Two are hardly worthy of the name, but the third is really nice – wide, about wellie boot deep, with a firm, gravelly bottom.

From Tregawne, past Tregustick and Tregolls to Trewollack, the names told me how Cornish this countryside was. My last lane ran from close by Trevithick to Trewolvas. This is a microcosm of typical green lane features. A smooth track runs through a copse. You can pick out the full width of the lane, now covered by trees and reduced to a single track. There is a little ford, just enough to wash the mud off the tyres. There is a little climb at the end over some loose rocky stuff. Nothing is very taxing, but it contains all the elements of some of the best lanes in the South of England more or less in miniature.

I joined the main road and whizzed the last ten miles home to St Columb Minor. I had been away for ages, it seemed to me, and I was very glad to be back. The difficult part would be getting on the bike for the last day's ride to The Land's End itself. I would worry about that in the morning. Tonight I wanted to talk to my family, enjoy some home cooking, a hot shower and my own bed.

Friday
Land's End

I was most reluctant to leave the comfort of my own bed. I lay in luxury till nearly six o'clock before forcing myself to get up. I knew I had to finish the ride on consecutive days or it would not feel like a single journey. The continuity was important to my picture of a green route from end to

Getting dressed for the final assault. (M. Thompson)

end of the South of England. I was on my way by seven, more lightly loaded today as I expected to be home early in the afternoon and certainly didn't plan to camp again.

The sun was bright and warm, while the air was cold and fresh. I could not have planned a better week for weather. I had been very lucky.

There is a whole network of green lanes around Goonhavern. Almost all of them serve private houses.

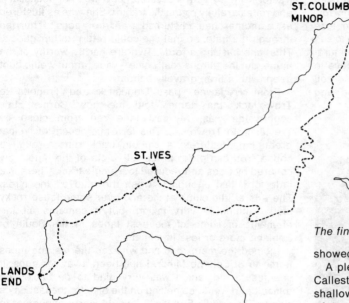

The final day's route to Land's End.

The lanes are lined with bungalows and cottages, each with their own little patch of ground, a few goats or chickens. It seems more like an old-fashioned corner of Belgium or France than part of England. The roads are firm surfaced but bumpy. You could drive a car along without difficulty, but you would be bounced around a lot. One of the impressive features of my French car is the way it will tackle this sort of green lane. It is designed to have the sort of suspension which will soak up these bumps, because so much of France is chequered with lanes like this. English cars are designed for smooth tarmac and tend to bounce your head on the roof unless driven very, very gently along green lanes.

The lane which serves my home was without tarmac until fairly recently. I heard the story of how it came to be tarmaced from a neighbour, a man who had been born in a cottage in the lane and now lives in a modern house a couple of doors away. The lane used to have a surface of stones – large pointed stones set upright in the ground, he told me. It sounded to me like the surface for which Telford became famous. It was smooth and well drained and never needed repair. It had served the householders well since before my neighbour was born. It survived the coming of the motor car, lorries and heavy farm vehicles, but it was destroyed by public utility vans. First the Electricity Board men dug it up to lay cables to all the houses, then the Water Board put in new water pipes, and the Gas Board put in a gas main. Each time a trench was dug along or across the lane, the carefully set surface of stones was disturbed, and it was never put back quite right. The lane developed potholes, wherever it had been dug up.

In the winter, residents took the long way round past the church to avoid the mud and puddles. At last the highway authority was persuaded to give the lane a new surface of tarmac. This has been in place for a number of years now and has survived many onslaughts from Gas men, Electricity men and Water men. They have been trained to repair a tarmacadam road. No-one ever

showed them how to deal with a Telfordised road.

A pleasant little lane runs past a string of cottages in Callestick. It splashes through two little fords, very shallow after a week without rain, but quite fun in the winter. A stony climb between wildly overgrown hedges seems to lead to a dead end. At some time, I cannot establish when, a little dog leg in the lane lost its protective hedges to make a bigger field. Now, you must do battle with a rickety wooden gate, tied up with yards of barbed wire and cross two hundred yards of ploughed and planted grain, before finding the final part of the lane, which follows two deep and well used ruts, past the Creegmoor farmhouse to the main road.

I galloped down the A30 to the Three Burrows roundabout. Just south of this lies the vast tangle of green lanes knitting up the Carnon valley, which once served the mining communities of the St Day district, west of Truro.

The tall, stone chimneys of deserted engine houses litter the skyline from here all the way to Land's End. Cornwall was once the mining centre of England. It was important many centuries before coal was mined in Wales or the North. From pre-Roman times, the Cornish have been exporting their mineral wealth. The Phoenicians sailed here to trade for tin to mix with copper in the Bronze Age. Tin, copper, gold and silver have all been mined here. When Cornish mines became worked out, Cornish miners took their skills abroad. They emigrated in their thousands to North America, Australia, Africa. A local saying for more than a century now is that anywhere in the world you find a deep hole being dug, you can bet there will be a Cornishman at the bottom of it.

There are still deep mines being worked in Cornwall, but their future is uncertain to say the least. It is a very expensive business to extract what metal remains. The mines must go ever deeper and the ore becomes ever more difficult to extract. The world's market place for metals is fiercely competitive. Most mines now form an open air museum of Cornwall's industrial past, waiting to be more fully exploited by Cornwall's modern industry – tourism.

I picked my way through the maze of lanes left behind by the miners. Most lanes are still in use by smallholders or dwellers in isolated bungalows tucked away among the spoil heaps and mine shafts. The main valley is lined with spoil heaps and pock-marked with shafts. Each shaft wears a conical hat made of steel tubing, to prevent anyone plunging to their deaths into the old workings. It is a strange, alien landscape, a world away from the crowded summer beaches of holiday Cornwall.

I climbed south out of the valley, past one of the

I picked my way through a maze of little lanes, left behind by the Cornish mining industry. (M. Thompson)

remaining working mines, though I don't know if it will still be working by the time you read this. A chain of green lanes took me southwards. There is a good ford near Gwennap. A friend of mine drowned a car here last winter. The water is knee deep and swamped the car's electrical system. My motorcycle has been designed to cope with this sort of ford. Nevertheless I collected a wellie full of water on my way through.

Everyone seemed to be out in their cottage gardens on the Polangrain track. The sunshine was making the weeds grow faster than the flowers. A weed is only a flower growing in the wrong place. The acres of colour I passed, growing free in the hedges, banks and copses of my ride, were the weeds of these carefully tended gardens. I prefer the wild abundance of the roadside to the chemical battle against nature waged in so many gardens. If a plant needs a fungicide to fight mildew, another to defeat blackspot, an insecticide to kill caterpillars and liquid fertilisers to make it grow, it cannot possibly be as healthy and natural as the wild flowers, which the chemical gardener kills with his selective weed killer. Perhaps the chemical gardener has never ventured down a green lane to see how nature manages her own garden when freed from the highway engineer's annual weedkiller spray, and the pollution of constant exhaust fumes on an overcrowded road.

My next lane begins as a farm track past a lone cottage

where an artist has his studio, judging by the debris in the back yard. The lane narrows to a single track. I recalled it being very wet on the last occasion I had ridden it. My companions had complained of the insanity of riding what they thought of as a stream rather than a lane. It appeared to have dried out since then.

No. I was wrong. Here was the water. I splashed through a puddle, which was up to a foot deep, and a quarter of a mile long. When I reached dry land again, I was at the fork in the lane. We had taken the right fork last time. This is sunk below the surrounding fields and lined with granite boulders which so narrowed the lane in places that the bikes needed to be manhandled between them. This was where Keith knocked a footrest off his Suzuki, and had to ride home with one foot resting on the engine casing. The right fork did not appeal to me riding solo. I could get through, but it would be hard work.

The left fork started with a very muddy patch. It had taken two of us to get the bikes through last winter. That was in the winter, however, and I was confident that the mud would be drier now. I took the left fork.

Round the corner was the muddy patch. I attacked it with determination. I blasted in. I was halfway through. I was stopped. The rear wheel was spinning round, but the front wheel had buried itself in the mud. As it span round, the back wheel dug downwards until it too was half buried. I stepped off the bike, and it stood upright by itself, supported by the mud. I tried to lift each wheel out of the mud in turn, but they were both immovable. I was well and truly stuck.

I removed the luggage and carried it back to a dry part of the lane, while I thought what to do.

I took out the tow rope and tied it round the front axle. I argued that I would be able to pull upwards more easily with the rope and so free the wheel. It did not work. The wheel did not budge. I succeeded only in making the rope muddy.

I peeled off my helmet and jacket, and tried direct action again. I heaved and twisted and shook the bike, but it was held fast. The mud sucked the wheels in and would not let go. All that happened when I tried to pull the bike up was that I sank down. My boots became buried in the mud and I had to use two hands to pull my boots clear.

I could hear a tractor in the field above me. I made my way over to the bank and waved to the tractor driver as he passed within twenty feet of me. He had seen this sort of thing before. Perhaps bikes were always getting stuck in this bit of lane. He certainly wasn't going to stop his work to help me out of the mess I had got myself into. With typical Cornish humour, he looked me straight in the eye, grinned and waved back, as he drove on round his field. I had no doubt that he knew my predicament, and he would enjoy telling his family about the young fool stuck in the lane and how he had waved to me. It would make a good story over lunch. I smiled wryly to myself and thought how I was to extricate myself without his help.

I concluded that I would have to dig the wheels out of the mud. But I was not sure how. I did not carry a spade, and there was nothing nearby with which to dig, just the overgrown hedgerow.

Inspiration came to me, I would use the peak from my helmet. It was not very big, but it was better than my bare hands. I set to work.

The mud was most strange. It was full of shiny flakes of mica, amid the brown goo. Where my wheels had spun,

Stuck! Lacking a spade, I had to dig the Yamaha out with the peak of my helmet.

the mud was runny, like thick porridge. Elsewhere it was firm textured, until you put your weight on it. Then it too turned to porridge.

I dug down a foot on both sides of both wheels. It took ages, but eventually they were both free.

Then I collected several bagfuls of stones from the dry part of the lane and packed them in front of the wheels. This, I thought, would give something firm for the tyres to grip, so that they could climb out onto the top of the firmer mud.

I started the engine, engaged first gear, and got nowhere. The stones were lubricated by the mud so that the back wheel span against the stones. It got more grip on the mud than it did on the stones. Carefully, I delved into the ooze under the wheels and removed the stones, one by one.

I would have to go back the way I had come. I saw I was about halfway through the muddy bit and it was quite a way back, but I had ridden in so I should be able to ride out. All I had to do was turn the bike round.

The lane was just wide enough to take the length of the bike, but it was full, from edge to edge, with mud. I would have to lift the bike round. I would never be able to ride it round.

I straddled the front wheel and grasped the spokes and lifted. It would not move. The mud had once more sucked it back into its grip. I found the back wheel was held fast as well.

I dug in again with the plastic peak.

I dug the wheels clear and moved the back wheel sideways onto some twigs growing on the edge of the mud where it would not sink back in.

I cleared a great arc of mud, peakful by peakful, so that I could swing the front wheel round on the firmer mud below the top foot of porridge.

I lifted the front wheel, up and sideways, three inches at a time, until it was pointing back the way I had come.

I climbed aboard and started the engine. I made three feet of progress and was stuck again.

I was now so determined to get out that I did not hesitate to start digging with my peak again. When I first rode into the mud, I had contemplated walking away from the bike and coming back the next day with some help. But now that I was so near to getting out by myself, even if

someone had come by and offered to help me I would have sent them away. I could do it alone.

Once more I climbed aboard. With big handfuls of throttle and mud flying in all directions, the bike slowly crawled forward. Faster and faster, scrabbling for grip, and then we were out.

I sat and rested, scraping layers of mud from my fingers. It had taken over an hour to get out of the mud and I was exhausted.

After a rest, a drink of water and a Mars bar, I was ready to go on. I rode back through the long puddle and paused to wash the mud from bike and clothes. Looking slightly less like the Creature from the Black Lagoon, I rode onto the next lane.

I needed to restore my self-confidence and this new lane was a different sort of challenge which should do just that. I rode through the stone pillared gateway to Clowance House. Muddy from head to toe, I chuffed brazenly between the luxury time-share apartments which were tucked discretely into the wooded grounds. I trundled confidently across the gravelled forecourt in front of the main house, and on to the green lane which ran through fields where the farmer was busy tractoring. Here was another confidence-boosting confrontation. Would he challenge my right to ride along his farm track?

He ignored me and got on with his work. I smiled a victorious smile. I had ridden from Dover along green lanes; I had dug myself out of the worst mud I had ever seen; I had exercised my right to use the public road through the grounds of Clowance House; nothing could stop me reaching Land's End now.

An easy, well used track took me into Leedstown. Most of the houses in Leedstown are on unsurfaced roads. Ten green lanes form the streets, with others radiating to outlying farms. I rode on, past the village hall, on a green track, freshly surfaced with gravel in places. I was confronted by a ''Road Closed'' sign at Truthwall Farm. It was a home made sign, not an official highway sign. It excited my curiosity rather than deterred me from proceeding. What reason was there for closing the green lane?

Several thoughts flashed through my mind. There could be a fallen tree, or possibly a landslip. The sign was new, so the lane could not be simply overgrown or waterlogged. On the contrary, it was well used, firm and dry.

I entered the farmyard and saw the reason for the sign. The farmer had contractors in laying a new farmyard. They had completed their work outside the cowsheds and were now concreting the area which crossed the green lane. In front of me was a three foot step up onto fifty square yards of wet concrete. This was a challenge I was not prepared to take on, much to the relief of the farmer's lad who stood watching warily from a barn. I picked my way over the part of the farmyard which had not yet been resurfaced, and rejoined the lane beyond the wet concrete.

The road may have been closed to ordinary traffic, but my bike had just escaped from a muddy grave and was not to be stopped by a patch of wet concrete.

I sped along the tarmac road to the outskirts of St Ives. Progress was much slower than I had anticipated, as a result of getting stuck in the mud. It was lunchtime and the best lanes still lay ahead. I had only just reached the Penwith peninsula, the oldest and most fascinating part of Cornwall. I stopped at the Spar shop to buy a snack for lunch. I was in luck. They had just taken delivery of a tray of hot Cornish pasties. They smelt irresistible. I bought one and popped it in my tank top bag. I would keep it until I found a picnic spot to do it justice.

I turned up Counthouse Lane. St Ives is slowly climbing upwards from its ribbon development along the coast. The green lane past the allotments is being lined with bungalows. The builders were erecting lap fencing around the gardens as I passed. The lane was still unsurfaced and climbed past a once isolated house with a gypsy caravan in the drive. A number of gypsy caravans still roam the Cornish roads, with canvas, barrel roofs like this one, pulled by patient, broad-footed ponies. Gypsies have found the verges of the old green roads excellent stopping places for countless years. They are seen less frequently these days, partly because their modern caravans and big cars are less suited to green lanes than the traditional, horse drawn caravan, and partly because there are now properly serviced sites at which they can stay.

I bounced to the top of the lane over the loose granite, and straight across on the tarmac road to Vorvas. Every house was called Vorvas. There was Higher Vorvas, Lower Vorvas, Vorvas Barn, Vorvas Vean and so on.

On the approach to Amalwhidden I passed a group of pony trekkers, fresh from the riding stables. The horses were plodding along sedately, but the riders were nervous. I went past slowly and quietly, and received a wave from their leader in thanks.

The narrow track over the ridge after Higher Amalwhidden was freshly churned by horses. Perhaps this was where the pony trekkers were heading. The surface was firm enough to cause me no problem. I stopped in the ford at the end to try again to remove some of the ingrained mud from my hands following the excavations with my peak earlier on.

Just along the road was one of my favourite stretches. I turned off the tarmac lane and climbed towards Lady Downs. A tractor stopped to let me come up. He was going home for his lunch, which reminded me of the pasty in my tank bag. It should still be warm if I stopped soon. This lane had been buried more than waist deep in sharp-pointed gorse no more than a year ago. Keith and I rode through it then, and it was hard work to say the least. It would have been impossible to walk through, but with the added weight and pushing power of sturdy four-stroke trail bikes, we had bashed our way onto the open heather moor.

A team of workers, sponsored by the government's Manpower Services Commission had been at work, clearing lanes on the Penwith peninsula and the new look lane was the result of their splendid handiwork. The lane had been transformed. They had cut a wide level track through the gorse once more, and cleared a drainage ditch to try to stop the soft, peaty surface from being eroded. The lane now provided a fitting entry to the high moorland.

At the top of the climb, I stopped for my long-awaited pasty. It was delicious, far more delicious than any shop-bought pasty had a right to be. This could hardly have been mass produced in a bakery. The ingredients were so carefully prepared that I would swear it was home-made.

I sat against a wall of granite boulders which was old when King Arthur was a boy. The moorland was cleared and walled for cattle pasture by the people who dwelt in the strange, Iron Age villages whose remains can still be seen nearby. Two miles from where I sat is the best excavated example of such a village, at Chysauster. You can buy a map and guide at the entrance hut where you pay for your ticket, then walk around the remains of eight or ten courtyard houses, built over two thousand years ago. Each house has a central space, or courtyard, with a series of rooms opening off it in the thickness of the surrounding wall. The remains of the walls are still quite remarkably high and give a real impression of what the settlement must have been like.

The most unusual feature of Cornish Iron Age villages is the fogou. This is a long, low roofed, underground chamber featured in many courtyard houses throughout the county. It was built by digging a deep trench, lining this with stone slabs which curved in at the top and was bridged by a ceiling of stone slabs. The stone tunnel was then covered over with earth. Each fogou had at least two entrances. Some experts believe that fogues were used as a place of refuge if the house was under attack, but others maintain, less romantically, that they were elaborate food stores.

Near the coast, on the lower, more fertile soil, the small fields, cleared of boulders in the centuries around the birth of Christ, are still in use, their outlines unaltered. The farmhouses have been rebuilt over and over again on the sites of the original buildings but the massive boundary walls of the fields have remained immutable.

From my vantage point, I could look over a landscape which, two millenia before, had supported a large community. Now the land looks wild and untouched, but, until the early tenth century, this was the Celtic kingdom of Dumnonia, fiercely independent, and wealthy because of the trade in tin through its ports to Europe.

A skylark landed twenty feet away. It looked big on the ground. It took off to sing incessantly, high overhead, like an invisible hi-fi. Vivid blue flowers sparkled at my feet where the young, green heather was sparse.

I got to my feet and climbed aboard once more. Off we went, following the narrow ruts cut through the black soil, avoiding the half-buried, mushrooming granite boulders which the ancient farmers had not cleared away. There are few landmarks nearby, and I relied on a feeling for the gentle slopes of the hilltops based on previous rides up here to guide me. If I were walking, on a clear day like today, I would have no doubts about my route, but the faster pace of a motorcycle can disorientate you on open ground, especially after almost a week of hedged or walled lanes.

Soon I reached a boundary wall, built of rough moorstone, and followed it until another wall came in on my other hand. The walls would funnel cattle from the open pasture in to the farm. I knew there was just such a farm ahead, because I had met the farmer on a previous ride.

I passed two goats, pegged out to feed among the grass covered hummocks of the wide drove. Then I saw Dave, my farming acquaintance, walking back from his goats to the farmhouse. I stopped to pass the time of day, but I could not get away with just a brief chat up here in such a lonely spot.

Over a cup of tea in the snug of Dave's rambling

farmhouse, he told me the story of how he came to be here. He related how he had bought the farm from an old gypsy woman nearly twenty years ago, and how he became the first of a colony on Lady Downs who had escaped the Rat Race to build a fresh and healthier life in this remotest part of Cornwall. I could read some of the struggles of the last twenty years in Dave's face, which was as weathered as the granite. He could turn his hand to most things and had needed to since moving up here.

He told me how the ceiling collapsed while he and his wife were relaxing with a quiet drink, nearly bringing their sleeping children down on their heads. He gave me an inkling of how hard it had been, having sunk all his money into the purchase price, to try to make the house fit to live in. He found the house he had bought almost uninhabitable. It was difficult to believe this now, but his twenty years' work had transformed a ruin into a cosy farm.

He took me to the back of the house. As usual there was a biting wind over the exposed ridge on which Dave lived. He was excavating a sunken garden to provide a sheltered sun trap to relax in, a spot for gentler plants to flourish on the wind-whipped moor. He had dug down ten feet and built up a sheltering bank, before deciding to stop. He would plant it with care, to provide a place of quiet refuge and recreation after the day's battle to make a living on the moor.

It was Dave who was able to confirm the existence of a green route along the peninsula. I had shown him some of my old maps of the area, and talked of an old road running along the high northern moorland. We traced the route on three separate old maps. Not only did Dave know the route, but he identified it as the old drovers' road which took cattle from St Just to the harbour, later the railhead, at St Ives, to be shipped off to markets up the country. Dave himself had driven cattle from St Just to St Ives on exactly this route about ten years ago. Our discussion confirmed that Dave knew most of the Penwith moorlands at first hand, having walked over it in all weathers at all times of the year.

I stopped just down the road to look at the old well Dave had just described to me. It used to be the water supply for all the cottages in this little community on Lady Down. It still ran, clear and bright, from a granite-framed opening. A square niche in the granite above the water intrigued me. Was this space for a plaster saint to mark the dedication of yet another holy well in Cornwall? Perhaps, in this remote spot, the water had been baptised into the Christian faith from an earlier belief. The plaster saint was the Christian version of the pagan water sprite, who had guarded the water supply and kept it fresh and clean long before the missionaries arrived from Ireland.

I rode on to the tarmac road, which I followed to a T-junction. Careful inspection revealed a narrow track running straight ahead across the open moor. This was all that remained of the drovers' road. I followed a rut, barely visible through the heather, and fell off on a hidden boulder. I stepped neatly off and picked up the bike in one movement. I was impressed by my own agility, in contrast to my difficulties on Bolter's Bridge in Somerset. Was I fitter now, near the end of my ride, or was it simply that the bike was more lightly laden?

I picked out the first granite boundary stone, carved with a large capital M for Madron parish. The drove road,

For centuries, cows were driven to market along the green drovers' roads. (M. Thompson)

I believed, followed the parish boundaries since these marked the dividing line, the watershed, between streams which flowed south to the English Channel and streams which flowed north to the Atlantic Ocean. I reasoned that this should provide the driest route throughout the year and was, therefore, a logical choice.

I bounced through thick heather and gorse along a criss-cross tangle of tracks made by grazing animals. They all went in more or less the right direction but strayed up to a quarter of a mile from the line of parish boundary stones. This did not seem an unreasonable width for a droving road across such open country, but it was hard riding through the tough heather. The bushes would yield to my passage, but unwillingly, and I was now always alert for hidden boulders, following my last tumble.

I came down to a dirt road at right-angles to my route. Ahead lay a large expanse of very rough grassland, pale yellowish and totally trackless. On the far side the heather moorland rose invitingly. I walked left and right, trying to find some track to follow, but there seemed to be nothing. The drove road disappeared into this mass of long dry grasses. I rode straight on, and discovered that the long dry grass rose out of a large bog.

The bog deceived me again and again. I would keep finding dry ground, and, believing myself to be through the worst, I pressed on further, only to sink once more, the back wheel spinning uselessly, into black slimy peat. The tufts of dry grass were as hard as rocks, and stood a foot or more above the surface of the mire. They were too high and too far apart to ride on, but to ride between them meant sinking into the bog.

Time after time I lifted the bike from the sucking grip of deep, black water.

I developed two techniques: One was to lift the bike out one wheel at a time. I would grasp the front wheel first and lift it up and sideways. Then I would grip the rear grab handle to heave the back wheel out and onto a dry tuft. The other technique was to push the bike over onto its side. The bog held it upright without assistance from me. The wheels would come free with an evil, squelch. Then it could be dragged across the ground on its side to more favourable going.

After an hour and a half in the bog, I was exhausted. I had decided to turn back some time ago, but was now too tired to make much progress.

A Royal Navy helicopter kept flying low overhead, about every quarter of an hour. Looking back now, I realise that it was most probably patrolling the coasts north and south, keeping an eye on the bathing beaches and on small craft. At the time it seemed to be monitoring my progress, or absence of progress. I thought about sending up a distress flare, except that I didn't have one.

I could see the following day's newspaper headlines:
"Helicopter Snatches Motorcyclist from Grip of Cornish Bog" Medals for bravery would be awarded to the intrepid aircrew, while I lay recovering from my ordeal in the nearest hospital. A team of navy divers would be sent in to hunt for my lost bike in the depths of the bog. Television crews from the news programmes would film the recovery of the slime encrusted vehicle winched free by special heavy lifting gear.

Real life is not so melodramatic. I must have been pretty shattered to entertain such a fantastic daydream.

Rescue came not from the air, but from the only house in sight. Someone had been watching me from the garden of Brook Cottage, half a mile away. I was so intent on my struggle with the bog, that I did not notice his approach until he was almost alongside me, having come across the bog from the cottage. Together we dragged the Yamaha from the last really boggy bit. I was then able to ride along a series of short stretches of slightly drier bog until I was once again back on the dirt road.

We rested and chatted for a while. He had a bike of his own back at his father's cottage, but he would never attempt to ride across the bog. He had sunk over waist deep in the mire, while walking across in the past. He told me of the last two bikes to be stuck in the bog. These were big, British roadsters. Neither of us could imagine how their riders had planned to hop across a bog on such unsuitable machinery. It needed a tractor to winch them out.

It was then he told me his best horror story. During the Second World War, the American army had used the area for tank training. One of their tanks had become bogged not far from where we stood. The tank crew had baled out, then stood and watched their tank sink slowly below the surface of the earth. All attempts at salvage had failed. The tank was still there now, twenty feet down!

I felt very glad to be out of that bog! My rescuer was able to point me on a safe detour round the bog and back on course for Land's End. I followed the dirt road at right-angles to my planned route and picked up a track a quarter of a mile away which circumvented the bog and led me on to the dry heather beyond.

I climbed towards the little community clustered around the derelict Ding Dong Mine, then swung right, past the Nine Maidens dancing in a stony circle. The maidens were staggering drunkenly and, perhaps it was double vision, but there seemed more than nine of them to me. Nine is a magic number, and most circles of standing stones have nine uprights. This one is said to have nineteen, but I did not stop to count them.

I pushed on across the open moorland until, once again, I picked up a pair of stone walls funnelling me into an exit lane. Here was where the farmers of Bosullow collected in their cattle from the moorland and drove them to their home pastures. Standing, lonely in a field, was the inscribed stone, Men Scryfa, which marked the upper limit of enclosed fields.

I was on a green lane between stone walls, thankful to be able to sit down in the saddle, after the standing concentration needed to cross the heather moor. At the end of the lane, I stopped, sat on the grass and rested by the roadside, glad to have made it, but reluctant to take on yet another bout of open moorland ahead. I had no wish to repeat my ordeal in the bog.

Just opposite where I sat was an old Victorian school. It had once served the scattered farmsteads of the high moor, but had clearly been superseded by an efficient school bus service into the towns. No schoolmaster lived here now, bringing his version of enlightment to the wild children of the hills.

The school had a sign outside declaring that it held an exhibition. An exhibition of what, I wondered? Who on earth would hold an exhibition up here in the middle of nowhere, and who on earth would come to see it? My curiosity was aroused, and I wandered across the road to investigate.

I pushed open the schoolhouse door and entered the Men-an-Tol Studio and print workshop of Ian Cooke, a member of the Newlyn Society of Artists. It was fascinating.

Mr Cooke was not at home. He had taken his three-wheeler to be MoT tested. His wife showed me round a tempting display of moorland etchings in the large main room, which had once been the classroom. Standing stones and the nearby Lanyon Quoit, the remains of a prehistoric burial chamber, particularly caught my eye. I was impressed by how well the texture of the ancient, course-grained granite had been captured on the acid-etched, metal plates.

Mrs Cooke came originally from Hong Kong, and I found her accent difficult to follow at times, but she had an irresistible charisma, which made me want to know more about how she and her husband came to be here. They had moved from London to Cornwall fifteen years ago, and discovered the old schoolhouse in 1980. She gave me some idea of just how much work they had needed to do to convert the derelict building into a beautiful home, workshop and gallery. The granite walls set off large quantities of glowing wood to give a rich, warm texture. Modern technology in double glazing and central heating transformed the cold, windswept perch of the old schoolmaster into a cosy nest, insulated from the harsh climate outside.

A staircase in the centre of the studio led to the open plan living room and bedroom. The old kitchen at the back of the school had been transformed to a smart modern galley looking out on a neat garden in place of the playground.

She explained the intricacies of making prints, using the large cast iron press operated by a huge bright red hand wheel. She produced some of her own prints, intricately worked arrangements of flowers and leaves, forming a striking contrast to her husband's harsh standing stones. Yet both styles came from the landscape in which they lived.

It was time to go, if I was to make Land's End today. It was not far now, but I knew little of the last green lanes ahead. I had to decline the offer of a cup of coffee, but promised to come back and look around the gallery again.

I felt ready for the final assault on Land's End. Only two more green lanes lay between me and my goal. Daisy chuffed cheerfully down the tarmac towards Great

From Carn Kenidjack I could see the end of Britain. (M. Thompson)

Bosullow, and on to the dirt track below Chun Castle, a hill fort which had once commanded the most westerly kingdom of Britain. I passed several walkers making their way to the castle. The track was well used, in contrast to the earlier sections of the St Just to St Ives drove route. It was easy, here, to follow countless other wheels, feet and hooves across the moorland.

I came to the last track, and had to make a decision. Should I play safe and ride south along the old road which climbed the hill by the air traffic control station? This was a smooth dirt road which I had used before. It would provide a gentle end to my green lane route, before the tarmac ride to Land's End itself. Alternatively, should I push straight ahead on the line of the old drove? I had never ventured along this part before and did not know what to expect. The most westerly bog in Britain, perhaps?

I chose the unknown, and plunged straight ahead into the mystery of St Just Common. The climb to Carn Kenidjack Tor was fine, a bumpy, little used track, but fairly obvious. From the high point of the tor I could see the Atlantic Ocean beginning to surround me. But I could see no road continuing ahead. There was an unbroken wilderness of heather. I followed a sheep track in roughly the right direction, but this kept swinging me too far north. I became totally disorientated and went round in almost a complete circle, first on tracks footrest deep and dangerous with granite boulders, then on a farm track.

What a way to finish! The last lane had been a fiasco of poor navigation and improper preparation. Ah well! I could never resist the challenge of a new lane, and it had proved my undoing yet again.

Down the road was the Land's End. What a tourist trap! I had to pay to park, which is something I object to strongly as a motorcyclist and will usually go to great lengths to avoid. Here there was no choice. I shuffled between coachloads of loud, elderly trippers. I tried the cafe, feeling I deserved a treat, and fell foul of the worst cup of tea I have ever tasted. It was incredibly weak, served in a thin, plastic cup, with a plastic stirring stick which broke when I tried to use it.

I turned my back to the trinket shops and their noisy customers and walked out towards the sea. It stretched, steely blue, as far as I could see. It looked huge. On the horizon were the Scilly Isles. I wondered what the green lanes were like there.

The cliffs on either side of me looked well worth exploring. They turned my thoughts to Long Distance Footpaths. Perhaps, another year, I would try a walk around the coast.

Perhaps there is a green lane route from Land's End to John o' Groats. It was something to be looked into.

At last I left the sea and the lowering sun, and headed home. The wind was behind me now. I had ridden for a week with it blowing in my face. I sailed along, hardly noticing the road. I had done it!

I HAD DONE IT!

I had ridden the long green lane from Dover to Land's End.

Chapter Seven

The North – Jedburgh to Derby

It was after I had finished the long green lane from Dover to Land's End that my thoughts first turned to writing a book. If I was to write THE green road book, I would need to find out more on the lanes in the North of England. I knew the South, the South-West, Wales, some of the Midlands and East Anglia, but the North was an unknown world to me.

Ideas creep up on me, they don't spring fully formed into my brain. I became aware that I was planning a trip to the North even as I promised myself that the Dover to Land's End trip had been my final big adventure. I knew I had to see the northern lanes for myself. It was not my style merely to write about the riding of others. I had to be there.

I would not ride a linear route. I would not try to join together as much green mileage with as little tarmac as possible, as I had from Dover to Land's End. In the North I would want to sample a few of the best lanes on offer in each area, and cover as many areas as possible.

In my mind, I had divided the North into five. The Borders, The Lake District, the North Yorks Moors, the Yorkshire Dales, the Peak District. Perhaps I should include Lancashire, North Wales or the Welsh Marches?

I realised that there was a very large area of Britain which I did not know. I could not ride it all. And to attempt to describe every lane in every area in the country would not make very interesting reading.

If my aim was to produce a green road book, I needed to sample some of the best areas and to describe my adventures in doing so. I would use the Whitsun holiday week of 1987 to ride from Jedburgh in the Scottish Borders to Derby. That was a realistic target. Well, only a shade over-ambitious. I would give it a try.

It was like planning the Dover to Land's End trip all over again, but with several differences. In the South, I already knew a lot of lanes. In the North I knew nothing. In the South, I was confident to find my own way on the ground. In the North, I wanted a guide.

Once again I called on the fellowship of the TRF to help me out. Postmen hurried from Cornwall to all parts of the North carrying my pleas for assistance, my maps to be marked up and my thanks for all the offers of help I received so readily.

At the same time I began a search for accommodation. I had refined my camping gear pretty effectively for the Dover trip, but I wanted to sleep under a roof occa-

Yamaha is hosed down in the back garden, ready for the next adventure. (M. Thompson)

sionally in the North. After much letter writing and several changes of plans, I took up offers of a bed for the first and last nights in the North, but chose the flexibility of camping for the rest of the week. It was not that flexible. I earmarked a particular campsite for each night, but booked nothing, so that if I did not make it, if I broke down or had to quit for some other reason, then I did not have to tell quite so many people.

My local guides for each of the five days riding were absolutely brilliant. Riding by yourself, you do see more. You can stop when you like and go at your own pace. But the right companion adds another dimension to the journey. He can tell you so much about what you see and where you go, as well as reducing the time you spend getting lost! Since I wanted to find out as much as I could about riding the northern lanes, a local guide was indispensable, and they proved terrific company.

Bike and body preparation began.

Weekly jogging sessions, interspersed with local trail rides got me marginally fitter. You don't need to be a Superman to ride green lanes.

I replaced the broken front mudguard and the rotted out silencer on Daisy, the trusty Yamaha.

Camping gear was dragged from the store cupboard, dusted off and checked over.

Supplies were bought, learning some lessons from last year. Beanfeasts were out. Good quality instant soup was in. I tried dried rice and vegetables from the supermarket instead of the expensive dried meals on offer from the

Camping gear. Sleeping bag, tent and air bed were the only items not crammed into the tank top bag.

Camping gear. Packed and ready to be loaded on board. There is room for essentials only.

camping shops. Extra rations of honey were packed in two small plastic jars. The staple diet was to be crunchie breakfast cereal and bread, the same as last year.

Riding gear was improved by the substitution of horse riding wellies in place of the more traditional type. Horse riding wellies look like expensive leather horse riding boots, but they are moulded in plastic. They are a better fit than ordinary wellies, and, most important, much taller. This meant that my waxed cotton overtrousers would not ride up above them, letting in the cold and wet. Ordinary wellies are fine if you are short, but I am long in the leg and horse riding wellies were just what I needed.

I watched the weather forecasts hopefully. I would go

at Whitsun whatever the weather, but good weather would help.

Almost before I realised it, Whitsun was here. On Friday night, I filled the petrol tank, checked the oil and the tyre pressures, and loaded my gear onto the tank and grab rail of my bike.

Saturday
Cornwall to Derby

I woke at five in the morning with a headache. I managed a bowl of cereal for breakfast, but felt too sick to eat anything else. Determined to start with a healthy breakfast I had made scrambled eggs on toast, but I could not eat it. I threw it into the kitchen bin. Even drinking a cup of tea was more than I could cope with. This was a great way to start the most challenging trail ride of my life!

Feeling pale and wobbly, I gave my wife a farewell kiss.

I was away, but only just. Within ten miles I was forced to stop by the roadside. I leaned against the bank for five minutes, retching and in a cold sweat. Feeling fractionally better, I continued on my way, only to find another bout of nausea attacking me ten miles later. This cycle continued for the first hour of my journey. I would ride for ten minutes, stop and gasp into the grass verge for five minutes and then ride on for ten minutes. I did manage to be sick at one point, which actually made me feel a little better.

When I crossed the Tamar from Cornwall into Devon, I began to feel better. Was it just nerves? I had been building up for this trip for a long time. I knew it was important to me and that there could be no second attempt at it. But nerves had never made me feel this bad before. I concentrated on feeling better, and pressed on.

By Exeter, my stomach was calm. By the time I stopped at Burnham-on-Sea to visit my parents I felt well enough to contemplate food. There is a superb baker's shop in Burnham. I have found nowhere to equal it anywhere in the West of England. I bought Eccles cakes and doughnuts from Curtiss the Master Baker to share with my parents, and called in at their bungalow for a cup of coffee.

It would be Mum's birthday on Sunday, so cards and presents were duly delivered. After a good chinwag, and something to eat and drink, I felt fully fit and headed northwards along the M5 motorway.

Just after Bristol, it started raining. It rained for three hours.

The motorcycle clothing market is full of cheap un-waterproof clothing. The manufacturers call it "showerproof". Showerproof is a euphemism for useless, when you find yourself in really wet weather. Motorcycle clothing is more difficult to design than, say walking clothing, because of the effect of speed. What may be waterproof and comfortable for walking in the rain can be cold and wet at fifty miles an hour on a motorcycle. The wind chill factor, the effect of speed on body temperature, requires extra insulation for the motorcyclist compared with the walker. The fifty miles an hour wind also makes the rain more penetrating, because the rain is hitting the front of your clothing much harder.

The long distance motorcyclist requires a suit which is warm, windproof, waterproof, hard wearing, comfortable and smart. It is possible to buy good waterproof motorcycle clothing. Top quality clothing can stay waterproof for two or three years if well cared for. My waxed cotton suit was waterproof when it was new, but that was ten years ago. Hours had been spent repairing the ravages of the years. Trail riding in the West Country involves considerable time spent in overgrown lanes. Belstaff claim their waxed garments are thornproof, which they are, but ten years of thorns had worn even Belstaff's tough cotton fabric. Holes were sewn up with heavy linen carpet thread. Reproofing wax was applied and both jacket and trousers warmed with a hairdrier to help the wax to soak into the fibres.

The repairs and renovation worked well for two hours, but by the third hour water was beginning to seep through the shoulders of the jacket and the seat of the trousers. This was not comfortable.

My hands stayed perfectly dry. I wore a pair of thermal inner gloves under a pair of unlined hide motorcycle gloves. The magic ingredient which kept my hands dry was a pair of loaf bags secured at the wrist with elastic bands. It was not elegant but it was very effective. No wonder plastic bread bags preserve plastic bread for so long.

Near Lichfield the world started to dry out. I parked near the site of the old abbey and wandered towards the city centre, glad to remove my plastic bags and feel the rain not hitting me in the face. Lichfield had been taken over by the annual fair. The whole city centre was full of giant rides, big wheels and rocket cars all glowing with hundreds of light bulbs beneath the black spires of the cathedral. Vast, old lorries had generators on their backs which were so noisy that they drowned out the loud pop music accompanying each ride. I learned that the fair was not yet in full operation. Monday was the main day and many of the side shows were still to arrive. There was also to be a procession of carnival floats on Monday.

The final leg to Derby was the only relaxed part of the day's ride. I felt well, the roads were drying and Dave Giles had provided a very detailed map to guide me to his home on the northern outskirts of Derby, where he had invited me to spend the night.

Dave Giles, my Derby host, inspecting a very green lane. The overgrowth is a result of underuse, yet a million people live within a dozen miles of this lane. (D. Giles)

David Giles' varied career has made him a unique asset to the cause of green lane motorcycling. Apprenticed to the aircraft industry in his home city of Bristol, he is a highly qualified technician. He worked for two years in Germany with the Dornier aircraft company, where he gained fluency in technical German. This was useful when he returned to Bristol Siddeley as a translator. He has devoted much of his life to youth work, including working in summer camps in America.

He put his two areas of expertise together at the Apprentice Training School in Bristol. Here, he was able to teach practical skills to craft apprentices and also to develop their initiative, self-confidence and reliability through an imaginitive General Studies programme. This involved rock climbing, canoe rolling, trampolining, expeditions and so on, in which he always took part, believing firmly in leading by example.

David's appreciation of the group dynamics of leadership are subtle. He told me the story of a youth expedition with Sir John Hunt, later Lord Hunt. David was one of the adult leaders of the youth party. Lord Hunt's approach to leadership was to be the first up in the morning. He would brew tea for the whole camp and take a mug of tea to each lad in turn. To be woken shortly after dawn in your tent in the high mountains by Lord Hunt bringing you a mug of hot tea had a remarkable psychological effect. If someone so important could make the tea, then it was no disgrace for a lad like you to help with the breakfast or to pack the tents. Lord Hunt's early morning chore set the pattern for each day and established his authority over the group in a quite remarkable fashion.

Dave is a long distance walker as well as a seasoned trail rider. While in Bristol he was secretary and local magazine editor of the Bristol branch of the TRF. His locally-produced magazine rivalled the national Bulletin in content and quality. Earlier in the year Dave had organised a National Rights of Way Conference in Derby, with guest speakers from the Countryside Commission, the Department of the Environment Inspectorate, Cambridge University and local government.

Dave has the gift of enthusiasm. He listened with avid interest as I outlined my plans for the week. After hearing me out he mentioned in his quiet way that he might well be free at the end of the week and perhaps he could come along on Friday when I rode through the Derbyshire Peak District. It sounded as if Dave was asking a favour, but of course it was· just the help I needed. Friday was the only day I would be riding alone, and his local knowledge was exactly what I needed to make the day a success. I wish there were more folk in the world like Dave Giles.

Sunday
Reaching the Start

I left Dave's house before 7.00 am. It was very cold and there was a stiff head wind out of the north. I had covered three hundred miles yesterday and had at least two hundred and fifty more to do today.

Sunday was not a day to remember. There were only two highlights to the day's journey.

The first was the Little Chef chain of roadside restaurants. On a bleak, cold grey day it is sheer pleasure to relax in warm, comfortable surroundings and savour a pot of tea. Motorway service areas are dreadful feeding stations. You feel as if you are on a conveyor belt. A Little Chef on the A1 is a far more attractive possibility.

The ultimate indulgence at a Little Chef is the Jubilee Pancake. These are unique to this chain of restaurants and I am addicted to them. A sweet pancake is filled with black cherries in syrup and a large cube of ice cream, folded over and sprinkled with sugar. Today's Jubilee Pancake was larger than usual. Perhaps they give larger portions in the North than in the South. It was fattening, full of sugar, thoroughly bad for me and delicious.

The second high spot of the day was the A68 road, north of Hadrian's Wall. This road crosses open, empty countryside in a series of twisting corkscrews and abrupt ups and downs that it could have been the ultimate ride at any fairground. It was marvellous fun, especially on a motorcycle. The road was dead straight in places, if seen on a map or from an aeroplane, but the "vertical curvature" was extreme. You would drive straight down a hill in a series of roller coaster swoops over blind crests, then feel the road push up against you as you climbed the next hill.

There were sections of sweeping curves over unfenced hillside and there were groups of hairpin bends into deep valleys. I learned later, and was not surprised, that it is used regularly by motoring magazines to test drive new cars. It is a road among roads.

After the Scottish border the weather became even colder and greyer. I had to keep stopping to restore the circulation in my numbed fingers. I was very glad to reach the campsite just north of Jedburgh.

The campsite was called Lilliardsedge Park and was on the site of one of the many border battles fought between English and Scots down the centuries. In this particular fight, in 1545, the Earl of Angus defeated an English army of some five thousand men. He hid his men in the woods and thickets on the steep slope overlooking the campsite. He used his cavalry to act out a mock retreat, and when the English followed his men fell on them from the trees.

An anecdote and a poem accompany the battle. The anecdote is not unusual in Border battles. The Kerrs, Armstrongs and Turnbulls had marched to the battlefield with the English army. When they saw the day was lost, they tore the red cross of St George from their sleeves and joined in the pursuit and plundering on the side of the Scots.

The poem tells of the bravery of a girl named Lilliard (hence the Lilliardsedge Park campsite). She followed her lover to the battlefield. On seeing him cut down, she rushed into the fray, picked up his sword and laid about the English until she too fell.

On the hill which bears her name is this inscription:

"Fair Maiden Lilliard
Lies under this stain,
Little was her stature
But muckle was her fame.
Upon the English loons
She laid monie thumps
And when her legs were cuttit off
She fought upon her stumps."

There was a monument on the hill behind the campsite, but there seemed to be one on each hill whichever way I looked. Which one bore the inscription quoted above I hesitate to say.

I pitched my tent in the lee of a coppice, planted long after Lilliard's fight. Behind the relative shelter of my flysheet and the trees, I lit the EPIgas backpacker's stove and cooked a hot meal. Camping and mountaineering shops sell all sorts of dehydrated packet meals, but they never look very tempting. I bought my supplies from my local supermarket, and that night's meal was really not bad at all. A packet of rice and dried vegetables, with a small tin of tuna, made tuna risotto. I thought I had done rather well with only a one third of a pint stainless steel saucepan.

The pan was washed up and re-used for coffee to accompany the dessert of a fresh orange, followed by cheese and biscuits. It was a thoroughly civilised meal, eaten sitting on the grass in a field.

I felt sure I had blown up my airbed before cooking the meal. Perhaps I had not blown it up firmly enough. I puffed into it again and snuggled into my sleeping bag for a cosy rest. I could HEAR the air escaping from the airbed. Within five minutes I was lying on the cold, hard Scottish earth.

This was no good.

I cannot sleep on the ground. I am too thin and bony. I have no natural padding to protect me from the bumps on the ground, and no layers of fat to insulate me from the cold. I need an airbed to survive in a tent.

I was miserable. I had reduced my camping needs to the minimum possible, as a result of last year's Dover to Land's End trip. Everything was just enough and no more, but I had to have an airbed.

Inspiration struck. I recalled the story of Allan Breck Stewart and David Balfour in Robert Louis Stevenson's "Kidnapped". When sleeping out on the Scottish moors they made beds fit for a king from heaps of heather.

There was a problem. I was surrounded by all sorts of vegetation, but no heather. This was not wild, Scottish moorland, but rich agricultural land.

I was not to be defeated. They had cut the grass on the campsite the previous day. I was surrounded by dry grass cuttings. I stuffed the two dustbin bags, used to keep sleeping bag and tent clean on the bike, with as much dried grass as I could find.

I packed the two bags under my sleeping bag to support by back and hips. I made a pillow from my waxed cotton suit.

Once again I snuggled into my sleeping bag. It was nearly ten o'clock and just getting dark.

Monday
The Borders

At 3.30 am, I woke. I was cold and the ground was full of lumps. My grass mattress had subsided under my weight during the night and now offered little protection from the coldness or the hardness of the ground. I was miserable. This was NOT a great adventure. This was pure masochism. Why on earth had I set out on such a foolish mission? I could be home in my warm, interior sprung bed with my electric blanket. What in heaven's name was I doing here?

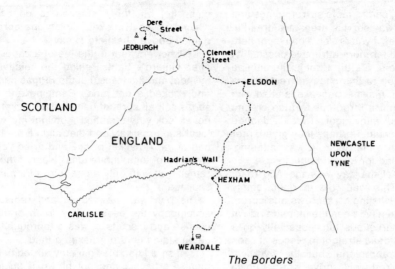

The Borders

I dozed fitfully for about an hour, then determined to warm myself with a hot drink.

It is possible, in a small ridge tent, to lie on your stomach in your sleeping bag, resting on your elbows, with your head and shoulders at the tent flap, to brew a cup of coffee. It is not particularly easy. It is not particularly comfortable. But it is possible.

After my coffee, I tried to get back to sleep. I was not due to meet my guide, Alan Kind, until 8.30, so I didn't need to get up early.

It was no good. I was too cold and uncomfortable to sleep. I would do better to get up. Moving around should start the blood flowing in my veins again and so warm me up. I sloughed off my sleeping bag and put on several layers of daytime clothing. I pulled on my boots and stood munching crunchie breakfast cereal, while the water heated for another cup of coffee.

The air was chill. The trees did little to stop the breeze cutting straight through me at that early hour.

At six o'clock I went for a walk in the wood behind the campsite. Paths had been cleared through the conifers and clearings made, large enough for a tent or a caravan. No-one camped in the gloom of the wood. The clearings were becoming overgrown. Brambles and honeysuckle were reclaiming the open spaces. Seedlings were spreading into the clearings from the feet of their parents.

As I approached the far edge of the wood, a deer, startled by my early morning presence, leapt into the open from her browsing place and took off at great speed across the green wheatfield. She zig-zagged at a great rate of knots, occasionally bounding into the air, her white rear flashing a signal for other deer to follow, but she was alone.

Her flight was instinctive, handed down from generations of deer hunted by men with bows. The zig-zagging and the occasional high leap were techniques to dodge shafts fired from a longbow. She stopped a furlong away, out of bowshot range, and looked back. Then she climbed the hillside towards Lilliard's monument and finally disappeared into woodland nearly half a mile away.

The wood was quiet as I trudged back to my tent. I had done two laps of the wood and was feeling a little warmer at last. It was gone seven, and a few other campers were beginning to stir and cough.

I washed and cleaned my teeth in the shower block. This is one of the main reasons for staying at a good campsite. Hot water and clean washbasins are luxuries which can be appreciated after a long day's travelling. On this site the facilities were kept immaculate by a key system. On arrival, each camper paid a pound deposit for a key to the washroom. Unfortunately, when I left there was no-one to return my pound deposit. I had no wish to wait for the reception office to open at nine, so I posted my key through the letterbox and forgot about the pound. I reasoned that the whole trip was an unnecessary luxury. I did not need to ride green lanes at all. The lost deposit on the key amounted to one per cent of the cost of the holiday. It was a sacrifice I could afford to make.

I rode through the empty streets of Jedburgh to wait for Alan Kind in the car park below the ruins of Jedburgh Abbey on the banks of Jed Water. Jedburgh is filled to overflowing with Border history. Here was the home of Mary Queen of Scots, declared a bright new signpost; there is where Sir Walter Scott lived; this way to the castle; that way to something else.

It was all too early in the morning for me. All I wanted to do was get started on the green lanes.

Alan arrived in the car park seconds after I did myself. We were both a quarter of an hour early for our planned rendezvous. Alan had ridden up from Newcastle-upon-Tyne and was, understandably, cold. We had a brief chat, while he thawed out. Alan took the obligatory photograph of the start of my ride, with me standing self-consciously between our bikes with the Abbey as a backdrop.

Then we were off.

We had exchanged letters, discussed over the phone and studied maps of the first part of the ride during the last six months. We were to use two of the three main green cross-border roads, then push down to Hexham and ride some moorland roads in Hexhamshire, before reaching Alan's father's holiday cottage in Weardale for the night.

We were to start just north of Jedburgh on Dere Street, a Roman road. Now, I had thought that Roman Britain ended at Hadrian's Wall, umpteen miles south of Jedburgh, but this is not so. The north-western boundary of the Roman Empire moved up and down across the Borders throughout the centuries of Roman occupation.

In the early days, the Romans controlled the North from their garrison at Eburacum (modern York). It was the job of the Ninth Legion, stationed at York, to maintain peace – the Pax Romana. We know the Ninth were in York in 107 to 108 AD because an inscription has been found recording the replacement of wooden garrison buildings by stone buildings constructed by the legion.

About 117 AD the Ninth Legion disappeared from the army list. Exactly what became of it, no-one is sure. The most popular explanation is that the Legion was surrounded and destroyed while marching north to quell a rebellion among the Border tribes. They marched north along Dere Street to their doom and were wiped out by an overwhelming force of tribesmen somewhere near Jedburgh.

Such a defeat would be bad news for the Roman administration. An entire legion of the invincible Roman army destroyed by a crowd of barbarians! It was unthinkable. The news would have been suppressed. It was not the sort of thing one handed down to posterity in one's written records. It is no wonder that no details of the massacre have been found.

The strength and the weakness of the Roman legionaries lay in their training and their equipment. Heavily armoured infantry, they were experts at fighting other infantry in open country and at assaulting fortified positions. The hilltop castles of Southern Britain were no real obstacle to Roman conquest.

Equipped with a short stabbing sword and two slender and well-balanced javelins, the legionaries advanced on the battlefield, shoulder to shoulder, with their long, semi-cylindrical shields held in a solid wall in front of them. When about thirty yards from their enemy, they threw javelins and surged in, thrusting their short swords into the bellies of their opponents with an under-arm action.

They were all but invincible in a pitched battle, but were too weighed down with equipment to pursue a lightly armed opponent. The Romans needed cavalry to chase a defeated enemy, to scout ahead, to act as a screen against surprise attack. In the moors and forests of the Borders, it must have been rare for the heavy infantrymen of a legion to catch a native tribesman, except when, through foolhardiness or desperation, he stayed to fight.

The Legion was vulnerable to hit and run tactics. In the far north, a long way from their base and their supply line, the Legion would be forced to march as a solid body. Any stragglers would be picked off by tribesmen hiding on the edges of the line of march.

Slowly the Legion would have been whittled down until its morale cracked and the Legion broke and ran, or it was totally annihilated.

Of course, there may be other explanations for the disappearance of the legion. Troops stationed so far from their sunny homeland, battling against the British climate and the hostile inhabitants, would not be easy to lead. If their morale sank too low they may well have rebelled without being attacked, killed their officers and made off into the wilds. Such things had happened elsewhere in the Empire.

Some less dramatic disgrace may have resulted in the disbanding of the legion and the redistribution of its centuries among other legions. It seems unlikely that we shall ever know the truth of the matter.

Rosemary Sutcliffe opted for the first explanation as the basis for her classic historical novel, *The Eagle of the Ninth*. The legion lost its eagle standard in a disastrous defeat by Caledonian tribes, but the eagle was recovered after many adventures by the son of one of the legion's officers. It is a great story, well worth a read.

We turned off the main road to Kelso onto a quiet green track. There was no sign of the Ninth. A wide, grass-grown road bashed south-eastwards through rolling farmland. Meandering along the Roman road was a single rut, which sometimes became three ruts, cut into the red earth by modern users of Dere Street. Evidence on the ground showed that these were mainly walkers and motorcyclists, with the wider spaced ruts resulting from the occasional Land Rover. There was no impression here of a wild frontier land. The road was lined by huge beech trees, centuries old, which gave more the feeling of a drive to a stately English home.

I was waiting for us to reach the end of the green lane, being accustomed to short lanes of less than a mile in the South-West, but Dere Street went on and on and on.

Just above Cappuck Farm, we came to Oxham Water. There was a narrow wooden footbridge for pedestrian traffic and a firm-bottomed ford. In 1927, this ford was regularly used by carts and cattle. In those days, this part of Dere Street was known simply as "The Drove", according to Jessie Mothersole, who walked the entire length of Dere Street in the early 1920s. On the south side of the stream is a steep sided mound, the remains of a small Roman fort, built to guard the river crossing.

The next couple of miles are tarmac now, but Jessie describes the road here as a track across fields "hedged in with beech on one side, and with hawthorn and blackthorn on the other. There is a ditch and mound on either side within the hedges. The surface is level and grassy. Where it is enclosed it has been made a scheduled road, for it was found that gypsies and tramps used to steal the fences for feeding their fires." She describes this delightful stretch in high summer, with the path lined with wild roses, foxgloves and honeysuckle in full bloom and "the afternoon so hot that the rabbits lay stretched out motionless on the grass, and had not the energy to stir" as she passed. What a difference a tarmac surface can make!

The underlying nature of Dere Street began to change. We were climbing steadily. After this short length of tarmac, the Roman road snaked away southwards over the empty hills. There was not a tree to be seen. The green road was defined by dry stone walls which stretched away to the horizon.

As we rode on the wall on one side of us first crumbled to a heap of rubble and then disappeared. The road still ran ahead over the rough grassland past sheep and past cattle.

Sitting in the road, next to the gate, was a huge, brown and white bull. Suppose this giant beastie took a dislike to us and our motorcycles while we were trying to unfasten the gate. If the gate were tied up, as so many were, we could be stranded in his field for several minutes. We would be feet away from him and unable to escape.

Alan volunteered to hop over the wall we were following, walk down level with the gate, climb back over and open the gate.

The bull sat, chewing contentedly, as I rode by, slowly and quietly. Then it was Alan's turn. I held the gate in one hand and the camera in the other. I wanted a picture if the bull did decide to turn nasty. The bull lifted his head as Alan approached. The little Yamaha two-stroke puttered past. The bull kept chewing and Alan kept on going.

It was a non-event. It might have been really exciting, but it was not. I have to admit that the few bulls I have found on public roads have all been as docile as this one, but it pays to play safe when dealing with so much muscle.

We came to a crossroads at Pennymuir. Here, the adventurous Jessie Mothersole found very comfortable lodgings with Mrs Scott of Pennymuir, dining on eggs, drop-scones and "curranties", while Mr Scott entertained them with Scottish airs played on his concertina.

There used to be a fair at Pennymuir for the sale of fat lambs from the hills around, but it is a desolate spot now. Pennymuir seems to have been a popular stopping point for the Romans, although it never became a permanent base. The rectangular earthworks of a series of three, perhaps four large marching camps are carved from the saddle of land between Oxnam Water and Kale Water, both flowing north towards Scotland. The camps look big enough to house an entire legion, the Ninth perhaps? Along the line of Dere Street to the south are other rectangular campsites, spaced at roughly five mile intervals across the high Cheviot Hills until a more permanent Roman castle is reached at Rochester in Redesdale.

We left Dere Street and followed the Kale Water northwards along the tarmac lane to Hownham. This remote village was the haunt of Covenanters in the Seventeenth Century. This Presbyterian Christian sect hid away here to worship in liberty, a strange, but all too common contradiction. Freedom of worship achieved only in secret.

We turned hard right onto a dirt road and climbed steeply over a loose stony surface from the village. The view behind us grew grander and grander as we climbed up and up. We passed through a gate and continued climbing, with a single grey stone wall on our left. We were looking for a turning to our left, but saw nothing.

Suddenly we discovered ourselves looking back down the valley towards Hownham. We had ridden in a semi-circle on the top of Windy Law and were now facing the way we had come. The wheel ruts we had followed were new ones, made by the farmer during the winter, bringing food up to the hilltop for his sheep. They led nowhere.

Alan had anticipated that we might miss our turning to the east and instead find ourselves on The Street. But we had missed The Street as well. The Street is probably much older than the Romans. They did not build it, but they certainly used it, hence its name – The Street. It runs parallel to Dere Street and was used for several centuries to bring herds and flocks from hill farms in Scotland to market in England. Its name suggests a Roman origin, but the only archaeological sites along its ten green miles are pre-Roman hill forts. General Roy's military map of 1755 names it not The Street but Clattering Path.

We back-tracked, peering over the stone wall, now on our right, for signs of a road. Climbing the distant hills

Exhausted mountain bike rider is caught by pursuing jeep.—A melodrama for the benefit of the camera.

was a streak of green of a slightly different shade to the hills themselves. It was heading east, so it must be the road we wanted. Then we found the gate we had missed. I had been so engrossed in the view up the valley that I had ignored the wall, obscuring the opposite view, and so had missed the gate completely. Beyond the gate, in the middle distance was a single, solitary tree and a small, stone cottage. This isolated building was marked "ruin" on our maps, and confirmed that the different shade of green was our road.

Once through the gate, the road was obvious. How could we have doubted it. It swept down to a stream crossing in front of the ruined cottage in a series of elegant curves. The road crossed the stream over a culvert, hand-built from moor stone. The curves to ease the gradient and the culvert to cross the stream made this more than a drovers' road. This had been engineered for wheeled traffic. It was undoubtedly a carriage road.

As we descended into Mowhaugh, we came upon two shepherds and a Land Rover. They were mustering their flock into a complex, dry stone sheep pen. We stopped at the end of the pen, since one large lamb had escaped and was running towards us chased by the younger shepherd. When the lamb's poor eyesight finally made out our shapes ahead of her, she made a U-turn, then jinked sideways to avoid the outstretched arms of the shepherd. With agility like that she would have made a good rugby stand-off. Unfortunately her sideways jink took her straight into the wall of the pen. She was cornered and scooped up by her pursuer, and dumped into the pen with her sisters.

We exchanged greetings with the shepherds and rode on to Mawhaugh. Alan explained to me that they were probably dipping the sheep at this time of year to rid them of various skin parasites. At the same time, lambs would be sorted out, identified and branded with dye. The

Roger Fogg stops for a chat while exploring in a Suzuki "Rhino".

lambing season came late to these northern hills, but it was now over and the farmer needed to be sure of the size of his crop.

An empty tarmac road took us south again in search of Clennell Street, the third green road across the border.

At Cocklawfoot, we crossed the stream and bore right through a farm gate, to climb the spine of Cock Law towards England. The road was wide open and green, stretching upwards for two and a half miles to where the border ran along the watershed between the nations. Here, in the brilliant morning sunshine, we paused to look back over the rolling hilltops of Scotland and forward to the rolling hilltops of England.

A farm gate marks the border, and stands on a spot known now as Cocklawgate but in ancient times as Hexpethgate. Hexpethgate was a meeting place of the Wardens of the Middle March. Here they would gather to discuss border problems between the great families on either side. All too often, such discussions became very heated and came to blows. It was in a "discussion", in 1585, that Sir Francis Russell lost his life at Hexpethgate. Russell's Cairn on Wyndy Gyle commemorates his name.

The border between England and Scotland was a flexible thing down through the centuries until the two kingdoms were united under King James VI of Scotland, who became James I of England in 1603 on the death of Queen Elizabeth I.

During Mediaeval times, the life of a Borderer revolved around raids on his neighbour and resisting counter-raids from his neighbour. Feuds went on between families down the centuries. Cattle rustling or "reiving" was an essential part of a cross border raid, and as often as not in raids on neighbouring valleys on the same side of the border.

Overlaid on this pattern of local squabbles, the Borders were a battleground for greater historical fame. King David of Scotland ruled part of Northumberland by right of conquest. King Edward I of England marched north into Scotland to conquer in his turn. Wallace and Robert the Bruce kept the history pot on the boil in the thirteen hundreds. James IV and James V led disastrous expeditions into England. Henry VIII sent an army into Scotland which was scattered at Ancrum in 1544.

Today the region still echoes its turbulent past. Each year the folk of the border commemorate their history in the Common Ridings "season". This begins at Hawick in early June and finishes in August at Lauder. One of the more spectacular events is the Jethart Callants Festival which is an excuse for the whole of Jedburgh to get drunk. The Ridings recall historical incidents and serve as reminders to all that once the now peaceful Borderlands had to be defended by strength. They also, incidentally, celebrate horsemanship and are both colourful and dramatic. It was a shame I was in the Borders in May, before the fun had begun.

We swung southwards into England and came upon the junction with the Salters' Road. I would have liked to explore the Salters' Road. Alan told me that it was one of the wildest, toughest and most demanding roads in the North today. It is a prehistoric routeway, which came into prominence in the Middle Ages when salt was exported from the salt pans at the mouth of the Tyne northwards to Scotland.

Salt is one of the most basic food needs of man. There are a number of salt roads across the Pennines, although obviously they would carry other traffic apart from pack horse trains of salt.

A superb Border road sweeps over the horizon towards England.

We passed a military Land Rover standing empty in the road. The area is heavily used by the military for all manner of troop training and manoevres. Not far away is a firing range where live ammunition of all sorts of calibres is fired off into the hills. This Land Rover, equipped with a mass of electronic hardware and a huge aerial bore the Belgian flag. We learned from a chap in the pub at lunchtime that there was a unit of Belgians training locally, and that it was not uncommon for foreign troops to fight mock battles up here.

We came down a couple of hairpin bends to a ford and a bridge across a stream. By the ford was a circular sheep pen. I think it was a sheep pen. It was fairly derelict. I wondered how archaeologists distinguished between an ancient sheep pen and an ancient hut circle. They used the same building technology. Dry stone walls are a very old form of construction. Superficially a sheep pen and a house must look the same, but I expect excavation would find the remains of a fireplace and perhaps the holes for the posts which supported the roof of a house. I wondered if there was ever a house in this lonely valley where the sheep pen now stood.

We came upon this deserted Belgian army Land Rover on Clennel Street. The area is a popular military training ground.

How do archaeologists tell a sheep pen from a prehistoric roundhouse? The technology of building here has not changed for millennia.

We splashed through the ford and rode on. The green part of Clennell Street was twelve miles long. Once again I was amazed at the size of green lanes in the North. It gave a different perspective to trail riding. These lengthy, open grassland tracks required a steady, leisurely gait to be maintained in order to see them at their best. In the West, we were used to short bursts of concentrated riding, followed by a spell of tarmac. I was really beginning to enjoy the North.

We passed a group of young soldiers, looking very pale and tired under their black camouflage greasepaint. Perhaps they were looking for their Land Rover. We reached Alwinton at the southern end of Clennell Street and pulled into the car park of the most aptly named Rose and Thistle public house to take refreshment after our border crossing.

Shortly after ordering pie and chips, I realised that I was not very hungry. Whatever had struck me down at the start of this adventure on Saturday had returned to plague me again. I had a headache spearing through one eye and a stomach very definitely disinterested in food.

The afternoon passed in a haze of discomfort and pain. Alan modified his planned route to take us more or less on a direct line to Weardale. His original route was most ambitious, and would probably have brought us to Weardale about ten in the evening. Alan is notoriously venturesome in his route planning.

The vast green dwarfs the church and pele tower in Elsdon village.

I remember Elsdon, not so much for its pele tower – a fortified house used as the rectory, and a typical example of the pele towers which were the strongholds of Border families, but for its vast village green. Village greens to which I was accustomed were small triangular affairs, but this one was a huge irregular rectangle.

I learned two facts about Elsdon:

When the church was being "restored" by the Victorians, they found over a thousand skulls, believed to be those of English soldiers who fell at the Battle of Otterburn. One hundred complete skeletons were also found within the church, and the remains of three horses, thought to be a pagan sacrifice to consecrate the church at some time in its past.

In the churchyard is the tombstone of Thomas Wilson "officer for the duty of salt" who died in 1778, a connection with the Salters' Road and a reminder of the importance of the transport of salt in the area.

We pushed southwards at speed along the tarmac. The green lanes we used grew steadily shorter, the further south we went. The green road to Great Bavington was over three miles long, across open grassland in huge stone-walled fields. The road used to be shown on the Ordnance Survey 1:50000 scale maps, but has been omitted from the latest edition. This makes a nonsense of the remaining path network, since the map now shows a

Winter's Gibbet near Elsdon (A. Kind)

bridleway ending in the middle of nothing. In fact, the bridleway joins the county road we were riding, which the Ordnance Survey now fail to show.

The green road across Hallington Reservoir was two miles long. The road has been built across the new dam when the valley was flooded to make the reservoir. The road before the dam was built was always a green road, so the new stretch across the dam was left green. It was a curious feeling, riding a wide band of tussocky grass over a modern dam.

We picked up a green road between Keepwick Farm and Cocklaw which took us across the fields, through a garden and up to Hadrian's Wall. The Wall is unimpressive at this point, buried beneath the modern road. The ditch to the north is clearly visible.

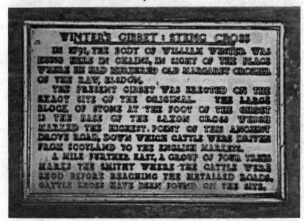

Inscription at the Gibbet foot.

This fallen tree will take more than a small chain saw to clear it from the road. (A. Kind)

The Wall was built long after the disappearance of the Ninth Legion. It formed an Iron Curtain between the civilisation of the Roman Empire and the barbarians who lived beyond its bounds. Attempts were made to push further north with the building of the Antonine Wall, between the Firth of Clyde and the Firth of Forth, across the narrow neck of Scotland, but this was not a construction on the scale of Hadrian's Wall and did not endure as a frontier for long.

Hadrian's Wall was begun in 122 AD and took ten years to finish. It was ten feet thick at its base and probably about sixteen feet high. It is difficult to estimate height after such a long time. The chronicler Bede, in the Middle Ages, says that it was standing twelve feet high in his day. Bede was a careful man who had surely been to look for himself, and that was some three centuries after it had ceased to be a frontier.

The western half of the Wall for some thirty-one miles was built of turf or clay at first, because of the local shortage of lime to make the mortar needed for a stone structure. This turf section was later replaced by stone.

For most of its length, the Wall was protected on its northern side by a ditch twenty-seven feet wide and nine feet deep. The wall and ditch presented a formidable barrier to the primitive tribes from the North, yet the Romans did not stop there. They built fortlets every mile along the wall, known as milecastles to house garrison patrols. Spaced between each pair of fortlets were two turrets. Then there were sixteen forts built into the Wall, housing regiments of auxiliary infantry and cavalry. All in all, this was an awesome frontier indeed.

I had visited one of the most spectacular bits of Hadrian's Wall last year, during a family holiday to Scotland. The major fort at Housesteads is definitely worth a visit. But not if you feel as rough as I did today.

A little over a mile of dry dirt road took us over Acomb Fell in the civilised land south of the Wall.

The shortest lane of the day was also the hardest. Just west of Hexham, Alan took me along a tiny short cut between Anick and Bank Foot. This was a West Country Lane! It was sunk deep between two banks and was becoming filled with tall, green summer vegetation. The reason for the undergrowth became apparent, when we found two small trees down across the lane, blocking the traffic of foot, horse and wheel, which would normally have trampled down the soft vegetation.

Alan had hoped that some of the local trail riders would have cleared the trees by now, but it was obvious they had not yet had time. We manhandled the bikes, on their sides, under the trees and rode into Hexham.

At the petrol station I admitted defeat. I told Alan we would have to make directly for his cottage in Weardale, because I neededto lie down pretty urgently. Reluctantly we abandoned the loop of lanes which made up plan 'C', or was it 'D', in Alan's list of alternative routes.

We arrived at the cottage in West Blackdene, Weardale sometime after 4.00. I unpacked my sleeping bag and went straight to bed, feeling as if this was the end of my trail riding for the week.

Alan made the most of the free time produced by my illness. He took out his paintbrush and set to work on the door and windows of the cottage with a pot of white paint. The cottage was up for sale and he was tidying it up whenever he had the opportunity.

I slept for over an hour, and woke feeling slightly more alive than dead. I took a bath and felt a little better again.

As my head slowly cleared in the warm evening sun, and my stomach began to return to its proper place inside my body, Alan talked of food at a restaurant round the corner. Feeling that he deserved a meal out after putting up with me all day, even though I was less than hungry, I agreed.

The entrance to the restaurant looked ordinary enough. Alan was well known here, and we were soon seated at a table in the most extraordinary room. The restaurant had been owned until recently by an enthusiast of American country and western music. Live entertainment was a regular feature, with barn dances, ho-downs and other "Wild West" delights. All the staff would be dressed in cowboy outfits and to complete the picture so would the restaurant and adjacent bars, especially the room in which we dined.

This lane in Upper Weardale is not far from Alan's father's holiday cottage where we spent the night. (A. Kind)

Cars are a rare sight on all but the gentlest green lanes. Car drivers are missing out on the best of our countryside, but could they gain access without damaging it?

Hosing down at the close of the day. (A. Kind)

The ceiling had been replaced by a great canvas arch – quite literally a wagon roof! We appeared to be sitting at our table inside a covered wagon crossing the deserts of Arizona. On the end wall, with his back towards us, sat the wagon driver. Beyond him, through the semi-circular opening in the canvas cover, could be seen the labouring backs of the team of horses trying to haul the restaurant along. The walls/sides of the wagon were festooned with cowboy paraphanalia. There were coils of rope to lasso steers, oil lamps and buckets.

Fortunately the food was more refined than cowboy beans. Alan was able to enjoy a vegetarian feast, while I sipped a bowl of soup, decided my appetite was returning, and ordered fish and a side salad.

We dined well in our make-believe world, and returned to reality to stroll up the valley to the cottage. Alan chatted away about the places we passed, painting a delightful picture of life on this warm May evening. Then he mentioned the flash flood which came down through the houses just up the valley a few years back, and how he used to be unable to stand upright in the winter winds while wading through the snowdrifts to take his children to school. You could see Nature in all her moods in Weardale.

Tuesday
Over The Pennines and Into The Lakes

A blackbird was singing his dawn song outside my window. I ignored him for as long as I could, but finally gave in and got up about five o'clock. It was a splendid song, but dawn is a little early for grand opera.

I felt alright. My head was clear and I was hungry.

I pulled back the curtains and peered outside into the grey light. I could just make out the dim outline of the house next door, some twenty feet away. Here was a different face of Nature – thick fog.

I washed and went downstairs. Alan joined me for breakfast and we went over the plan for the day.

We would tackle Grasshills Causeway which ran south-westwards from the head of Weardale, but Cross Fell was not a good idea in fog like this. We would make a more northerly and more varied loop, taking in some of the old turnpike road between Alston and Penrith. Alan would leave me on the main Penrith road, and I would make my way to the head of Haweswater to meet John Gillett, who was to be my guide in the Lake District.

Alan locked up the cottage and we were away into the fog. I could just about keep Alan's bright red rear light in view at fifteen miles an hour, as we threaded our way along the lanes from West Blackdene and up Ireshope Burn. The tarmac lane swung west towards Burnhope Reservoir.

The wet cotton wool continued to shroud us as the road turned from tar to rock. This was the highest green county road in England. It reached a spot height of 674 metres, 2210 feet, while the famous Walna Scar road in the Lake District only just touches the 2000 foot contour. What a view there must be from the top on a clear day! Alan's rear light grew fainter as he pulled away from me over the stony surface.

At about seventeen hundred feet, we climbed out of the mist into brilliant sunshine from a cloudless sky. It was magic! What a difference a little water vapour can make!

We stopped at the top, a little over two thousand two hundred feet above sea level. The high point was marked by an old gateway – Galloway Gate. To our right rose the crest of Jagger Hill. The map labelled the pass Coldberry End.

Galloway cattle were driven south from Scotland along this road in the eighteenth and nineteenth centuries. Hence the name Galloway Gate. The old drovers had a reputation similar to the cowboys of the United States.

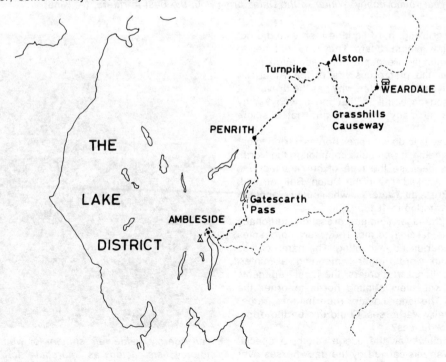

Over The Pennines and Into The Lakes

Trail riding is a year round hobby. Winter in the Dales brings out the best in riders. (A. Kind)

They were hard drinking, hard fighting men who did not always hold the law in high regard. They were not men to tangle with unwittingly. Perhaps their reputation is as much a myth as the glamorous life of the American cowboy. If their lives were similar, why has the drover not been immortalised on celluloid like the cowboy? Why have their been so many Westerns and not a single Northern?

The Jagger Road is to do with pack horses. I tried to get to the root of this name. It was quite common in the North. Alan said it was because the type of horse used was called a jagger. I linked it with the Dutch, Belgian and, especially, the Prussian "jagers", who fought Napoleon at the battle of Waterloo in 1815.

The history of the jager soldiers, dressed traditionally in green uniforms, fascinated me. They were companies of gentlemen experienced in hunting. The name comes from the German word "jäger", meaning a hunter. Instead of conventional trumpeters, the jäger regiments had "hornists" who blew hunting horns to order the troops in battle. The jäger cavalry rode hunters, rather than trained cavalry warhorses. Could this be the origin of the jagger pack horses?

Another possibility was the Jaeger cloth, a special woollen cloth. Was this carried by the pack horses over these passes from the cottage based clothing industry

Trail riders provide refreshment for weary walkers. The motorcyclists acted as marshals for the Weardale Marathon – a long distance walking event. (A. Kind)

which was the basis of English wealth for centuries before the Industrial Revolution?

Or did the name Jaeger for the cloth come from the special weave used for the green hunting jackets of the Prussian jägers?

In my search through the dictionary for a solution, I came across "jag – 16th Century dialect word, meaning a load for one horse; origin unknown."

Coldberry End suggests the site of a Roman earthwork, though I spotted nothing obvious around me. "Cold" usually refers to a Roman road, as in Cold Harbour; while "berry" or "bury" means an ancient earthwork or fortification.

Who knows how old this road is? Alan assured me that it was used regularly by ordinary motor cars until twenty years ago. The surface was firm and dry all the way today, although rather potholed and littered with loose rocks in places, damaged by frost and flood.

The view from Galloway Gate to the west was like a fairyland – a scene from a Tolkien novel. The valleys were filled to overflowing with dense white mist, which poured from valley to valley over the lower hill slopes. The hills rose, bare and green, basking in the sun. Further away, beyond the hills, the whole landscape disappeared beneath the mist. On the horizon, a darker, higher level of mist was visible over the sea on the coast.

We waited for weird knights to gallop out of the mist and over the ridges, pursued by hobgoblins and purple-winged dragons, but perhaps it was too early in the day for them. Or perhaps they only rode these hills at night, and the dawn had chased them back to their underworld hideouts.

We came down to the main road high in Teesdale. Here there was no mist, but the thin haze which promised a hot summer's day.

We followed the tarmac road to the head of the dale. Crossing the watershed, we were at the head of the South Tyne valley. This ran northwards, again filled with dense white mist. We were in the clear, several hundred feet above the mist, when Alan spotted the point where the pre-turnpike road to Alston left the modern turnpiked road.

At least, he thought he had spotted it. There was the derelict barn where the green lane started, but, somehow we were the wrong side of a post and wire fence. We seemed to be following wheel ruts through the grass, but they were turning the wrong way. What had gone wrong?

We walked up and down the fence line. Had the gate been removed? Surely not, because the fencing wire was old and rusty. There was no sign of any recent alterations.

Reluctantly we climbed on our bikes and headed back towards the tarmac to try again. We didn't reach the tarmac. Climbing over a mound we spotted the lost gateway. We were ten yards too far north, when we left the tarmac road. Which goes to show that a miss is as good as a mile when you are trail riding.

This was another green county road which the Ordnance Survey map failed to show. The roadway was cut into the steep side of the narrow valley. It was smooth and well engineered with a gentle gradient. It was surfaced with grass but there were a couple of awkward washouts, where the road had all but completely fallen into the stream below.

On the west bank, we came across the ruins of a mining community. All the hills around here had been worked for lead. Most of the humps along the horizon were hand-built spoil heaps from before the days of mechanical mining. Below us were a series of drift mine entrances, burrowing horizontally into the valley sides, lined with rough moor stones. A smooth green track ran up to the ruins of a stone house.

All was quiet now. The miners had long ago gone to search for richer pickings. The hills were deserted.

The cobbled streets of Alston were deserted. It looked old-fashioned – perhaps the 1930s. A teenager in baggy trousers and a flat cap lounged in a corner of the market cross, drawing on a cigarette. The buildings were dark stone with dark windows.

It was still early. Perhaps Alston would soon bustle with light and life. But I doubted it. Alston claims to be the highest market town in England. It had no wares to offer us this morning.

Bayles Moor Road runs above the Penrith road. It was a rocky road made bumpy by heavy farm vehicles. A heavy vehicle thumping into a small pothole creates a larger hole. Each time a tractor passes, the hole gets bigger. This was the first green lane I had come across in the North showing any signs of intensive agricultural use.

A cock pheasant sat, dozing, on the stone wall as we rode past. It was 7.30 and he was sure no-one would be hunting him so early.

A grey cat crammed itself flat against the grey stone top of the wall, pretending to be a stone. His eyes flashed at me as I trundled past.

After two miles of bumping through the potholes, Alan's luggage fell off. Travelling twenty yards behind him, I stopped to retrieve it. The bag was very heavy. He had enough tools in there to open a garage.

Alan waited at the end of the lane, unaware of his lost luggage until I handed it to him. We hunted for the elastic luggage straps that had secured the bag to the rear mudguard. They had not fallen off with the bag. We found them, shredded and wrapped round the rear wheel. Their useful days were over. They would strap no more luggage in place.

On inspection, we found that one of the rear flasher brackets had all but sheared through on Alan's bike. I didn't mention that Alan had carefully cleaned and tidied this Yamaha DT175 and was about to advertise it for sale. It had been pressed into service for one more trail ride. The effects of the careful cleaning were no longer apparent, of course, and now a bracket had all but broken off. I felt guilty about all this, since but for me, Alan's bike would be standing, gleaming, in his garage this morning, awaiting a queue of potential new owners.

Alan produced a roll of heavy duty plastic sticky tape from his weighty tool bag and set about strapping up the wobbly indicator with several yards of the stuff. After some rearrangement of the luggage in the rucksack on his back, we were off again.

The main road from Alston to Penrith had been turnpiked twice. On the second occasion, the survey and construction work were undertaken by none other than John Loudon McAdam, the man who invented the modern road surface.

The work was carried out on behalf of the Royal Greenwich Hospital for Seamen who were large land-owners in the area. The arguments put forward for road improvement were compelling. The roads were in a most

HEXHAM, 27th August, 1823.

My Lords and Gentlemen,

YOUR approbation of my propositions for the improvement of the Roads, through the Hospital's property in these Counties, conveyed to me by your Minute of the 9th Instant affords me much satisfaction ; and your consent, to my proposal, that the Hospital should subscribe Five Thousand Pounds towards the undertaking, has given great confidence to those Gentlemen who are interested in its completion.

Notwithstanding the heavy rains, Mr. M'Adam and his Surveyors, have been indefatigable in laying off the proposed Lines of Road, and having ascertained, with sufficient accuracy, the whole extent of the undertaking, which on maturer examination we considered necessary to be accomplished ; a second Meeting of the Trustees was held here this day, when the subject was further examined in detail, and the two Trusts united in a Resolution, to apply to Parliament next Session, for the purpose of being incorporated, and to obtain the necessary powers for carrying the measure into execution.

Mr. M'Adam reported to the Meeting, that the improvements which, we have been induced to recommend, to their adoption, will cover an extent of One Hundred and Twenty Miles, of which upwards of one half will be new Road ; and he took this occasion to state his opinion, that if the sum of Twenty-Six Thousand Pounds is now raised, and laid out with proper skill and economy, no further Loan will be required for the completion of the whole undertaking.

The Trustees concurring in our proposition, that the more enlarged plan should be adopted, have resolved to increase the sum to be raised by Loan, to Twenty-Six Thousand Pounds, and directed Mr. M'Adam, to complete the Survey with all practicable expedition.

I cannot conclude this letter without expressing my very sincere acknowledgements for the zealous support of Lord Viscount Lowther, who again presided at our Meeting of this day, and also to Messrs. Wailes and Brandling the Receivers, who have co-operated with the utmost cordiality in conducting these arrangements, affording me their personal assistance and information, and giving every facility to Mr. M'Adam, and his Surveyors, in these long and laborious Surveys; nor should I lose the present opportunity of declaring my increased confidence in the judgment and ability of Mr. M'Adam, and my persuasion that under his personal control and superintendence, these extensive improvements will secure very important advantages to the inland Commerce of all these Northern Counties.

I have the honour to enclose Copies of my Correspondence with Mr. M'Adam, and of the Minutes of the two Meetings of the Trustees held at this place, on the 29th July and 26th Instant, and I have requested Mr. M'Adam to forward to me a more detailed Report for your information, so soon as the whole of his Survey shall be completed.

I have the honour to be,
My Lords and Gentlemen,
Your most faithful and obedient Servant,
EDWARD HAWKE LOCKER.

To the Right Honourable and Honourable,
The Directors of the Royal Hospital
for Seamen at Greenwich.

Extract from a letter about a new turnpike road to be built by John Loudon McAdam.

deplorable state, according to the surveyor. I quote from McAdam's report:

"With respect to the construction of the Roads, they are altogether the worst that have yet come to my knowledge, – not only have the old defective methods been followed in the formation, stoning, and subsequent repairs of the Roads, but the work has been done in the most slovenly careless manner, without method, and regardless of expense. No pains have been taken to preserve the Roads from the winter floods, by keeping open the waterways. They are washed out so as to present the appearance of a bed of rocks, rather than an artificial road. Under such circumstances it must be obvious that the traffic required by the Commerce and Agriculture of the District must be carried on with difficulty and at great expense".

He was a canny chap, McAdam. Notice the stress laid on needless expense and the emphasis on economic advantage. He knew how to appeal to the hearts of his employers.

He estimated the roads around Alston were carrying 14000 tons of lead and lead ore, 3000 tons of coal and some 3000 tons of timber and other heavy goods annually. All this on roads which resembled rocky stream beds!

The alternative transport systems of canals or railways were considered impracticable because of the high Pennine ridges that had to be climbed over or tunnelled through.

In places the old road rose at a gradient of one in seven. McAdam declared that "Hartside Fell may be crossed at a rise of one foot in thirty from Aldstone to the summit and at one foot in twenty from Melmerby to the summit."

The old turnpike lane was smooth and straightforward despite McAdam's complaints, until we came upon a ewe and her lamb. We had encountered endless sheep since leaving Jedburgh, and I was to slow for sheep to scamper or dawdle from my path throughout the week, but these two were the silliest of a very silly race.

They ran past all the obvious gaps in the walls on either side. They ignored a gate into a field full of mothers and their lambs, they seemed bent on diving into the main road ahead. They were kamikaze sheep, determined on self destruction.

On a smooth lane, with silly sheep, the final solution is to overtake. You have to go quickly, but once you are alongside, the sheep will stop and then trot back quietly down the lane.

Unfortunately, the nature of this lane changed as we approached the main road. The smooth surface was replaced by hugely churned tractor ruts, eroded by rain

A bleak warning on the Hartside pass. This is McAdam's improved turnpike route giving easier gradients for the heavy traffic from the local lead mines. (A. Kind)

The old Hartside Pass turnpike crosses the new at right angles, heading straight for the summit.

The pre-turnpike Alston to Hartside road is even steeper and wilder than either of the turnpiked roads. (A. Kind)

to a depth of a couple of feet into the rocky soil.

The sheep trotted out onto the main road, to be tooted at by a passing car which swerved to avoid their death wish, and I bent the brake pedal in a rut. The brake lever was straightened with a stone age hammer – a large rock.

We reached the summit of Hartside Fell. There was a large cafe and an even larger car park, both deserted.

The new turnpike swept down the fellside in a great hairpin bend, half a mile long. We rode straight down and onwards on the steep, pre-turnpike green road.

We found a green lane with Byway signs at either end. "Public Byway to Five Lane Ends" declared the first sign. I had never seen such a sign before and stopped to photograph it. The number of green lanes being given byway status under the 1981 Wildlife and Countryside Act seems to be diminishing. It is an ideal name for a green lane, but the legislation is so complex and so over-burdened with political and individual prejudice and self-interest that it may never become the normal green lane title.

We rode one more green lane, again the first generation turnpike. Alan led me back to McAdam's handiwork on the main Penrith road. Here we were to separate.

Alan had proved a great riding companion. He was a skilled and dependable green laner, with a fund of local knowledge which he put at my disposal. He was patient and good humoured, when I kept stopping for photographs or just to look at the view. I could only hope that my other "native guides" would measure up to Alan's high standards.

Alone, I headed for Penrith and then along miles of country lane to Haweswater. I stopped at Bampton for petrol. Already it was clear that I was in the Lake District. This was a holiday area. Visitors were the norm. Even in this out of the way village, few turned to stare at my odd and rather grubby motorcycle loaded down with camping gear. Beyond Bampton seven miles of tarmac ended in a small car park.

It was ten minutes after nine. Already there were half a dozen cars here. Some were empty, while the occupants of others were lacing up heavy walking boots and shrugging on their rucksacks, before striding off into the hills. They were heading straight on, trudging up past Small Water to the Nan Bield Pass which provided an alternative packhorse route into Kentmere from the Gatescarth Pass I was hoping to ride.

Ten minutes after I arrived, John Gillett bowled up. I thought he had been holidaying in the Lakes and was merely popping round the corner to meet me. But he had ridden from his home in Lytham St Annes in Lancashire two hours away this morning. Throughout my time in the north, I was impressed by how willing my fellow trail riders were to put themselves out to help me.

John had hoped that a couple of other Lancashire riders might have joined us. We waited a while, but no-one turned up, so we went through the gate and started our assault on Gatesgarth.

The gradient was ferociously steep. Despite all the heavy stuff packed in my tank bag, I was struggling to keep the front wheel on the ground much of the time. Large white rocks wriggled incessantly beneath my wheels as the steady chuff, chuff of Daisy's engine lifted me ever upwards. There were easier bits, then more hard climbing up and up.

John had pulled some distance ahead of me and stopped. I caught him up and we rested for five minutes to catch our breath and cool down. Looking back, we could see that we had taken a rather more direct route than the original road. Faint green lines could be seen looping back and forth across the mountainside. The road was mainly used by walkers these days, and, as a walker I

A friendly sign clearly marks the start of the Public Byway, a green lane, to Five Lane Ends.

know, on foot you tend to go straight up despite the gradient.

The sun burned down on us as we continued climbing. Black waxed cotton motorcycle jackets are excellent absorbers of the sun's radiant energy, I noted, as the sweat trickled down my back. John told of the rider who collapsed in tears on the Gatescarth Pass, unable to struggle up any more, and I recalled the guy in Wales who had thrown his bike down and stormed off swearing, equally unable to cope. This was much more demanding that Wales. John told me it was even more interesting when there was ice on the rocks!

The best bit was near the top of the pass, where a series of seven closely packed hairpin bends were smothered in loose rocks and washouts. After conquering this section I was ready for anything!

Although this road was mainly used by drovers and pack animals, there are written records of coaches climbing the pass. The thought of climbing the road I had just ridden, perched on the box of a coach and four was too much for me to contemplate.

If the ascent had been rough, the descent was even rougher. I would much rather go up than down. Going up relies on throttle control, while going down uses the brakes. Clearly my braking technique needs improving.

Exhausted by the effort of keeping my balance through rocks and gulleys, hummocks and washouts, I fell off on a boggy patch at the foot of the steepest part of the descent.

I made a soft, three point landing. Nothing was damaged. We rested a while, and watched a farmer in a tiny four-wheeled buggy make his way up the pass like a fly climbing a window pane and turn off onto the fellside to find his sheep.

I was told later, that the pass had had a good, firm surface, until it was used as a training ground for caterpillar-tracked Bren gun carriers in the Second World War. These vehicles had broken up the hard surface and started the erosion which had made the descent so difficult today.

In T. West's *Guide to The Lakes*, published in 1778, the climb from Haweswater over Gatescarth was one of the most ferocious in the Lake District. "The path soon became winding, steep, and narrow, and is the only possible one across the mountain." This must mean the only one practicable for a vehicle, since the Nan Bield Pass was an acceptable alternative for an adventurous horse rider.

On the Longsleddale side, things were easier in West's day. Much of the lower road has been made up to serve the slate quarry at Wren Gill early in the eighteenth century.

We soon came to this easier road, enclosed by stone walls. It was still steep in places, with some tight bends, but we had left the worst behind us. We descended steadily until reaching tarmac at Sadgill Bridge.

A petition written in 1717 was got up to promote the construction of the bridge:

"The inhabitants of Long Sleddale, Langdale, Grasmere, Rydal and Loughrigg, Ambleside, Troutbeck, Kentmere and several other townships in the Barony of Kendall, show that the great road and highway between Hawksyde, Ambleside, Shap, Penrith and Appleby, very much used by travellers, drovers and others having occasion frequently to pass and repass to and from the said markets with cattle and other goods, in which public highway there is a water or rivulet called Sadgill which by the violent and sudden rain there is often raised and overflows its banks so that no passenger dare venture to cross the same and many times travellers are forced to

John Gillett knows what lies between us and the summit of Gatescarth pass in the Lake District. The rock behind my rear wheel, preventing the Yamaha slipping backwards, gives some idea of the gradient.

stay two or three days before they dare venture to cross and often are in danger with their cattle of being lost in crossing the said water to the great prejudice of trade, and pray that a bridge may be erected over the same.''

A little hamlet has grown up around the bridge that was built to cross the stream in spate. We waited for the red Post Office van to finish his deliveries, before we could tackle the climb up behind the houses on the green road to Stile End.

The main drovers route out of Lakeland from Ambleside and Troutbeck and all the places listed in the petition for the bridge, was over the Garburn Pass, the Stile End, and then either south down Longsleddale or north over Gatescarth. This route is also known as an ''assize'' road, because it was the road used to reach the Assize Court in Appleby.

After the initial steep climb, the road was pretty straightforward. The descent to Stile End was over remarkable slate cobbles, laid on end. I could not decide whether these were a natural outcrop or a man-made surface. Bearing in mind the heavy use of the road in the past, I tend to favour the latter.

We dropped down steep tarmac into Kentmere, before the third part of the green drovers route – the Garburn Road. This starts climbing steeply straight away, surfaced with large, loose rocks like the start of the Gatescarth Pass. I tried to ride feet up, but I was getting

Only Cumbria can boast views like this! The tarmac pass snakes alongside the river, thousands of feet below my rocky perch.

tired and resorted to paddling more than once.

Ahead of us I could see a large group of walkers. Dressed in summery white and pastel shades of green and blue, they sat or leaned or stood on two outcrops on either side of the road. They are waiting to ambush us, I thought.

We were managing little more than a walking pace against the rocks and the steep climb. I was breathless, but I tried to raise a smile and a word of greeting as I panted by the ranks of pedestrians.

Their ''ambush'' was a mass hostile glare! Their leader, whoever he was. had clearly told them to disapprove of vehicles on the Garburn Road. Perhaps he hadn't read its history?

Without exception, everyone else we met was friendly, as people should be who are enjoying the countryside, whether at work or play. It was sad that this great gang of walkers, trudging upwards in each others noise and dust could find no pleasure in others sharing the countryside with them.

The next two walkers we passed begged us, jokingly, for a lift. We passed their two young sons, near the top, who ran (!) ahead to open the gate for us. Those two boys were fit! We collapsed in a hollow of green, sheep-cropped grass at the summit, but the boys strode on past us with a smile. They looked about ten or eleven years old. I wish my parents had taken me to the Lakes when I was that age.

We didn't want to stay too long and encounter the unfriendly gang again. The descent was much easier than the climb. We gave the boys a wave as we passed them. The view down the valley to Windermere was superb. This was the Lakeland I remembered from so many walking holidays alone or with my wife. When the air is clear, there is nowhere else in England I would rather be than on the Lake District fells.

Robert Orrell crossed Garburn with two packhorses in the journeys described in his recent book *Saddle Tramp in the Lake District*. He notes that the local magistrate, Benjamin Browne, ordered the pass to be repaired in 1730 because ''it is so utterly much out of repair and in decay that a great part of it is not passable for neither man nor horse to travel through the said ways without danger of being bogged in the moss or lamed among the stones.'' Nowadays the problem of maintenance is more subtle. Robert Orrell, like myself, would hate to see Garburn ''improved'' by a layer of tarmac, yet to draw the line between adequate maintenance and over-improvement of historic routes is very difficult.

We took the back road from Troutbeck into Ambleside. Here we really were in the heart of the tourist industry. There was a traffic jam the whole length of the one-way system through Ambleside. We were able to slip through without much trouble. A motorcycle has an obvious advantage over a car when the traffic gets really heavy. We passed hundreds of stationary vehicles, too wide to go through the gaps we were using.

We followed the roads round the northern edge of Lake Windermere to the campsite at Low Wray. This was a National Trust campsite in the grounds of Low Wray Castle, and I really didn't know what to expect. I had never stayed at a National Trust campsite before. My hopes were raised by the fact that it allowed no caravans and no advance booking. There should be space there for my little tent, but would they accept motorcyclists? Many campsites listed in my AA guidebook had banned motorcycles because of trouble in the past.

We turned into a farm drive before reaching the castle, following a fingerpost to the campsite. We stopped opposite the reception office, converted from a room in the farmhouse. No sooner had we dismounted than the campsite Warden strode past.

"Are you looking to camp here?" he called aggressively.

"Yes please," I responded, sweetly.

"Pitch your tent over there, and no hassle!" he shouted. "I've had my fill of bikers over the Bank Holiday just gone."

With that friendly welcome, he climbed into his National Trust Land Rover and drove off.

I felt I knew where I stood with this gentleman – somewhere lower in the pecking order than a cockroach.

Being certain that I would give him "no hassle", John and I rode quietly in the direction he had pointed, parked and started looking for a suitable spot to pitch my tent.

John sat astride his bike and watched with dry amusement as I criss-crossed the camping field, apparently inspecting each blade of grass.

Choosing the right pitch is important, as I explained to him. You want a flat spot, but not in a place where a puddle will form. You need to avoid rocks and thistles and the like. You want to try to catch the morning sun, but avoid the prevailing wind. You need to be aware of where others may pitch; there is nothing worse than someone arriving late at night after an evening in the pub and erecting their tent within feet of where you were once sound asleep.

Having found the optimum site, I pitched the tent and dumped my camping gear. John and I headed back to Ambleside to hunt for a replacement airbed. There was no way I was sleeping on the hard ground again, after my experience at Jedburgh.

Not one single shop in the whole of Ambleside could offer me a cheap plastic airbed. I warn all future campers of this fact. Shops sell everything for the climber, the rambler, the canoeist. You can buy barbecues and frame tents, igloo tents and emergency flares. What you cannot buy is a lightweight airbed.

I bought a heavyweight, rubberised canvas, Lilo bed, and we headed for an eating and drinking house for lunch. Local TRF expert, Pete Deeley had recommended the Skelwith Bridge Hotel as a handy place for lunch and so it was. We bought a drink, ordered a sandwich and sat outside in the sun.

It was boiling hot. Everyone around us was dressed in shorts and tee-shirts, and even they were too hot. We sweltered in layers of protective clothing. There are times when riding a motorcycle has disadvantages.

We sat and chatted while waiting for my sandwich to arrive. When you ordered your food you collected a numbered ticket. Mine was 74, and I waited eagerly as 70 and 71 were announced by the waitress, clutching steaming plates of pies, fish, pizzas and chips. 73 came, then 72, then 75, 76, 77. All I wanted was a sandwich. Time passed and still no number 74 appeared. When it got to 82, I went to investigate, and found my lonely sandwich sitting on a bench near the bar.

It was a very tasty sandwich, but I am not sure that it was worth waiting quite so long for.

As we sat in the sun. John persuaded me that I didn't want to ride Walna Scar that afternoon. He did this in his subtle Lancashire way: "You don't want to ride Walna Scar this afternoon, Ian."

Well, yes, actually I did. I had been looking forward to it, especially after the success of this morning. However, there was more behind John's subtle hint. I did not wish to abuse his generosity in giving up a day of his holiday to show me the Lakeland passes so far from his home. He did look tired. John had joined the TRF in 1975. He had been a leading light in trail riding in Lancashire ever since. I can remember reading his brief but colourful run reports for years. He had been rights of way officer for Lancashire for ten years, and was handing this role over to someone else in the autumn. He felt he had done his duty to promote and preserve green roads. Now he deserved the right to pick and choose a little what he did and when and where he rode.

We were baking in the afternoon sun just sitting still. It was not really the sort of weather for yet another long, hard climb. Perhaps I had done enough for one day.

I agreed that I could leave Walna Scar for another time. John accepted another drink. I promised not to mention John falling off on the Garburn road. It was just a funny coloured, motorcycle-shaped rock I had ridden past. We sat enjoying the sun for over an hour, but John finally had to leave for home.

I returned to my campsite by the castle, carrying my new airbed, and thinking over the reports I had heard of Walna Scar.

Pete Deeley had written to me before I set off and described Walna Scar as "very rough and steep almost all the way to the summit on the eastern side. The western side was O.K. until almost at the bottom when there are some large boulders which need care. The views are sensational in fine weather." I was disappointed to have missed the views.

Andrew Lennie from Teeside described it as the high spot of his weekend in the Lakes in 1981. He said the descent was very hard and he collected a puncture.

Rosie Swindells' comments were more detailed. She said "It was alright except for the bits where you had to carry the bikes! The first mile or so was a piece of cake – a really nice rocky lane, rising slightly but mainly following the contours around the hill, and with a beautiful view, I then noticed that Terry had stopped some yards in front of me, so rather than plough on regardless, I thought I'd better stop and see what was going on. I soon found out . . . boulders, boulders and more boulders, and rock steps up a narrow gully. The lads struggled up but Ann and I decided that discretion was the better part of valour and waited a while before heading for the pub."

I found a nice description by Pete Deeley in an old magazine. "You can use all the green lane superlatives on Walna. It is rocky, steep, very difficult, scenically sensational and from the top, on a clear day, you can see the Isle of Man. But on this occasion it was drizzling. Have you ever tried riding in drizzle while wearing glasses? Unbelievable! I could just about see my front wheel, let alone the Isle of Man. The dreaded rock step provided the usual problems about how to get up it, but sadly there were no spectacular attempts.

"Then Roger's bike had a flat tyre, so we set to and fitted the spare tube. This was easy. After all we had 6 tyre levers, 27 spanners, 3 pairs of pliers, 4 screwdrivers,

I gave this one a miss. I must go back and ride Walna Scar. Everyone else seems to have such "fun" tackling it. (R.Marston)

3 tins of WD 40, 6 spring links, 2 half links, two pumps, one of which was broken and a Sammy Miller catalogue. Three quarters of an hour isn't bad, is it?

"The next incident was rather like that Gerard Hoffnung thing about the builder, a barrel of bricks and a pulley, because on the way up we met Reg from Kirkby Stephen, on his way down — backwards! Poor Reg. This was only his second 'real' trail ride. Just before Christmas he had badly wrenched his shoulder after falling from his bike, and in the past week he had been involved in a car smash as well. By the time we got to him his backward motion had ceased but he was very tired. We got his bike to the top and had a rest. It took a long time to get down to the valley below and once there Reg decided to call it a day."

I mulled over all these colourful comments while I sat under a tree at the campsite. The sun was hot and I was glad of the shade. The tree was on the shore of Lake Windermere, and I was watching the lake steamer cruise past and people messing about with dinghies and sailboards. I became convinced I had made the right decision. It was great to be in the Lake District, and I would definitely be back. Next time, I would tackle Walna Scar. Definitely. But this afternoon I would enjoy a rest on the beach.

Wednesday
Into The Dales

It was a golden dawn. The land glowed pinkish-orange in the first of the sunlight. I had slept well on my new Lilo and made a leisurely start. Some other folk were walking about the campsite before I had finished strapping the tent onto my bike.

I chuffed off down the empty roads through sleeping Ambleside. On the outskirts of Windermere I stopped to check my route along the back lanes out of the Lakes. A chap in yellow oilskins on a well-used trail bike pulled up alongside. His bike had little paint left and was equipped with various serious green road goodies, like a tyre inflator and a spare inner tube.

"You must be Ian Thompson!" he said. "Good morning! I'm Pete Deeley!"

It was a chance meeting indeed! Here was the expert on Lakeland green lanes, the man who had marked up my Lake District Tourist Map for me and written two pages of detailed route notes on the best lanes to use. We could have talked for an hour, but we managed only a couple of minutes. Pete was late for work. I will look him up next time I come to the Lakes.

And I will climb Walna Scar.

I followed narrow lanes along the lowest edges of the fells north of Kendal, and picked up the main A6 above Garnett Bridge. The main road climbed up towards the high pass at Shap, a gap between the Lakeland fells and the Pennine spine used by road builders from the Romans, through the turnpike age, the rail roads of Victorian times to the motorway builders of today.

At a sharp left-hand bend, I turned right, through a gateway and searched for my first solo green lane of the holiday.

A diesel roller stood in the field ahead of me. It was being used to improve the track running down Borrowdale, designated a bridleway. My road lay at right angles to this, straight up the fellside into the mist and low cloud.

I went through a gate and crossed the beck. The road was deeply etched into the ground above the stream. Too deeply etched! It was a bog! This was not the road but the

Green road users in the early morning.

Into The Dales.

drainage channel on the high side of the true path. I backed out and tried again, this time riding the high bank, separated from the fell by the ditch.

A rusty iron gate, tied up with the usual orange string was awkward to open on the steep gradient. I had to find a suitable rock to keep the bike steady while I untangled the knots and heaved the gate back on its broken hinges.

Dew sparkling on the short grass helped me pick out the faint shape of the road over the pass. The sun could not quite burn off the mist, rolling up from the east.

Before I knew it, I was at the top of Breast High Pass. It had been a steep climb for about a mile over open grassland. I looked back, but Lakeland was lost in the mist. I headed on eastwards towards the Yorkshire Dales.

Near the foot of the pass, the sun finally cleared the mist. The lane ran by a stream. Clear water sparkled by white stones. Below the surface, brown weed turned the stones almost black. Trees grew by the stream, lessening the starkness of the landscape of hills, stone walls and grassland.

My meeting place with Gordon Thackray, my Dales guide, was Tebay Services. This was a hole! It would have looked quite smart on an industrial estate in a big city, but here it was an eyesore. A vast corrugated steel construction like a warehouse fitted between the Old Tebay road and the M6 motorway. It was a truck stop, a transport cafe with a small corner set aside for cars.

I would make the most of what they had, I thought. At least I can get petrol and a cup of tea. But I was out of luck. There was a power cut in Tebay. The petrol pumps would not pump petrol and tea could not be brewed in the cafe.

I was an hour early for Gordon, having tackled Breast High with so little trouble. I sat on the grass (there wasn't much to sit on) and ate dates and sultanas to the sound of the auxiliary generator whining powerfully to keep the Shell offices working, but not the Shell petrol pumps.

Gordon Thackray was, without doubt, the most colourful of my week's guides. He was staggeringly knowledgeable about the vast network of lanes throughout the Dales. He knew every gate, every twist in the road. At times he seemed to anticipate every bump and rut, picking the easiest line through, not by looking ahead, but far in advance, from memory.

He was an expert on the legal side of rights of way, explaining to me the niceties of "ratione tenurae". This was an arrangement whereby the farmer agreed to maintain the public highway in exchange for a reduction in his rates, instead of the highway being maintained directly by the county. This strange arrangement was popular in the more remote corners of Yorkshire, where the locals would rather look after their own roads than have some official from the town interfere with them.

Gordon was involved in a motorcycle accident in 1977. An almost head-on collision with a car left him lucky to be alive, but with one arm gone and a messed up leg. He limped badly but rode brilliantly.

His bike had been specially modified. The throttle, clutch and front brake were all on the left handlebar. The right handlebar carried a special peg to plug into the end of Gordon's artificial right arm. The rest of the bike was a wreck. It was the remains of a Yamaha DT80. The lights had been removed, because they had packed up. Everything that was still attached showed signs of the hard use Gordon made of the bike. He rode green lanes more than once a week throughout the year and that was enough to wear out any bike.

When not riding a motorcycle, Gordon rode a pedal cycle. His fellow cyclists would complain that, when Gordon led them for a day's cycling, he included too many green lanes, but he maintained that this was the best way to see the Dales. He had "worn out" his current pedal cycle through hard use and was negotiating for a replacement.

Gordon's signalling system had clearly evolved to a fine art. I would have thought flashing indicators would have been a priority for him, but he had discarded all such luxuries. Right turns were indicated by a waved right foot, a leg signal in place of an arm signal. Left turns were usually arm signals, but occasionally the left wellington boot was called into play.

Gordon apologised for the lack of speed of his diminutive 80 cc mount, but had planned our route accordingly. The distance between green lanes was kept to a minimum, and main roads were avoided where a quieter alternative route, more suited to a relaxed pace, was available. As with Alan Kind on Monday, we adopted a simple system for gates. Gordon opened them and I closed them. There turned out to be an awful lot of gates in the Dales.

We headed north, then west from Tebay to find our first green lane at Fawcett Mill. This started as two tarred ruts with a grass centre. There was an old, grass-grown bridge over Rais Beck by the mill. The bridge had a high, slender arch, looking too fragile for modern traffic. We used the newer, less graceful bridge alongside.

At the end of the lane, we followed a quiet road up the Lune valley, on the opposite side to the A685 trunk road. Once again we were following the older generation of road, replaced by the modern road, but in this case both generations were tarmac.

From Newbiggin-on-Lune the road turned green again, between widely spaced, dry stone walls. Beyond Friar's Bottom Farm, we dropped down to Smardale Bridge. This struck me as an incredibly well-made bridge to serve a green lane. It would repay some research into the reasons for its construction.

Looking back from the top of the steep climb onto Smardale Fell, I saw a deserted farmhouse, a disused limestone quarry, a large, square limekiln and the road bed of the dismantled railway, on the opposite side of the valley, above Smardale Bridge. All were intricately inter-connected in some recent past, but I had not the key to unlock their mystery.

We rode on into an ever-widening landscape of open grassland, full of sheep. Smardale Fell was not marshy and tufted with bog cotton, as I had imagined, but acres of short grass and hundreds of ewes and lambs.

A narrow lane took us under the railway, past Greengate, to Croop House. The boundary between the tarmac lane and an open paddock on our left was defined by an electric fence. Here we turned sharp left, through a gap in the electric wire secured by a piece of fine orange twine.

"It's an amazingly effective fence," said Gordon. "In all the years I've known it, that fence has never been switched on, but the horses in the paddock never stray onto the road."

The horses were tricked by their experience of real electric fences into believing that this single strand of wire marked a painful boundary to their world, and not one of them had ever put it to the test.

The green road ran across open grassland at the foot of Wharton Fell above the River Eden. Here, I saw a pair of curlews. They flew across in front of me at little more than head height. I could clearly make out their long, downward curling beaks and the brown streaks on the underside of their bodies, like a smudged version of a thrush's markings. I had never seen curlews before. They

Massive walls define the route of so many northern lanes. Walls are as precious and as fragile as the rich hedgerows of the south. (M.Cowling)

You have to stop and drink in a view like this in Wensleydale. (M.Cowling)

are not a common bird in the South.

A plover stood in the grass. The tuft on its head and the irridescent green on its back marked it out as the lapwing or peewit, the commonest of the plover family. I had grown up in Northamptonshire surrounded by fields full of peewits. They were as common as crows. They were unusual in Cornwall, my present home. Here, among the sheep they were, again, a common sight.

One other difference in the bird population between North and South was obvious. The gulls were different. I was used to great big, greedy herring gulls, with faces like penguins, standing on the cliff tops or soaring without effort on long, glider-shaped wings. Here, the much smaller, more delicate, black-headed gull had first pickings of anything fit to eat between Scarborough and Blackpool.

I had come a long way to ride the next lane. The High Way is that sort of road. It is not difficult as green roads go. It is long, about eight miles, I estimated. It has charisma. Something about it makes it special. To me it is partly the continuous, sweeping panorama available from a road which runs along the high edge of the limestone moor. It is also the history of the lane, the feeling that you are following so closely and at times so obviously on the heels of travellers from the past.

Until 1825, the High Way was the main road south from Kirkby Stephen. The new turnpike road scuttles along the valley floor, alongside the Settle to Carlisle railway. The High Way strides along the fell edge, three to four hundred feet above.

This was the road used by Lady Anne Clifford on many of her tours about her northern estates in the seventeenth century. She was quite a lady by all accounts.

Born in 1590 in the family castle at Skipton in Craven, she was the only daughter of the third Earl of Cumberland. By rights she should have inherited her father's vast landholdings throughout the northern counties, but her father's will left them to his brother. Lady Anne invoked a deed from the reign of Edward II to prove that the land was hers. She fought for years for her inheritance. She argued with lawyers, with the

Hell Gill Bridge on High Way looks innocent enough unless you look over the parapet at the startling drop below.

Archbishop of Canterbury, with King James himself, that the lands were hers.

Her uncle died in 1641 and the properties passed to his son. When he died three years later the deeds should have passed, at last, to Lady Anne. But, with England in the middle of the Civil War between the Roundheads and the Cavaliers, she had to be patient for a further six years before she could travel north to claim what was hers. After waiting thirty-eight years, she finally came into her inheritance.

At the age of sixty, she set about sorting out her estates, building, repairing and enjoying them. She travelled in a style little short of regal as she progressed through her "kingdom". She reclined in a horse litter. Her ladies-in-waiting were in a coach drawn by a team of six horses. Her women servants were in another coach. Her estate officials and menservants were on horseback. Her furniture, carpets, tapestries, mattresses, silverware and glassware travelled from house to house ahead of her. It is claimed that at times her train totalled over three hundred people.

She continued to journey about her estates in this splendid manner until she was in her eighties. She kept a day book of her travels giving details of the places visited and events on the way. She knew the High Way and most of the other Dales roads well.

We climbed from The Thrang onto Mallerstang Common, treading in the footsteps of countless drovers and packhorse trains, as well as the wheel tracks of wealthier travellers.

We paused at Hell Gill Bridge, which marks the boundary between Cumbria and Yorkshire, and also the boundary of the Dales National Park. The narrow bridge spans a deep cleft in the limestone. There is a high parapet today, kept in very good repair, but the narrow crossing of the deep ravine must have been quite tricky in a horse-drawn carriage. The present bridge was erected in 1825. It replaces an earlier bridge which was repaired in 1676 at a cost of three pounds ten shillings. There was a magnific... of Wild Boar Fell on the far side of the Eden val... ...uted to be the spot where the last wild bo... ...nted down.

We stopped to let this horse rider pass on a narrow lane near Austwick.

There is a string of farms along the High Way – High Hall, High Way, High Dyke. The road to High Hall set Gordon a puzzle to avoid dropping off the true route and descending to Shaw Paddock at the head of the turnpike pass. He had ridden the High Way only recently, while leading a group of trail riders on the annual John Ebbrell Memorial Run, but they had been travelling in the opposite direction. Occasionally we caught glimpses of wheel marks in the softer ground.

Near High Way farm there is the ruin of a small building within a walled enclosure of about four acres, known as Horse Paddock. This was an overnight stop for pack horses, where the horses could be turned out into the paddock and their loads stored in the security of the building overnight.

High Dyke is a large and complex ruin. It was once an inn, much frequented by drovers and packhorse trains as recently as 1877.

From Cotter End we rode down the ridge to the boggy section at Cotter Riggs. Even this was dry today. I was not to sample a northern bog, it seemed. On this last bit of High Way, we passed two men and a boy repairing a dry stone wall. The only way to make a proper repair is to dismantle the wall and rebuild it, or so it appeared. It looked like a long job.

The road above Cotterdale to Hardraw had been on the agenda, but we missed it out in order to take on fuel in Hawes.

From Hawes we went through Gayle, waited for a flock of sheep being driven along the High Street, then turned ... through a treacherously slippery ford of dimpled ... ne pavement. The limestones by the side of High ... dimples which sparkled in the sunlight like ...

... dirt beyond the farm at Bands. We ... and were on the road to Cam ... The Pennine Way joined ... northwards ... ery step ... that lot? ... remember ... d to end of ... n a pack a ... s part of the ... that you must ... rder to use a

Elevenses at ...
me to hot dogs a...
excellent hostelry.

We were following not just a packhorse road but a coach road, an eighteenth century turnpike road. Soon we were joined by the Roman road from Bainbridge, known as the Cam High Road, and the Dales Way long distance path. For a green lane, it had quite a busy time.

We crossed the dry river bed full of rocks, near Gearstones, where there used to be a notoriously rough inn. It was the scene of cattle fairs where the cattle driven down from Scotland would be sold to English buyers. According to the Honorable John Byng in 1792, this was not a pretty sight. He found the place crowded with noise, animals and rough-clad people, and "at the conclusion of the day's squabble, the two nations agreed in mutual drunkenness."

We gave the inn a miss, and called in at the hot dog stall at Ribble Head. The fast food van was surrounded by cars, scattered over the unenclosed grassland. The beautiful views from here made it a "honeypot" for holiday makers on a fine day. The cheerful, red-faced stall owner was well known to Gordon. Clearly this was one of Gordon's regular dining spots when out in the hills.

We tucked into hot dogs and cups of coffee, sitting in the sun. Gordon dangled his feet in the water under the bridge. All was right with the world, this morning.

We were off again. Three miles of tarmac brought us to Selside. We squeezed past the cars and minibuses of potholers, preparing to get wet, cold and dirty in a hole in the ground. Trail riding often leaves me wet, cold and dirty, but it does keep me in the fresh air. I don't fancy potholing.

We went through a gate and followed the slight trace of a road across the fields. Soon the road was invisible in the grass, cropped close by sheep. Gordon's uncanny local knowledge did not falter, and we were soon riding on a natural causeway, formed by the limestone rocks. Limestone grows in great, rectangular blocks. Here we rode below a shallow limestone cliff about four yards high and above a much deeper limestone cliff, on a natural shelf.

The cliffs or "scars" are a tremendous sight. Gordon knew the best of them. We came to a wooden fingerpost, where walkers crossed our route at right angles. They missed the best view of the limestone cliffs. I would have missed it too, but for Gordon.

We followed the low cliff above us on our right until a stone wall joined us from the left. Gordon parked his bike, and we walked over to a small gate in the wall. We were looking over a precipice into a great, semi-circular amphitheatre of limestone cliffs. Below us was a large expanse of bare limestone pavement, deeply criss-crossed with black gulleys. Beyond the pavement, the ground disappeared over another limestone precipice, and we looked straight down the valley towards Austwick in the distance. Here was yet another sight which was worth travelling from Cornwall just to see.

We threaded our way between the cliffs all around us. We passed pairs of walkers, teachers on holiday, judging by the gaunt, tired air about them.

From Austwick we rode lower, more enclosing lanes, with stone walls tight on either side and sycamore trees overhead. We stopped to let a girl on a horse come by. The lane was very narrow, but with our engines switched off, the horse went by quietly. The smile and the "thank you" from the rider made it well worth our while to stop.

The lane to Bark Houses started tarmac, but soon turned to dust and rock. I dropped back to allow Gordon's dust time to settle before I reached it. We followed a group of pony trekkers, fresh from the stables. They were going very slowly and some of the riders seemed barely in control of their mounts. We stopped on a rise and waited for them to ride clear of the end of the green lane. We waited for ten minutes, watching, as they were instructed on how to ride in traffic on the quiet tarmac lane they were about to join.

The horse riders had just cleared the end of the green lane when rider number seven toppled slowly sideways from her seat. She was the tallest girl in the group and had been given the biggest horse, so it was a long way to fall. She was back in the saddle by the time we reached the tarmac and turned the opposite way to the trekkers.

Within a few minutes, we were at the campsite. The grey stone farmhouse and reception area with its slate roof stood high up overlooking the camping fields leading down to the River Ribble and the deep, black pool below the waterfall of Stainforth Force. A group of teenage lads were making much noise about daring each other to jump into the pool, but only one of them, the quietest, and presumably the best swimmer, had actually got his swimming shorts wet.

Gordon helped me pitch the tent in a sea of vari-coloured canvas. The tent dried out as we watched. The heavy dew from this morning's start in the Lake District at last had a chance to dry out, free from the black plastic dustbin bag which protected it from the grime of travelling on the back of my bike.

We had an hour's riding left, if I was to be back in time to buy food at the campsite shop at five-thirty.

We rode Long Lane, from Helwith Bridge, over loose stones and grass and through gates. At Churn Milk Hole, a young woman was shovelling limestone chips beside a miniature excavator and a large coil of green plastic draining pipe. She was putting the finishing touches to the repair of erosion damage caused by the thousands of feet trampling up the ridge to Pen y Ghent.

The mountain rose four-square before us, challenging conquest, and I could see why so many people would want to reach its summit. It was on the Three Peaks Run and, of course, the Pennine Way, but it was not on our route. We swung right, to Rainscar, then zipped along the unenclosed tarmac road to dive into Helton Gill.

Horse Head Pass rose invitingly before is, but time was short. We turned down Littondale, to climb Cow Close, heading back parallel to the way we had come. After a gate, the lane climbed splendidly steeply with lots of loose rocks. I was thoroughly enjoying myself. This was not an awe inspiring climb like the Lakeland passes, but it was just challenging enough to make you feel you had accomplished something.

We came to an enclosed stretch. I closed the gate after Gordon had set off, and a young rabbit started up in front of me. It sprinted a quarter of a mile, ahead of me along the walled lane to the next gate. Before Gordon could open the gate, the rabbit scuttled between his legs. It continued over the next hill, still following the rutted track over the open grassland.

I held the next gate for some early evening walkers, who seemed to think we were being lazy by riding instead of walking. They looked clean and fresh, beside our dusty bikes. We came to their cars, parked at the edge of the tarmac, a quarter of a mile away.

There was no time for more, so we dashed back to the campsite with five minutes to spare before the shop shut. I bought bread, cakes, biscuits, yoghurts, crisps and agreed to meet Gordon before nine the next morning.

Thursday
Still in the Dales

The day started grey and overcast with occasional bouts of drizzling rain. It was not cold, but the weather appeared to be on the change. After three days of sunshine, I could not complain. The English summer is rarely more than three or four days long.

I packed up and waited for Gordon in the TV lounge. This was the converted hay loft above the stables of the farm. I watched the weather forecast on "Breakfast TV" with interest, although I had been told by everyone I met in the North that the weathermen in London knew nothing of the weather in the northern hills. The official forecast was "sunshine and showers".

Gordon arrived through the mild, grey gloom and we headed south for Settle. We puttered round the steep narrow back streets and onto the aptly nick-named "Water Lane". This started as a long, shallow ford, and was then a narrow walled lane, used as a footpath to the town from the outlying houses. We passed a woman off to do her shopping, wearing a blue plastic mac against the drizzle and clutching two multi-coloured shopping bags.

The road to Lodge Farm was tarmac. Beyond the farm the lane was carpeted with grass from wall to wall.

The tarmac road to Stockdale Farm was designated a bridleway, according to the map, but it was another of the rate rebate-maintained roads. Then it was bare limestone; no need for tarmac here. We passed close below Great Scar, the limestone crags looming up suddenly through the mist.

There was little to see in the mist. We were following

Someone should write a book about gates. This one pivots on the most contorted stone gatepost and is close by a large weight on a spring.

Gordon's nose, as much as the faint marks in the grass, to navigate from gate to gate. Every gate was different, so if you knew your gates you couldn't get lost. Someone really should write a thesis on "English Gate Fastenings". Orange bailer twine would undoubtedly be the most popular fastening, but the variety of fastenings evolved by local farmers and local blacksmiths would be a fascinating study. Some were simple loops of heavy gauge wire, while others were complex designs incorporating safety catches fit for modern mountaineering equipment. The sprung bar type of latch, common in the lowlands and ideal for a horse rider to open from the saddle, was a rare sight in the hills. Most fastenings up here were intended to be opened on foot. Even more rare were the self-closing gates of the West Country, either as a pair of gates blown closed alternately by the wind, as on Exmoor or the rising hinge gate, which needed a Cornish blacksmith's ingenuity to design. A little extra

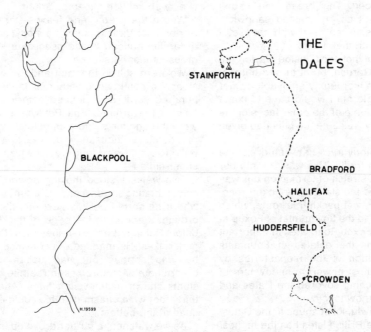

THE
DALES

STAINFORTH

BLACKPOOL

BRADFORD

HALIFAX

HUDDERSFIELD

CROWDEN

H.19599

Still In The Dales.

thought and you have a self-closing gate which will open either way. It was not just nostalgia for the West Country that made the rising hinge gate my favourite, it was the engineering nicety of the system – harnessing the force of gravity in just the right way to solve an age-old problem.

We threaded our way through the Grizedale crags, with me hoping Gordon would not lead us over the edge of anything, and turned west towards Langcliffe. Here again we rode open grassland through the mist. The road became less green as we approached Jubilee Cave and Victoria Cave. Here, the road surface was repaired with black stone chips to give confidence to car drivers wanting to shorten the walk to the cave entrances. Closer inspection revealed that the chips were in fact old tarmac, broken up and re-used. Where we joined the proper tarmac, the sign on the black, steel gate said, ''No through road for motor vehicles''. It wasn't true, as we had just shown.

The unfenced, tarmac road climbed up to Cowside, where we turned left, following Gordon's outstretched left wellington boot, down a double rut over the grass. Soon we were riding between walls, then the surface changed to gravel, loose and slippery after the firm grass. We passed a group of walkers, starting their day's assault on the hills.

We were back in Stainforth, only a quarter of a mile from my campsite of last night. Gordon parked in the High Street and declared that it was time for breakfast. He popped into the village shop and sub-post office and asked if they were open for food yet. Clearly this was another spot where Gordon was well-known. The postmaster agreed to open up the cafe which had once been the living room at the side of the shop. Gordon and I entered and sat down. He ordered a full fried breakfast of bacon, sausage, eggs, tomato and so on. I had eaten my breakfast at breakfast time and settled for a toasted cheese sandwich. I joined Gordon for a pint mug of coffee.

Bad news was announced. The bread van hadn't arrived yet, so they couldn't do my toasted sandwich. How did I feel about a toasted tea cake with cheese? I would be perfectly happy with that, I said.

We would need plenty of hot food inside us for the lanes ahead, according to Gordon, but it turned out that the dry weather made them thoroughly enjoyable rather than endurance tests. He told me I would have to come back in the winter and see some of the other faces of the Dales, to offset the warm dry welcome the hills had given me so far.

Moor Head Lane was a stony track between dry stone walls, rather cut up by farm traffic. This was put into our itinerary to avoid too long a stretch of tarmac on our way to Horton in Ribblesdale and the start of the Foxup road.

The Foxup Road is a wild, wet packhorse route, which climbs north of Pen y Ghent to the tiny hamlet of Foxup at the head of Littondale. The Foxup Road was an important line of communications for the estates of Fountains Abbey. Before the dissolution of the monasteries by Henry VIII, they were the most powerful landowners of the North. Their sheep ranching covered the Dales and created the landscape we know today.

Even today there are an awful lot of sheep in the Dales. Except for New Zealand, the British Isles has the highest density of sheep in the world – on average about two

Hull Pot gapes hungrily at this pensive walker, almost swallowed by the mist.

hundred sheep to every square mile. There are some twenty-six million sheep in Britain.

Where the green lane leaves Horton, it is known as Horton Scar Lane. It climbs a stony, stone-walled lane to a derelict building, once used as a shooting box in the grouse shooting season.

We were still in the mist and the way ahead was not clear. Gordon headed off across the grass for a couple of hundred yards and stopped before the most enormous hole in the ground. Hull Pot was a giant swallowhole, worn through the soluble limestone by the acid rainwater of countless thousands of years. We could see the bottom, but it was a long way down and all the sides were sheer cliffs.

Two walkers stood looking down. Perhaps they were contemplating a descent. Gordon said that this was where he sorted out his new recruits to trail riding. He brought them up to the edge of the Pot to have a look, before telling them that they had to jump it on their motorbikes! He managed to convince some of them that he was serious but had never let anyone try it. Unfortunately, motorbikes in real life cannot perform the stunts shown in television films. Attempting to jump a thirty foot wide chasm like this could end only one way – dead at the bottom.

As we watched, a farmer drove up in a Land Rover and walked around the edge of Hull Pot. We could hear the plaintive bleating of a lamb separated from its mother. Eventually we traced the sound to an isolated pinnacle of rock rising up from the floor of the Pot. Somehow the lamb had managed to jump onto the tuft of grass on top of the pinnacle, but didn't know how to get back.

There was nothing we could do for it at the moment. Any attempt to get close to the lamb would make it try to get away from us, as any hill sheep would do. In other words it would jump off the pinnacle of rock and fall to the ground far below. The best thing seemed to be to let it find its own way off in time. If this failed, perhaps it could be rescued when it was more tired and less frisky. The farmer said he didn't mind too much just now, because it wasn't his lamb!

We rode back, away from the edge and turned up through a gate on the true course of the Foxup Road. Wild and wet it was, even on this mild morning. I managed to get stuck in the only patch of wet peat bog of the holiday. Gordon found a way round most of the boggy bits which littered the road at one stage, but we just had to ride across one bit.

What I did wrong, he explained, as he helped me to drag the bike out, was to try and ride up the hard bank at

Photographer in a bog. Mike usually takes pictures of other folk in the mire. (Cowling/Crone)

the edge of the bog. He had ridden further through the bog to find a shallow exit point. My back wheel had not broken through the bog surface until my front wheel had rammed the bank. I didn't have another opportunity to put this theory to the test, but I would imagine your bog riding technique would soon improve if you used roads like this in the wet season.

We came down a series of steep bends into the valley at Foxup. The bridge across the beck in front of us looked strangely familiar. It was being repaired today. The parapets were untouched but the single arch had the road surface removed to reveal the old stonework underneath. I had been here before. I remembered that bridge from 1973, when I had ridden in the Round Britain Rally. We had to navigate our way round every county in Britain, and the navigational target for the West Riding of Yorkshire had been the bridge at Foxup, Littondale.

We now took the road out of Littondale that had attracted me on our early evening excursion of yesterday. From Halton Gill we climbed Horse Head Pass. This is a continuation of the Foxup Road, taking packhorse trains from Horton to the markets of Askrigg and Hawes in Wensleydale.

This road between Littondale and Wharfdale was used regularly between 1807 and 1833 by the incumbent rector of Halton Gill to take Sunday services at Hubberholme, which was a chapel of ease to the mother church at Arncliffe. A chapel of ease, as it's name implies, was built to serve the outlying district of a parish which lay too remote from the parish church for weekly service.

The rector must have had a very fit horse. It was one hell of a climb! The track zig-zags upwards through open sheep pasture, with a surface of loose stones and dirt. It was best to use the rather grassier centre rut, which would be where the horse trod pulling a light trap over the pass. It would take more than one horse to pull a normal farm cart up here. The Dalesmen had especially small farm carts built to cope with the steep gradients. (This also explains why they could get away with such narrow gates on carriage roads in the Dales.)

No sooner were we at the top, at Horse Head Gate, than we started to go down the other side, which was nearly as steep as the climb up had been.

We trundled gently down the remoteness of Langstrothdale, through Hubberholme, looking for more fun. The Norse names of the upper reaches of the valley show who settled here, far from their homeland in Scandinavia. To a Viking, these windswept hills and steep-sided valleys must have looked like his own country.

Starbotton was steep hairpin bends and slippery limestone steps. Fun!

In Starbotton we found the fun I was looking for. A series of steep hairpin bends climbed the fellside over slippery limestone steps, covered with loose white rocks. It seemed to climb up for ever. Gordon told me they used this hill in the annual Alan Jefferies Trial. Bearing that in mind, I think I climbed it rather well!

At Cam Head, we passed a couple out walking who smiled and waved. They looked slightly puzzled as we seemed to come back past them, but we had made a sharp right-hand turn and were now on a different track down the backbone of the ridge to Kettlewell. This is known as Top Mere Road and becomes a walled green road lower down towards the village.

Now we headed for one of the most famous lanes in the Dales. Mastiles Lane has for years been the centre of controversy. The authorities have frequently pressed to have its surface waterproofed with tarmac, but everyone who knows and loves the lane wants it left as it is. Walkers, cyclists, climbers, motorcyclists and all other country lovers united to oppose the highway planners. Mastiles Lane has been saved so far, but the threat will hang over it for many years to come.

Mastiles Lane is one of the most famous monastic roads in Britain. The monastic grange at Kilnsey was built during the latter half of the twelfth century and served all the Fountains Abbey estates in Wharfdale, Littondale, Airedale and parts of Ribblesdale.

The road starts by the inn, below the towering ramparts of Kilnsey Crag. Gordon had approached Kilnsey from Kettlewell on the quiet lane to the east of the

River Wharfe, rather than the busy main road on the west side. This gave me a chance to see Kilnsey Crag from a distance, rather than to pass directly beneath its overhang.

The old name for Mastiles Lane is Street Gate, which suggests a Roman connection. The outline of a Roman marching camp has been found at the western end, but I could make little sense of the bumps in the ground when we reached them. The route of the monastic road is marked by the bases of stone crosses, the crosses themselves having disappeared long ago, but, like the Roman camp, I saw no trace of these. We seemed to hurry through today, and missed quite a lot. As always, this road would repay a second visit at a more leisurely pace.

My thoughts had turned to cycling along Mastiles Lane with my family, until we came across a group on special mountain bikes by the side of the road. Two of the mountain bikes were up-ended while their riders tackled punctures. Mountain bikes are fitted with extra-heavy duty tyres to cope with rocks. If even these had been defeated by what appeared to me on my motorcycle to be a pretty smooth green lane, I did not fancy the family's chances on our lightweight "racing" cycles.

On second thoughts, I am not so sure. Perhaps it would be something worth a try on some of the greener, grassier roads in the Dales. Gordon's choice of bicycle was the cheapest "ordinary" three-speed bike he could find. He felt that they would all fall apart in no time at all, so why spend hundreds of pounds on buying a new mountain bike. It was an argument with some merit, I felt, looking at the little group of mountain bikers.

Just before Mastile Gate, which marks the highest point of the lane, I stopped to look back eastwards, taking in one of the classic views of the typical Dales green lane, its twin white walls threading their way into the far distance over the rolling green hills.

As we pressed on, the lane became greener, though clearly well-used for recreation and farming throughout its length. At the western end, beyond the indistinguishable Roman camp, we came to Street Gate, which marked the limit of the tarmac encroachment along Mastiles Lane. Here we turned north-east over Cote Moor. This was a superb ride over open grassland for miles and miles. Mastiles Lane may be the classic green lane, but this unenclosed track was more typical though less photogenic. We stopped by a lime kiln, built into the hillside high above Cote Gill and watched a black rabbit trying to merge into the tussocks of grass on the far hillside. It was significant that we could only pick out the black rabbit. The genetic fault that had upset his colouring made him visible and vulnerable while his normal coloured brothers and sisters were camouflaged and invisible.

We sat here for some time, going over the two days I had spent in the Dales and enjoying the afternoon sun, which had, at last, replaced the mist and low cloud of the morning.

I still had quite a way to go before reaching my campsite in Derbyshire, and Gordon wanted to fit in one more lane so that we could finish at yet another of his treasured eating stops in Burnsall.

The last lane of the day left the B6265 at an acute angle and ran north and east to Linton. It was a walled lane, but running across lower ground, was shaded by the full

Mastiles Lane was used by the monks administering the great sheep ranges owned by Fountains Abbey.

I was urged to sample the dales in winter. It looked interesting! (M.Cowling)

leaves of early summer sycamores, a few horse chestnuts and a handful of limes. It was a pleasant way to finish.

Burnsall was busy with tourists in cars and coaches. The road ran right down by the river, and there was a village green to wander about, but our interest was focussed on the large cafe. It was fairly empty as we entered. It was too late for lunch, but not too early for tea.

I ordered lasagne and chips to go with my cup of tea. Gordon, having been well set up by his late breakfast, settled for just a drink. He was not so far from home in Otley now, and, I expect looking forward to tea at home.

I said goodbye to Gordon, the third of my guides. I had been very lucky, so far, with my companions. Tomorrow I should be joined by Dave Giles, if all went according to plan. I headed south into the urban sprawl of Leeds, Bradford, Halifax and a dozen other overlapping towns.

I had not really thought this part of the journey out. There was no obvious route through, and, the worst mistake of the whole holiday, I hadn't packed a decent map of the area. I was navigating through the back streets of Huddersfield using a small map of the whole of Britain.

After hours of wandering in roughly the right direction, I stopped for petrol and to ask directions in a filling station on the Huddersfield ring road. I was told that I was within two hundred yards of the road I wanted, which would take me to Holmfirth, then out of this urban morass onto the heights of Derbyshire.

I climbed the great pass over Holme Moss. The climb was steep and hard. I passed lorries crawling their way upwards, grinding through the gears. The descent was fast and open. The road was lined with wooden marker posts over six feet high, to guide the snow ploughs when they cleared the road in winter.

Just over a mile from the foot of the pass, I pulled off into the haven of Crowden campsite. The lady in the office was just going off duty for the night, but I was able to book in. The campsite was all but deserted. There were two groups of Pennine Way trampers – young men too tired by the day's hard slog to do more than eat their supper and sleep.

I pitched near a solitary tent containing a man and his young son. The man was dressed in full Pennine Way gear – breeches, boots and woollie hat, but young son sat in the tent huddled in sleeping bags and extra blankets. They had overdone the healthy outdoor thing and were waiting for mum to come and rescue them in the car. All son wanted was his own warm bed and his teddy to cuddle.

My pitch was sheltered behind a copse of young trees, providing a perfect windbreak. I looked out onto black scree slopes of hard, dark stone on all sides. It was a beautiful evening, out of the wind. I was hungry and set about my supper.

"Easy opening" sardine tins, designed to be opened with a rotary can opener are not, I proved, designed to be opened with my multi-purpose camping opener. I chimbled an opening in one end of the tin and spooned mashed sardines onto slices of bread. Instant chicken soup, with noodles and croutons was delicious. It had been a good idea to buy the most expensive packet soup. The cheap stuff was all salt and monosodium glutamate. Dessert was a Mars bar, accompanied by a mug of coffee.

I felt like an after-dinner stroll, so I scrambled up the hillside above the campsite, to see what I could see. Signs warned me to keep to the footpath, which seemed odd on such a steep and rock strewn slope. At the top I came to "Open Country", according to a very official notice board. Dire penalties were threatened if I was naughty in open country. Worrying the livestock, damaging the trees, stealing the rocks, polluting the water, were all catalogued crimes. I knew why.

This was the open country access gained after long battles, both physical and political by the forerunners of the modern Ramblers Association. The big landowners had no intention of allowing ordinary folk onto their "private" hills for air and recreation. The hills were for grouse, not for people, they claimed, and they enforced their ideas through wardens armed with clubs and guns, supported when need be by the police.

The essence of green lane riding is having time for a chat. (M.Cowling)

The struggle for access was hard won, and this sign was a memento of the landowners' arguments against it. The crimes listed make strange reading alongside the usual "Country Code".

I turned back down the hillside to the isolated phone box by the roadside. I called Derby, to check that Dave was still available to guide me through my final day. Having received a satisfactory confirmation, I returned to the campsite and snuggled down to enjoy a good night's rest.

Friday
Derbyshire

It rained during the night, but the morning's sky was clear blue. The sun reached the campsite just ten minutes before I packed the tent. Then it disappeared behind gathering clouds. There are disadvantages to camping in a deep valley.

Sleepy Glossop was still tucked up in bed. It looked a compact, sandstone town surrounded by green hills. In the 1820s, the Duke of Norfolk planned to turn it into a new cotton mill town. In 1784 Glossop had a population of a few hundred and just one cotton mill. By 1850 there were sixty mills in the town and the population had grown to 26000. If anything, the population of Glossop today is less than this. The boom town of the nineteenth century became a slump town of the twentieth century as the cotton trade withered in the wind of depression.

I climbed up and up the Snake Pass. I thought the road into the campsite last night had been wild and bleak, but the Snake Pass was even more so. Leaving the green fields of Glossop, suddenly there was nothing but cold, black heather, cold air and low, grey cloud. The road twists up a westward flowing valley and twists down one that is eastward flowing, yet it is named not after its serpentine nature but after a pub. A high pass like this would need a change of horses at the summit for mail coaches. There was scope for an entrepreneur to cash in on a new market. Weary travellers would need food, possibly a room for the night, while horses were changed or rested. When the whole Manchester to Sheffield turnpike was complete in 1821, the Duke of Devonshire built an inn at the top and called it The Snake after the serpent on his family coat of arms.

The western side of the pass was grassier and gentler. The soil was less acid. The sky was clearing of the menacing clouds that had threatened me as I left the campsite at Crowden.

This northern part of Derbyshire is known as the Dark Peak. A type of sandstone called millstone grit replaces the limestone of the Yorkshire Dales. It is millstone grit because it was used for making the mill stones for windmills and watermills in the days when wheat was ground into flour by the local miller. I looked for signs of millstones, but only spotted one during the whole day. That was used as a decoration outside a renovated mill on the Staffordshire border.

South of the Dark Peak, limestone becomes the predominant rock again. This is the White Peak.

The Dark Peak is wild and threatening, challenging anyone who dares to venture into it. The White Peak is a pretty landscape of narrow valleys and high plateau, scarred by too much quarrying.

I sat by the Ashopton Viaduct over Ladybower Reservoir, soaking up the sun from a pale blue sky with tiny, white clouds scudding south-eastwards.

There was a battered van parked on the verge nearby and, shortly after I arrived, a police patrol car came to investigate. The police officers were in good humour, because the sun was shining, but were concerned that the broken down van could be a hazard at night on the busy main road. They radioed for a truck to come and tow it away.

Fishermen began to arrive and unload wicker baskets

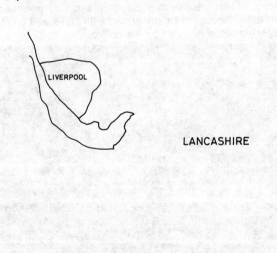

and coloured umbrellas from their cars, setting up camp for the day on the banks of the reservoir.

I wandered along the quiet, minor road which ran above the shoreline. I had walked no more than two hundred yards when Dave arrived. I strolled back to greet him. Yes, was my reply to his obvious question, it had been a great week so far. I was looking forward to what today would bring.

Without more ado we were off, riding up the valley alongside the reservoir. This was not really one reservoir, but a succession of three. The uppermost, the Howden Reservoir, was started in 1901, and was followed shortly afterwards by the larger Derwent Reservoir. The third and largest, the Ladybower Reservoir, was opened by King George VI on 25th September 1945 and was the largest earth-dammed reservoir in Britain at the time.

Dave knew where to turn off into the forestry plantation which edged the reservoirs. This was just as well, because the turning was not easy to spot from the map. The forest track climbed diagonally up Hagg Side, and I rode most of the way up looking backwards at the superb view down the flooded valley behind us.

We came out of the woods on the ridge, and the view ahead was just as good. We were in the open here. We rode high above the A57 which had just come down the Snake Pass. The cars on the main road were a negligible clutter of Matchbox toys, way below us. The hills were big, dark green, merging into black rock and heather. The valley bottom was filled with the brighter green of cultivated fields, and the lower slopes of the hills were patched with the evergreen of fir plantations.

Dave rode slowly, relaxed, giving us plenty of time to soak up the scenery. His pace was deceptively easy. We covered a lot of ground while seeming to just dawdle along. It took me a while to adjust my pace, after a week zipping along rather faster. I didn't mind slowing down at all. I was in no hurry. My trip would be over soon enough, without my rushing.

We dropped down to the modern road along the valley floor, crossed it, and climbed on to the Roman road. The Romans had taken a rather different route through the Snake Pass. Now, where the A57 followed the shore of Ladybower Reservoir, the Roman road climbed the ridge to the south, aiming for the fort at Brough. The climb on to the ridge was strewn with loose rocks. I am sure the surface was better in Roman times. Dave held the farm gate open for a jogger, or perhaps he should be called a fell runner up here. The chap ignored him as best he could, considering Dave stood in front of him in a bright yellow motorcycle helmet, and climbed over the stile. I suppose the up and over of the stile was more of a challenge than the gate, but it left Dave looking flummoxed.

We were now on the ridge opposite our first lane above Hagg Side, and once again the views were splendid. They must have been even better before the Forestry Commission covered the northern slope with fir trees. I came upon a strange stone monolith, which I at first took to be a signpost. It stood over six feet tall with a flat, square cap on the top. On each edge of the cap was a name – Glossop, Edale, Sheffield, Hope. Just under the cap, on the main part of the pillar, was the date 1737. This was not at a crossroads, but on a high ridge, so I reasoned this was a viewing platform, pointing out the main features in each direction. Unfortunately, the Forestry fir trees obliterated half the modern view.

Ahead of us the view was dominated by a huge chimney streaming a great plume of white smoke. It didn't look at all pretty and we were heading straight for it.

Our green road came down from the ridge into the village of Hope, just north of the Roman camp of Brough, or Navio as the Romans knew it.

Almost at the foot of the giant chimney, which, I discovered, was the property of Blue Circle Cement, our road turned green again. Or rather it faded from battered tarmac to white earth and loose rocks. We climbed a deep, narrow valley, overhung with rocks and known as Pin Dale. The sides of Pin Dale had been quarried to feed the cement works in the past. The wheel tracks criss-crossing our road told me that now the quarry was used mainly for trials riding practise by motorbikes and pedal cycles.

Dave pottered gently upwards, and I found myself struggling to keep my balance. We were going too slowly on the tricky bits. My heavier bike needed more gyroscopic effect from the wheels to keep it upright and straight. Alternatively, I wasn't much of a rider compared with Dave, who made it all look so easy.

The top of the road was a source of confusion. We came to tarmac rather sooner than we had expected. We eventually agreed that my map was out of date and a new road had been built. We managed to unravel the road we wanted from the maze and pushed along Dirtlow Rake. This could have been a beauty spot, but it was a long, shallow quarry, sad and semi-derelict. It was being worked by a lonely earth mover and a solitary dumper truck in a half-hearted sort of a way. None too soon we left this eyesore and followed a white farm track onto tarmac by Rowter Farm.

Within a mile we stopped at one of the most beautiful spots in Derbyshire. We had climbed through the narrowest of saddles in a high ridge to look down on the fairytale valley of Edale. You have to stop, because the suddenness of the panorama demands it. In a car this is difficult, because the road is narrow and steep. On bikes we just pulled up, dismounted and looked.

Edale is an abundant green valley, packed with neatly walled fields, below the towering dark moor. There are trees in all the field boundaries, and I think it is the trees which give Edale an air of civilisation, contrasting with the bleak landscape to the north.

Edale marks the start of the Pennine Way long distance trudge. Somehow Edale has survived the influx of long distance walkers, and of ordinary trippers who have been flocking here ever since the railway was put through to give access to the hills from the industrial cities all around. Now they come by car and by coach, but Edale does not bend much to accommodate them. It is a farming community, with a few simple shops scattered along the valley road.

We did not ride to the valley bottom, but swung westwards to climb back past Rushup Edge on the old road to Chapel-en-le-Frith – the road known as Chapel Gate. This would have been an easier route from Edale to the markets west and south of the valley than the tarmac saddle by which we had entered the valley. But Chapel Gate has never been christened with tar. It has received precious little maintenance of any sort judging by what I encountered.

Pausing to catch my breath and to look at the panorama of Edale below Chapel Gate.

Chapel Gate is a favourite lane of every trail rider who has ever tackled it. There are two choices. You can ride the gully eroded into the hillside, which varies between two and ten feet wide and is filled for most of the climb with loose rocks and stray boulders. You can ride the outer bank, perched between the gully and the steep drop down the hillside to the bottom of Edale. The bank is made of sharp rocks, lightly covered by soil and grass, with a few loose rocks to make it more interesting.

Dave recommended the outer bank for most of the climb, but said both routes were popular. I followed his wheel tracks and watched him steadily pull away from me. His trials riding experience showed as he rode slowly, keeping his balance, over every obstacle. I sweated along behind, trying to keep my feet on the footrests and the front wheel aiming forwards. The rocks were angular and unexpected, trying to catch me out and flip me off. I fought them. I had not come this far to be knocked off by a few lumps of limestone. Mother Earth should not have me. The forces of gravity could be beaten. The handlebars writhed against me. The saddle kicked up at me from behind. But Daisy's heart thumped steadily, chugg, chugging me to the top, where Dave waited, grinning.

Riders climb Chapel Gate all the year round. I had just made it up in the summer in the dry. I recalled the

following dramatic description of a winter assault!

"The light was worsening as we attempted the most difficult climb of the day. Paul and Steve put their previous trials riding experience to good use over the rocks where grip was at a premium. The normally easier route of riding a path above the gully, on the edge of a huge drop, was extremely difficult as the ice forming under spinning back wheels tried to force you over the edge. Mick demonstrated that there isn't much friction between waxed cotton and snow as he tobogganed down the drop on his back. Gwyn's bike tried to follow suit and it took four of us to haul it back onto the ridge. We were glad to reach the top of this one and were certainly a lot warmer for our exertions!"

The descent to the main road held a few more surprises in the shape of massive, white rock steps. Limestone grows in rectangular blocks, which is fine if you want to quarry it for building, because it is already cut to shape. It is not so fine when the rectangular blocks form the roadbed and are as big as these. I was glad we were going down, not up. I could use the brakes to drop one wheel at a time over each two foot step. Riding up would have relied on the back tyre finding enough grip to scrabble up the vertical part of the step, and I doubted my ability to find that sort of grip.

Thankfully we reached the new gate at the lane's end, but we had gone only a few yards before we turned through another gate on the old road to Hayfield. This seemed nice and smooth, a pleasant rest after the furious struggle with Chapel Gate. It lulled me deceptively, and I was puzzled when Dave climbed up the bank instead of following the smooth road ahead. Dave was not given to showing off. Why was he taking the apparently more difficult high level path?

Ah! It was because of a long series of those limestone steps. I bumped down them one after another, and the next time Dave rode high on the bank, I followed him.

Some strange mental process made me doubt Dave's wisdom again. I know he knew these lanes well, but the lower level route didn't look that bad, and I hadn't come all this way to take the easy way out. At the first opportunity I was back in the bottom, assailing the rock steps again.

Dave waited ahead and waved me down. If I planned to ride down the next bit, and he advised against it, he wanted time to get ahead and photograph me doing it. Could it really be as difficult as that, I wondered?

We did something I rarely do. We parked the bikes and walked the lane to evaluate its rideability. This is a technique essential in a competitive trial. You must try to memorise every rock and plan every inch of your path, if you are to win. But I was a trail rider. I was riding the public road. You should not have to inspect every inch of the public road before you ride it.

The steps here were gigantic! No vehicle but a motorcycle could get down those. And I was not so sure that a motorcycle could. But my spirit was soaring high. I would have a go.

Dave positioned himself on the bank high above, and I trundled forwards.

"I'll not stand on the footrests, even for a photograph!" I called up.

"I don't expect you to," said Dave, reassuringly.

Slowly, one wheel at a time, Daisy and I made it over the steps and loose rocks. Dave took his photograph and

My guide advised a detour round this series of giant limestone steps on the road to Hayfield, but I wanted to have a go. The steps went on and on! I was glad I was going down. Coming up these steps would be more of a challenge than I wanted at this stage of my journey. (D.Giles)

rejoined me on the lane.

There were more rock steps and long stretches of loose rocks. It was a very long lane, and well-used, but by motorcycles only, judging by the evidence on the ground.

We both agreed that we deserved a cup of tea. Would Dave turn out to be a connoisseur of cafes like Gordon? The cafe we found in Chapel-en-le-Frith suggested that he might. It was clean and bright, with chrome behind the counter and waitresses in smart green uniforms. Chapel-en-le-Frith is famous for the Ferodo brake factory, but I saw few other tourist attractions. We missed out the garden shed where Herbert Frood first developed his brake shoes in the 1890s. We did pass the large modern factory, still churning out brake linings for the British motor industry. Then we were out of the town and hunting for the next green road.

We turned right in Brook Houses, climbed above Spire Hollins and took the left turn to Wythen Lache. (What splendid names they have in this corner of Derbyshire!) This proved to be a dusty track over open grassland.

At Wythen Lache we came to yet another Roman road. This one was heading for Buxton, for the Romans were the first to exploit the warm mineral springs of "Aquae Arnemetiae", the North's rival to Bath in the South-West.

When the Romans left, the spa town fell into decline, but was popular again in the later Middle Ages and on into Tudor times. Queen Elizabeth's advisor, Lord Burghley, came here for a health cure as did Mary, Queen of Scots. The healing properties of the mineral water were exploited more and more, reaching a peak at the end of the eighteenth century and into the early nineteenth century. When the railway came in 1863, the town was given another boost as a watering place for the upper and middle classes of Victoria's England. Today it is a staid, rather old-fashioned town, genteel apart from the quarry lorries.

Our route out of Buxton took us over one railway line, where all that was visible was the grass-grown roadbed. The railway age is over. Railway tracks are being turned into long distance recreational routes for walkers and cyclists.

Within a hundred yards on either side of the green railway and the deserted goods yard were two roads. We were on the old road, wide and well used with a surface of hard-packed white stones. Opposite us ran the modern road, the A54, along which a stream of huge petrol tankers thundered towards Buxton. Once upon a time such cargo would have been on a train. Once upon a time perhaps a hundred horse drawn wagons could have hauled such a load along our quiet road.

A walker came past heading home for lunch. The far end of our road came out into a picnic area and car park at the head of the Goyt Valley. Since the river was dammed in the 1930s, the Goyt Valley has become steadily more popular with visitors. Once a remote and empty place, though very beautiful, now it is so busy that the roads have to be closed at Bank Holiday weekends to prevent over-crowding. A minibus service takes folk to the picnic spots, alongside the river or the two reservoirs, or drops the more energetic off to explore on foot.

The Goyt Valley has been opened up to the public by the Peak Park Planners. Our destination was a modern secret in comparison. We were heading south for Three Shires Head. Buried deep in a steep sided valley, an ancient packhorse bridge marks the junction of Cheshire, Staffordshire and Derbyshire. Three shire counties and four green roads meet at the bridge. Our road to the bridge bore a modern sign forbidding entry to all vehicles "Except motorcycles and mopeds". I wonder what traffic used to use it before the motor age.

Three Shires Head was a magical spot. The elegant bridge crossed the River Dane immediately above a great waterfall. The parapet of the bridge was no more than knee high to give clearance to the wide packs slung across the trains of pack ponies. This must make the bridge crossing a hazardous one for a horse and rider if either are nervous, especially when the river is in spate.

Once over the bridge, we passed through a gate and climbed up a narrow tributary valley towards Blackclough. We passed several more green turnings on our green road. A whole network of green roads funnelled into the bridge at Three Shires Head. We passed a school party out on a field trip, clipboards and questionnaires in hands. Someone else, apart from us, had found this secret place. No doubt their teacher was busy unravelling some of the mysteries of the travellers who used to come this way, as well as pointing out the flora associated with a spot little disturbed by modern

The day was warming up. I paused after closing the gate to take off my sweatshirt. The sheep-cropped grass was dotted with trees, like parkland. (D.Giles)

poisons designed to produce profitable monocultures. The vegetation here lacked the colour, variety and abundance of the West Country, but it wasn't bad.

We stopped at the appropriately named "Travellers' Rest" for a drink, but unfortunately, no food. This was yet another pub claiming to be the highest in England. I doubted its credentials, but liked the tables made from old, cast iron, treadle sewing machines, with oak tops inlaid with old pennies. We drank our beer over the heads of Victoria, Brittania, Elizabeth and a couple of Georges.

Ignoring our hunger, we skirted the edge of the National Park to reach a network of green lanes around the remote village of Hollinsclough. The name brings back memories to all who followed motorcycle trials in the post-war years. Ralph Venables, the long-serving newspaper reporter on all things relating to trials, described the climb at Hollingsclough as the hardest trials section in England. It is no more. It was filled in and bulldozed smooth several years back, though it is beginning to erode back to its former glory.

Before Hollinsclough we took a packhorse track to Tenterhill. The road had been cobbled across part of its width to give the pack animals a firm footing. The surface had lasted well. It was not exactly smooth. It was steep. But it had not eroded away to the great limestone steps of the earlier lanes.

The bridge was wide enough for one packhorse at a time, with an even lower parapet than the one at Three Shires Head. While the Three Shires bridge was also designed for wagons, at Tenterhill, wheeled traffic went through the ford. We were wheeled, so through the ford we splashed.

The climb out was steep and rocky, starting along a side stream bed, before drying out, still strewn with rocks to the top. There were no neat cobbles here. Derbyshire green lanes were full of unsolved riddles. Here was another. Why laboriously cobble only one half of the road? Was there another route out from the ford? I could not see one.

Hollinsclough village seemed to be built on scrap. Every house seemed to have its own piece of waste ground littered with scrap metal. Rusting tractors, old cars, strange agricultural machinery no longer recognizable under layers of rust, were tucked into corners everywhere.

Dave took me along a string of green lanes in and out of Hollinsclough, including the once-terrifying trials lane. The best of them was the one which ran south from the village. This was narrow and steep and filled with loose rocks. I was not surprised when Dave told me that this was the new trials testing section, replacing the bulldozed one.

The infant River Dove led us down a wide valley. We took a green lane down to the bank opposite Pilsbury and splashed through a nice wide ford. I bet this is quite a challenging crossing in the rainy season! Now we followed the left bank of the river to Hartington.

Here we found mud, at last! The North seemed to lack

The packhorse road to Tenterhill was surfaced with cobbles set on edge to help the horses keep their feet on the steep gradient.

The packhorse bridge was built without a parapet, to give clearance for the packs slung on either side of the ponies. Wheeled traffic used the ford.

Fording the River Dove near Pilsbury.

railway line, relic of the nineteenth century steam age, had been converted to a recreational cycleway for the twentieth century age of leisure.

A long tarmac lane took me out of the Manifold Valley to Wetton, then down to cross the Manifold by Weags Bridge and up again to Grindon.

Only the main road through Grindon was tarmac. We took the road behind the houses, which was filled with lush grass, and turned left on two miles of green farm track to Waterfall.

Here my green road ended. It was time to find my bed. First we filled up with petrol since we were not sure of a garage between Waterhouses and Brian Smith's house at Ballfields. We had been looking for petrol for several miles before reaching Waterhouses and found nothing. After filling up we passed another six garages.

Brian and his wife had prepared a feast to celebrate the end of my journey. I was royally entertained, with a four course dinner, accompanied by wine and completed by coffee and chocolates. And I didn't get to do the washing up.

In a warm, soft bed, I realised how lucky I was to have found the comradeship that goes with the exploration of green lanes. Our whole island is still covered with a secret network of untarred roads. I had picked out the most spectacular ones to ride in the North, but from the Scottish border to the Isle of Wight there were thousands of ordinary green tracks, threading their way between the fields. How lucky I was to have found a way to enjoy this hidden heritage, either by myself or in the best of company.

It is a long way to Cornwall. On the last day of my journey, it rained all the way home, but I didn't care.

mud, something the South has in abundance, even in the driest summer. Even Hartington only managed a little bit of mud, then we were on a nice green lane between white stone walls again. A similar road took us towards the Dale End, but we turned right at a crossroads of four green lanes.

Within a mile we were descending steeply into Beresford Dale and fording the River Dove once more. The far side of the ford was a day trippers "honeypot" and we drove out of the water into a melee of cars and dogs and children.

I found a millstone at last, made from Derbyshire millstone grit. It was leaning against the wall of Westside Mill, which had been converted to a rather splendid private house.

A tarmac lane took us to the Top of Ecton and then turned green. It turned completely green. There were no traces of wheel tracks. There was just close cropped grass covering the narrow floor of a steep-sided V-shaped valley. The green lane was confined by the valley sides, not by stone walls. It was an idealised green lane on which to end my ride. It was a green lane through a landscape which bore no obvious evidence of man's presence – an undatable landscape.

My time machine brought me back to the twentieth century as we reached the Manifold Valley. Here the old

A totally green lane through a valley unchanged in centuries.

Conclusion

Green lanes are a way of thinking. Once you become involved in exploring them, your view of the landscape in which we live changes radically. Never again will you be able to drive past a gap in the hedgerow without a sideways glance to see if it leads anywhere interesting.

There are so many different facets to exploring green lanes:

I start, more often than not, with a map. You can buy a map in W.H.Smith's which will give you more information about your local lanes than any book. Visit your County Hall or your local trail riding group to find out the proven rights of way, then you are in business.

But this is only half the story of maps. The county archives contain an immensely rich variety of old maps. When you start studying these, you peel back the layers and find the origins of green lanes.

A collection of maps covering your area down through the years is not difficult to acquire. Ask for photocopies of county maps from the archives, one inch to the mile or larger is best. Anything up to 1835 will prove immensely useful. Buy the First-Series Ordnance Survey maps from your book shop. Originally published between 1809 and 1820, they are re-published by David and Charles and are beautiful.

A classic Derbyshire green lane – wide, grassy and smooth, lined with dry stone walls. Why is it here? Who built it? Who uses it? Will it be here in twenty years? (D.Giles)

I have taken to hunting antique shops and second hand book shops to find maps from the early part of this century. They can still be found quite cheaply – less than the cost of a new map – and they show how the use and standard of maintenance has altered. Cycling and motoring maps are fascinating, as well as the more obvious Ordnance Survey editions.

Green lanes have changed my view of natural history. The immense abundance and variety of flowers which cover, and on occasion engulf, some lanes would force anyone to take notice of natural history.

I have never seen so many wild mammals – deer, foxes, hares, rabbits, stoats and voles, anywhere as often as on green lanes. The quiet lanes provide homes and food and, I suppose, a sheltered route from place to place for so many of our native species.

To see and to hear small birds, the walker has the advantage. No matter how hard they try, the manufacturers have still not produced a bike quiet enough to allow you to hear the gossips of green lanes. Bird song is drowned by the chuff and rattle of the internal combustion engine. This is a good excuse, if one is needed, to stop, switch the engine off, and to look and listen.

If you explore green lanes, you are bound to learn a great deal more about agriculture. So many of our lanes survive only because farmers need them to reach their fields. Even in open country, farming is an integral feature of green lanes. The burning of bracken – swaling – to promote the growth of sweet grass, the problems of rustlers and the hard economics of rearing ponies on the high moors are brought home to you when you explore away from the tarmac.

When you start to explore further, regional variations become apparent. Compare the intense acres of crops in the south-east with the animal husbandry of the north and west. Worry about the terrifying problem of hedge destruction, now at last being recognised for the threat it is. Our hedgerows are the largest nature reserve in Britain – definitely sites of special scientific interest (SSSI's).

Inevitably, local history will become part of your hobby. Why is the road there? What purpose did it serve? Trace its progress from prehistory to the coming of the Roman road builders. See it as a Saxon military road, a Medieval saltway, a Tudor lead mining road, a Georgian turnpike, and a modern byway. Follow the passage of carriages and kings, of armies and pack horses, of drovers and pedlars and tinkers and salesmen. The mail coach and waggon, the dog cart and the gipsy caravan, all knew these lanes before the first cough of a motor car was heard.

I have walked many miles of green lane. I enjoy walking. But I have to say I prefer walking in a thousand other places. We do not have unrestrained freedom to roam on foot in Britain, but we do have many tens of thousands of miles of hard won public footpaths to walk, and access to open country in many of the most beautiful

areas of the land. By contrast, our surviving green lane mileage is pathetically small. I choose to walk where I like best, the cliff tops and hills and to explore green lanes, in general, by wheel.

I have driven four wheels down a fair few green tracks. It can be fun and is certainly a good way of taking friends into the countryside. Choose your season and your lanes carefully. Soft winter mud can entrap a normal car all too easily, while a carelessly used four wheel drive vehicle can destroy the delicate surface without really trying.

I don't feel the same closeness to the countryside in a car as I do on a bike. (Being thwacked in the face by a bramble is more memorable that being hit in the windscreen!) More importantly, I think a motorcycle, properly maintained and used, has far less impact on the environment of green lanes than a four wheeler.

I leave the reader free to choose his own way to travel. Explore before it is too late. Green lanes are disappearing all the time. The Devon "Adopt-a-lane" scheme needs to be spread nationwide. People must care for our green lanes or there will be none for future generations to enjoy.

The message of this book is go out and explore and enjoy the endless variety of our green lanes. But take care! They are our heritage, our childrens's heritage, and our children's children's heritage.

Alec Dale caresses a rock at Middlehope Lane near St. John's Chapel. (G.Wilson)

Appendices

Appendices A and B are a catalogue of the green lanes used on the two week-long rides described in the book — from Dover to Land's End, and from Jedburgh to Derby.

Each lane is identified by the 1:50000 Ordnance Survey map number (or numbers if the lane is on two maps), followed by the six figure grid references for the start and finish of the lane. Each lane is identified by a name or the name of a nearby landmark.

The description given is very brief and in many cases should not be relied on. A lane which I found dry and smooth in the summer could well be a sea of mud in the winter.

Semi-colons are used to divide the description of different parts of the same lane. E.g. Tarmac; smooth dirt; ford; steep rocky climb, means that the lane starts tarmac, so don't look for a green track at the junction, it then becomes a smooth dirt farm track to a ford, then after the ford there is a steep rocky climb.

Appendix A
Dover to Land's End

179 319474 323444 Roman Road to Dover.
Cut by new A2. Take bypass to next lane

179 275434 276421 Chilton Farm.
Farmyard: open meadow; woods.

179 262415 256410 Maggot Farm.
Hedged ends; ploughed middle.

179/189 248418 241423 South Alkham.
Climb to hill fort; green lane.

179/189 235419 240411 Drellingore.
Narrow muddy descent with tree roots.

179/189 175399 163407 Lyminge
Open meadow; long single track

179/189 134418 126420 Stowting
Steep muddy narrow; wider, then tarmac

179/189 112418 100426 Brabourne
Well marked "North Downs Way"

179/189 080444 088451 Nature Reserve
Steep muddy climb

179/189 088466 085486 Crundale Downs
Beautiful woodland ride

179/189 065468 056469 Wye
Wide dirt road

189 984479 964494 Pilgrims' Way
Well used wide track

189 957499 921522 Pilgrims' Way
Narrow headland track; beanfield

189 921522 916524 Pilgrims' Way
Tar; dirt road

189 912524 901528 Pilgrims' Way
Hedged green lane; open field; tarmac

189 900529 894331 Pilgrims' Way
Three ruts, well used headland track

189 875534 845554 Pilgrims' Way to "Pilgrims' Rest"
Mainly hedged, some open fields

188 765598 751602 White Horse Stone
Wide, smooth; very muddy

188 697620 685628 Cemetery
Single track – horse use

188 685628 652612 Pilgrims' Way
Very narrow; wide and smooth

188 635609 626602 Pilgrims' Way
One track, dry and smooth

188 593595 582594 Pilgrims' Way
Heavy ruts from farm vehicles

188 5775664 586564 Oldbury Hill
Very steep up; very steep down

End of First Day

198 165099 125090 Steyning Round Hill
Chalk and downland

198/197 110088 034122 To South Downs Way
Blank fingerposts. Well used

197 970151 956152 Dogkennel Cottages
Climb over wet leaves

197 954158 878166 South Downs Way
Downs; muddy under trees

197 875166 813159 South Downs Way
Good climb; miles of chalk

197 782184 749195 South Downs Way
Muddy in woods; tarmac

197 749195 746203 Cart Road to Buriton
Muddy steep descent; farm track

197 700215 710197 Leythe House
Climb chalk scarp to hill fort

197/185 705191 683189 Tegdown Hill
Muddy most of the way

185 675191 666209 Wether Down
HMS Mercury; used by bikes

185 666209 668231 Henwood Down
Muddy

185 626236 615252 Warnford
"Conservation Area"

185 615252 605266 Joan's Acres Wood
Green in wood; tar after farm

185 605266 589272 Source of River Itchen
Three ruts between barbed wire

185 588280 580304 Hinton Marsh
Three ruts, drier

185 573327 532361 Itchen Stoke Down
Smooth dirt; dry, grassy

185 514364 483363 The Lunway
Wide green drove

185 484355 460356 South Wonston
Very wide, well used chalk

185 460356 450354 Worthy Down
Dry dirt; ends by oil well

185 448358 414372 Crawley Down
Wide chalk; grassy three ruts; look for right turn

185 350351 339353 Meon Hill (Roman road)
Smooth grass, single track

185 337353 323343 Houghton Down Farm
Smooth, fast and dry

185 323343 317324 Broughton
Muddy, churned up; smoother and drier

185/184 305328 276321 Clarendon Way
Bare chalk, smooth and grassy

184 267324 251327 Roman Road
Smooth sunken grassy lane

184 236331 224331 Roman Road
Holloway under beech trees

184 224331 184331 Roman Road
Three ruts; wide field; causeway

End of Second Day

184 090315 980346 Grovely Hill Ridgeway
Wide avenue; wide chalk; milestones; concrete road

184 980346 939342 Chicklade Bottom
Very wide green; single track; open meadow

184 919346 898339 Cold Berwick Hill
Wide green farm track

184/183 901328 873326 Holdens Farm
Wide hedged track; field ploughed out

183 853338 825344 Charnage Down
Wide, green with milestones

183 825344 786352 White Sheet Hill
Dual carriageway green lane

183 786352 773354 Long Lane
Smooth green holloway

183 665334 657315 Pitcombe
Well used dirt road

183 654313 647320 Priddle's Hill
Very good descent and climb

183 621337 589334 Bolter's Bridge
Open fields; ends tarmac

183 566309 557295 Cross Keys Inn
Very muddy hedged lane

183 557295 552309 Keinton Mandeville
One track, recently cleared

183 528291 512291 Windmill Hill
Smooth, loose stony descent

183 521285 518298 Windmill Hill
Good climb; stony track

183/182 505327 492328 Compton Dundon
Bumpy twisting descent

183/182 492328 490321 Compton Dundon
Bumpy farm track

182 42446 479435 Godney Moor
Rutted grassy track; steep bridge

182 469436 473451 Drake's Drove
Rutted grassy track; steep bridge

182 465454 460437 Northwood Drove
Peaty farm track; steep bridge

182 455437 460454 Dagg's lane Drove
Smooth, potholed; steep bridge

182 454452 448432 Lytheats Drove
Smooth, potholed; steep bridge

182 442432 448451 Weston Drove
Smooth, potholed; steep bridge

182 443336 439475 Mill Lane
Grassy in summer, very muddy in winter

182 427472 427465 Madwoman's Lane
Impossible!

End of Third Day.

181 193361 167354 Parson's Lane
Tarmac; stony climb onto Quantocks

181 167354 110416 Quantock Ridgeway
Heavily used open track

181 103408 105402 Lower Weacombe
Smooth dirt; tarmac

181 096393 089395 Woolston
Wide smooth; beware summer growth

181 036376 046363 Woodadvent Farm
Single track with good views

181 46362 036364 Sticklepath
Old tarmac

181 025358 014360 Leigh Barton
Pass farm; climb over deep valley

181 999368 005377 Druid's Combe
Through farmyard; climb and descent

181 014376 016389 Croydon Hall
Holloway, climb over loose stones

181 016389 006385 Felon's Oak
Tarmac; rough track

181 996407 010421 Hill Lane
Open climb; descent over loose rocks

181 998427 980425 Dunster Park
Climb and descent through woods

181 963455 956432 Grabbist
Climb and descent through heath and wood

181 943412 952396 Pitt Bridge
Steep climb; muddy groove

181 951387 930388 Kersham Lane
Tarmac; ford; steep rock climb

181 899400 905387 Trottsway Cross
Smooth with drainage channels

181 905387 903380 Luckwell Bridge
Rock climb; muddy groove

181 902375 909361 Ison Lane
Bare rock; farm track

181 895363 873386 Kemps Lane
Steep climb; farm track; gates; tarmac

181 867387 854405 Exford Common
Stone gateway; rock steps

181 843391 836391 Downscombe
Ford; very steep climb

181 843351 812319 Porchester's Post
Open moorland

181 847313 860313 Tarr Steps
Tarmac; loose rock descent; wide ford

181 912344 907333 Edbrooke Hill
Steep rocky climb; farm track

181 911311 915280 Dulverton ridgeway
Well used track

181 936298 930294 Oxgrove
Steep; awkward bend

181 937287 944275 Bury Hill
Descent over leaf mould and rock

181 945272 951258 Bury
Very steep climb on bare rock; descent; blocked 1986

181 927193 924191 Carscombe
Rough stony climb

181 917193 913190 Quoit at Cross
Smooth dirt

181 912194 903211 Iron Mill Stream
Tarmac; loose rocks; water; long climb

181 898200 902188 Coleford Bottom
Stony, muddy, wet

181 866171 869158 Tidderson
Tarmac; farm track

192 846119 848107 Chapple Farm
Tar; steep descent; ford; short climb

192 836105 852094 Puddington
Tarmac; farm track; ford

191 819971 828962 Oldridge
Ford; farm track

191 823921 795906 Westland
Tar; steep descent; ford; climb; tar

191 783914 777900 East and West Down
Tarmac; grass descent; woodland

End of Fourth Day

191 743899 741887 Fingle Bridge
Six hairpins on loose stones

191 729835 722825 Langdon
Single track between stone walls

191 723788 730775 Bell Tor
Steep, rocky climb; moorland track

191 716769 698778 Widecombe in the Moor
Tar; granite blocks; open grass; loose rocks and rock steps

201 456729 454728 Lumburn
Loose rocky climb to pub car park

201 391694 388688 Cleave Farm
Tarmac; loose stony climb; mud

201 385660 373647 Mellion Golf Course
Tar, road under construction; farm track

201 345650 324654 Hammett
Gate; grassy track; tarmac

201 312647 306646
Tar; narrow between high banks

201 303642 288640 Hepwell Bridge
Climb; narrow muddy; farm track; tarmac

201 300585 284580 Lydcott Wood
Stone bridge; climb, three hairpins; tarmac

201 273574 267579 Bin Down
Tarmac; smooth dirt descent and climb

201 260582 248574 Plashford Farm
Smooth wet farm track

201 235580 206572 Gillhill Wood
Tar; stony descent; bridge; climb; tar

201 199576 183571 Crooksball
New gate; open fields; single track; ford; tar

201 152582 148584 Kingston House
Dirt farm track; loose stony descent

200 115575 110591 Lanwithan
Farm track; rock steps; tarmac. "Impracticable for Cars"

200 071596 057618 Helman Tor
Green road; tarmac

200 999643 002652 Withielgoose
Farm track

200 005656 001661 Tregawne
Tarmac; farm track; ford

200 961658 956654 Rosenannon
Wide grassy track; open fields; tarmac

200 934638 936633 Trevithick East
Smooth, narrow; ford; climb

End of Fifth Day.

204 790530 786510 Caernkief
Mainly well used dirt

204 775502 779488 Callestick
Two fords, stony; ploughed out; tar (Turn right to cross field)

204 740463 756452 Penstraze
Well used dirt road

204 755441 752439 Kerling
Loose rock descent; ford

204 752433 747429 Rising Sun
Climb; cross tarmac; descent in orchard

204 747429 759422 Hale Mills
Wide, well used

204 759422 749413 Wheal Clifford
Bumpy climb; three farm tracks to Cathlowena

204 746407 749398 Sewage Works
Wide track; deep ford; tarmac

203 706325 702338 Polangrain
Farm track; rocky climb; concrete

203 652331 656345 Blackrock Chapel
Farm track; water; bog; farm track

203 638349 620349 Clowance
Tar through holiday village; green headland track (not in woods)

203 620349 613345 Leedstown
Well used track

203 602344 592346 Carzise
Well used; gravel; farm track; concrete

203 523387 515382 Counthouse Lane
Tar; good rocky climb

203 490371 485370 Arnalwhidden
Tar; stony single track; shallow ford

203 481373 457362 Lady Downs
Loose rocks; thick gorse; moor; tar (Don't get lost!)

203 451360 408344 Drove road
Open moor; Beware! Bog!

203 409336 385331 Chun Castle
Well used track

203 395331 ?????? Carn Kenidjack
I got lost in the gorse and heather (Use alternative to 407318)

End of the Sixth Day – Land's End.

Appendix B

The North – Jedburgh to Derby

Monday:

74/80 661241 755143 Dere Street
Look out for the lost Ninth

80/74 779191 814206 Hownam to Mowhaugh
High hills and superb views

80 853186 911062 Clennell Street
Superb long green road

81 002837 983803 Great Bavington
Unfenced green track

81 983769 965774 Hallington Reservoir
Green between walls

81 944715 952694 Hadrian's Wall
Dry tractor ruts; through garden

81 947687 954676 Acomb Fell
Dry and green

81 953654 954651 Bank Foot, Hexham
Tree down; overgrown

Tuesday:

91 848384 8813351 Grasshills Causeway
Highest road in England

91 774364 757384 Slack's Rigg
Old lead mining road. Start is hard to spot.

86/87 712463 699439 Bayles Moor Road
Bumpy, well used

86/87 676423 657423 Old turnpike road
Smooth; badly rutted

86 646418 623425 Hartside Cross
Steep dirt road

86 622426 603420 Five Lane Ends
Green byway

86 614402 628411 Old turnpike road
Green lane

90 469106 484056 Gatescarth Pass
Ferocious climb and descent; stony track

90 483055 464050 Stile End
Steep climb; rocky track

90 457041 412026 Garburn Road
Rocky climb; beware walkers; good views

Wednesday:

90/91 552035 584046 Breast High Pass
Steep climb; gentler descent

91 636065 654057 Fawcett Mill
Note the old bridge

91 707052 746072 Smardale Fell
Open grassland

91 771045 779030 Croop Ho
Open grassland

91/98 783004 841921 High Way
Superb long high lane

98 864890 829834 Dodd Fell Road
Grass with boggy bits

98 829834 785803 Cam High Road
Well used green road. Look out for walkers

98 782757 769686 Selside
Largely invisible in the grass

98 721687 789675 Wood House
Walled single track

98 790677 791693 Bark Houses
Gates, scars; tarmac

98 813695 842714 Long Lane
Loose stones and grass

98 898743 855729 Cow Close
Good climb; long green lane

Thursday:

98 820631 818620 Water Lane
Shallow ford; walled lane

98 818620 834630 Lodge Farm
Tarmac; green walled lane

98 836630 880649 Stockdale Farm
Tarmac to farm; rock; open fields

98880649 829653 Jubilee Cave
Green open fields; black chippings

98 839685 822673 Cowside
Two rut farm track

98 833685 813695 Moor Head Lane
Stony walled lane

98 809724 871767 Foxup Road
Mind the pothole and the bogs. Wild, wet lane

98 879766 905786 Horse Head Pass
Loose stone zig wags

98 952748 971753 Starbotton
Steep rocky hairpins

98 971753 972724 Top Mere Road
Open grass; walled lane

98 974678 904656 Mastiles Lane
Long walled road

98 904656 947705 High Cote Moor
Open green lane

98 985624 994626 Linton
Walled, leafy lane

Friday:

110 181884 152893 Hagg Side
Forest road; open ridge

110 152893 166853 Roman road
Ridge road with excellent views

110 161824 156819 Pin Dale
Rocky track through quarried gorge

110 155821 127826 Dirtlow Rake
Past quarry; farm track

110 113843 093824 Chapel Gate
Fierce climb; down rock steps

110 092823 045859 Old road to Hayfield
Down evil rock steps. Try it the other way!

119 033788 018794 Spire Hollins
Dusty track on open grassland

119 018794 043747 Roman road to Buxton
Mainly tarmac

119 037724 018715 Old road to Goyt Valley
Well used dirt road

119 003681 010685 Cut Thorn to Three Shires Head
No entry except motorcycles. Pretty valley

119 010685 023683 Black Clough
Climb valley by stream

119 062686 051671 Tenterhill
Cobbles to packhorse bridge

119 062667 056664 Hollinsclough
Short climb; dirt road

119 054658 061661 Hollinsclough Moor
Dirt road

119 061661 064665 Hollinsclough trials section
Smooth whith a few loose rocks

119 064665 063657 Hollinsclough south
Steep climb with loose rocks

119 112628 117633 Pilsbury
Steep descent; wide ford

119 126600 132603 Crossland Sides
Green between stone walls

119 134603 137593 Dale End
Walled green lane

119 132587 117570 Beresford Dale
Steep descent; ford; tarmac

119 104571 098557 Wetton Mill
Quiet green valley

119 091543 083519 Grindon to Waterfall
Long farm track

Bibliography

Title	Author	Publisher
The Old Roads of England	Addison	Batsford
Archeology of Somerset	Aston and Barrow	Somerset County Council
Lorna Doone	Blackmore	Pan
Wiltshire	Cheetham & Faber	Faber
Derbyshire	Christian	Batsford
Rights of Way	Clayden & Trevelyan	Open Spaces Society
Archeological Sites of Britain	Clayton	Weidenfield & Nicholson
Roads & Trackways of Wales	Colyer	Moorland
Peakland Roads & Trackways	Dodd and Dodd	Moorland
Walking Ancient Trackways	Dunn	David & Charles
The Roadmender	Fairless	Duckworth
The Journeys of Celia Fiennes	Fiennes	Cresset
The Wind in the Willows	Grahame	Methuen
Archeology of Exmoor	Grinsell	David & Charles
The Yorkshire Dales	Gunn	Century
The Drovers' Roads of Wales	Godwin & Toulson	Wildwood
English Villages	Hadfield	Michael Joseph
Old Cornish Bridges	Henderson & Coates	Bradford Barton
Journey Through Britain	Hillaby	Paladin
Roads & Trackways of the Lake District	Hindle	Moorland
The Green Roads of England	Hippisley Cox	Methuen
The Making of the English Landscape	Hoskins	Pelican
Along the Pilgrim's Way	Jennett	Cassell
The Walker's Companion	Jones	Ex Libris
Along the Green Roads of Britain	Peel	Cassell
Portrait of Exmoor	Peel	Hale
Green Roads in the Mid-Pennines	Raistrick	Moorland
Roads & Tracks of Britain	Taylor	Dent
Ancient Trackways of Wessex	Timperley and Brill	Phoenix
The Shell Guide to Wales	Vaughan Thomas & Llewellyn	Michael Joseph
Book of the British Countryside	Various	Automobile Association
Fellwanderer	Wainwright	Westmorland Gazette
Around Historic Somerset & Avon	Wintel	Midas
Roads & Trackways of the Yorkshire Dales	Wright	Moorland

Index